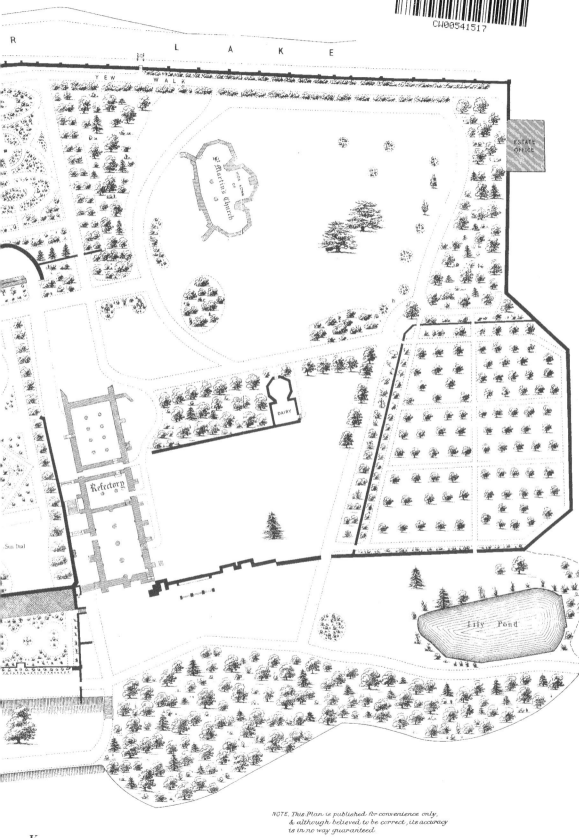

R LAKE

YEW WALK

Ruins of
St Martins Church

DAIRY

Refectory

Sun Dial

Lily Pond

NOTE. This Plan is published for convenience only,
& although believed to be correct, its accuracy
is in no way guaranteed

K

BATTLE ABBEY

AND

THE WEBSTERS

BATTLE ABBEY

AND

THE WEBSTERS

Two Hundred Years of
Ambition, Profligacy and Misfortune

ROY PRYCE

Roy Pryce has lived in East Sussex for most of the past 40 years. A former professor at the University of Sussex he has published books on *Heathfield Park* (1966), *Rotherfield Hall* (2001), and *Heathfield and Waldron: An illustrated history* (2000). He read history at the University of Cambridge where he obtained a Double First and a Doctorate: he was subsequently a Research Fellow at Emmanuel College, Cambridge and St Antony's College, Oxford.

First published in 2005 by Roy Pryce,
Stone House, Cade Street, Heathfield, East Sussex TN21 9BS

Designed and produced by Accomplice Ltd,
The Old Courthouse, High Street, Hailsham, East Sussex BN27 1AU

ISBN 0 9528093 1 1

Typeset in Classical Garamond.
Printed and bound in Great Britain by Dunnsprint Ltd,
Clarence Works, Clarence Road, Eastbourne, East Sussex BN22 8HJ

End papers: Plan of Battle Abbey, 1901 Sale particulars

Contents

Preface & Acknowledgements   *i*

1   The Webster family and the Abbey   1

2   An ambitious arrival   5

3   Born with a silver spoon   25

4   An unfortunate rake   35

5   A disastrous profligate   59

6   Two Websters at sea: A reluctant sale   85

7   A period of nobility   103

8   The Websters dispersed   117

9   Return to Battle: Triumph and tragedy   127

10   Hanging on: Lucy, Evelyn and Godfrey   151

11   The 1976 sale   177

12   Postscript: From private to public ownership   193

Notes   209

Index   223

Preface

The Webster family's period of ownership of Battle Abbey, though lengthy and remarkable, has so far received rather scant attention in the literature about the Abbey. This book sets out to remedy that gap.

I have exceeded the strict bounds of the Webster period in two ways. The first is a chapter dealing with the years between 1858 and 1901, an interregnum in their ownership, when it was owned by the Duke and Duchess of Cleveland. This was a glittering episode in the Abbey's history when, unlike the Webster period, money was not in short supply. For this I have drawn extensively – though not exclusively – on the Duchess's own account in *History of Battle Abbey*, published in 1877 (and long since out of print) which is also a valuable source about the Websters themselves.

The second addition is a postscript dealing with the aftermath of the Websters' departure in 1976 and the transition to public ownership, taking the story up to 2004 when, the last of the Websters connected with the Abbey having left the scene, a group of their family portraits, restored by English Heritage, was brought back and re-hung in the library. This seemed the most appropriate moment at which to end the story.

As the book is intended for the general reader, I have banished the rather extensive notes to the end of the book. I have not attempted to provide present-day equivalents for the sums of money which were either owned or owed by the Websters at various points in the story, but I hope the orders of magnitude involved – usually huge – will be clear from the text.

Acknowledgements

I embarked on the book at the suggestion of Christopher Whittick, Senior Archivist at the East Sussex Record Office (ESRO). He generously made available not only his unrivalled knowledge of the Battle Abbey archives, but also drafts of his extensive essay on the Webster family for the *Oxford Dictionary of National Biography*. In the midst of a hectic professional life he also found time to read, comment on – and correct – early drafts of this book. I am most grateful for all his help.

A great deal of the research for the book was carried out at the Record Office in Lewes where a substantial part of the Battle Abbey archive relating to the Webster period of ownership has been on deposit since 1961. Other documents, relating to the first Webster baronet, his forbears and immediate successors, are to be found in the Henry H Huntington library at San Marino, California: they form part of the huge archive of the Battle Abbey estate, covering both pre- and post-Dissolution periods, which was sold by the debt-ridden fifth Webster baronet in 1835, most of which was acquired by the Huntington library in 1923. Microfilm copies of some of the early monastic and manorial records from this archive are available at ESRO, together with two invaluable calendars covering the whole collection compiled by Christopher Whittick. I made extensive use of the second of these volumes which deals with the post-Dissolution deeds.

The documents in the Battle Abbey archive at ESRO come from a variety of sources. Most of those relating to the Webster family were deposited during the 1960s by Evelyn Webster and the Official Solicitor acting on an order of the Court of Protection on behalf of Miss Lucy Webster, then life-tenant of the Abbey estate. After she surrendered her life interest in 1969, ownership of these documents was asserted by the Trustees of the Battle Abbey Estate, who were however persuaded to allow them to remain on deposit at ESRO.

In September 2003 I made contact with Lady Alexandra Roche, then Chair of the Trustees, to seek permission for the use I intended to make of information provided by those documents. This set in motion a quite unexpected train of events. Lady Roche and her co-trustee, Mr Angus Gordon, who were in process of winding up the Webster family trust, had not at that stage realised that the documents deposited at ESRO were still part of the estate and liable to tax. Fortunately the course they chose was to offer the archive to the government in lieu of this liability. A lengthy procedure was set in train which involved Christies, the Inland Revenue, and the Museums, Libraries and Archives Council as well as a ministerial recommendation to accept the proposed deal. This was made public in July 2005: it is hoped that the document will remain on deposit at ESRO.

The decision taken by Lady Roche and Mr Gordon ensures the continued availability in this country of this important archive: I am also most grateful to them for the help they gave me with my own study, including the information they provided about the later Websters.

I have an equal debt to the staff of ESRO, both past and present. The pioneering Catalogue of the Battle Abbey Estate archives by Judith Brent, a former Senior Assistant Archivist, who completed work begun by Brenda Chapman when she was Assistant County Archivist, was my constant companion. I have taken the liberty of reproducing, with some minor changes, the Webster family tree which is included in the Catalogue. As always, the staff of the Research Room – often under heavy pressure – were unfailingly helpful and efficient. The current County Archivist, Elizabeth Hughes, has kindly given permission to quote from, and in some cases to reproduce, material from the Battle Abbey (BAT) collection: references to specific documents will be found in the notes at the end of the book.

To supplement the information available from these and other written records, especially for the final period of Webster ownership and its aftermath, I have consulted a wide range of those who knew the family or were involved in the affairs of the Abbey. I have a particular debt to Ralfe and Nick Whistler, whose family connection with the Websters goes back to the early 18th century, for their sustained encouragement and very practical help in a variety of ways. I have a similar debt to Ann Moore who, as a County Councillor and spokesperson for the 1066 Trust, was heavily involved in the struggle over the fate of the Abbey once the trustees decided to sell in 1976. She provided a great deal of valuable information about that as well as subsequent developments. Others, including Margaret Chester, Julia Bolton Holloway, Maureen Millar, Paul Petrovitch, and Patricia Roberts gave me lively first-hand testimony about Evelyn and Godfrey. Sir John Lovill and Bill Lanning added their recollections of the role of the East Sussex County Council in the transition to public ownership, and Peter Mills, now Town Clerk at Battle, told me about the tasks facing English Heritage, for which he was then working, when it took over the Abbey in 1983. I am grateful to Ivor White for information posted on his website (www.battle-abbey.co.uk) and for space on it.

Several members of the present staff of English Heritage have also provided invaluable assistance in a number of ways. They include Jonathan Coad (currently Senior Properties Historian), Rowena Willard-Wright (Senior Curator, South East Region) and two former staff members of the now disbanded Conservation Studio in Regents Park, Adrian Buckley and Graham Barraclough, who were responsible for the restoration of the gigantic Battle of Hastings painting and the Webster family portraits now re-hung at the Abbey. I am grateful to English Heritage for permission to reproduce a number of these in this book.

I am also much indebted to Roger Clark, Headmaster of Battle Abbey for his support and assistance, and permission to reproduce several photographs from the school archives. Other members of staff, past and present, have also been most helpful. June Parker (Headmistress 1968-82) added to the information given in her invaluable history of the school; Monica Steward, a former Deputy Head and now honorary keeper of the archives, greatly facilitated my search for illustrations, as did Tony Paton, Deputy Head, who has also contributed two of his own photographs. E J Westnedge (a former chairman of the governors), and Michael Sechiari, whose father was solicitor to the school, also provided helpful recollections.

Another invaluable source of information was Battle Museum of Local History. I am particularly grateful to its archivist, David Sawyer, who responded with great efficiency and unfailing good humour to my many requests, and to Anne Ainsley the Chair of its Executive Committee for permission to reproduce items in the collection.

Other illustrations have been drawn from a wide variety of sources: John Farrant generously helped me identify many of them. Special thanks for their assistance and permission to reproduce material are due to the Hon. Mrs Charlotte Townshend; Victoria Williams, Curator of the Hastings Museum and Art Gallery; and Emma O'Connor of the Sussex Archaeological Society. For permission to reproduce other illustrations I am grateful to the British Library, the Illustrated London News, the National Portrait Gallery, and the West Sussex Record Office.

Melanie Davies and Jim Tipler of Accomplice Ltd have been responsible for the design and production of the book: it has been a great pleasure to work with them again, and to benefit from their national award-winning professional skills.

I also wish to record my special thanks to three family members: Susan Milnes for proof-reading, Jeremy Raj for research, and – above all – my wife Sheila who has patiently read and re-read successive drafts and proofs of this book, has made many good suggestions to improve it, and as on previous occasions has given the sustained support and encouragement an author and publisher needs to see the job finished.

Roy Pryce

WEBSTER FAMILY TREE

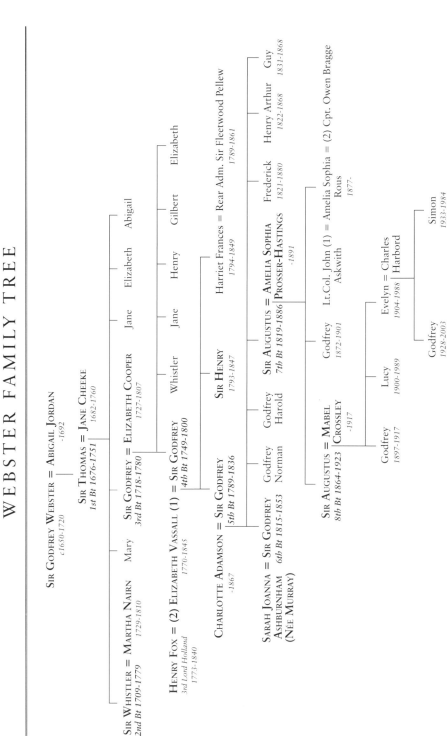

Sir Godfrey Webster = Abigail Jordan
c1650-1720   -1692

Sir Thomas = Jane Cheeke
1st Bt 1676-1751   1682-1760

Sir Godfrey = Elizabeth Cooper
3rd Bt 1718-1780   1727-1807

Mary   Jane   Elizabeth   Abigail

Sir Whistler = Martha Nairn
2nd Bt 1709-1779   1729-1810

Henry Fox = (2) Elizabeth Vassall (1) = Sir Godfrey
3rd Lord Holland   1770-1845   4th Bt 1749-1800
1773-1840

Whistler   Jane   Henry   Gilbert   Elizabeth

Charlotte Adamson = Sir Godfrey
-1867   5th Bt 1789-1836

Sir Henry   Harriet Frances = Rear Adm. Sir Fleetwood Pellew
1793-1847   1794-1849   1789-1861

Godfrey   Godfrey   Sir Augustus = Amelia Sophia   Frederick   Henry Arthur   Guy
Norman   Harold   7th Bt 1819-1886 Prosser-Hastings   1821-1880   1822-1868   1831-1868
                                -1891

Sarah Joanna = Sir Godfrey
Ashburnham   6th Bt 1815-1853
(Née Murray)

Godfrey   Lt.Col. John (1) = Amelia Sophia = (2) Cpt. Owen Bragge
1872-1901   Askwith   Rous
                                1877-

Sir Augustus = Mabel Crossley
8th Bt 1864-1923   -1917

Godfrey   Lucy   Evelyn = Charles Harbord   Simon
1897-1917   1900-1989   1904-1988   1933-1984

Godfrey
1928-2003

1

THE WEBSTER FAMILY AND THE ABBEY

The Websters owned Battle Abbey for over two hundred years between 1721 and 1976. Their story is a family saga as melodramatic as the plot of a Gothic novel. They were the longest-serving and most tenacious of the Abbey's private owners but they had a great capacity for self-inflicted misfortune. The wealth with which they acquired the Abbey was dissipated by a period of reckless and profligate behaviour followed by chronic debt, family disputes and prolonged court cases. Sexual adventures led to importunate mistresses, illegitimate children, disease, lunacy, suicides and early deaths.

Not surprisingly, the family's problems meant lengthy periods of neglect of the Abbey itself. But this did not prevent it gradually assuming over their period of ownership a much more prominent place in the national life. The famous battle of 1066 has always occupied a unique place in British history, but when the Websters arrived its site and the ruins of the Abbey built to commemorate it were only of antiquarian interest. By the time they departed both had been recognised as an important part of the national heritage, visited by a hundred thousand people each year. It was a profound transformation, paving the way for the purchase of the Abbey for the nation.

At the time the first Webster baronet bought it in the early 18th century, the Abbey had already been in private hands, and used as a country house, for almost two hundred years. Sir Thomas Webster arrived on a steeply-rising curve of material and social success backed by a fortune accumulated through hard work, entrepreneurial enterprise and lucrative government contracts as well as a very profitable marriage. But affluence had a corrosive effect on the family fortunes. Two later Webster baronets squandered the wealth they inherited by profligacy on a prodigious scale. In the middle of the 19th century the Websters were forced to sell the Abbey and what remained of its estates.

That might have been the end of the story. But the family had become deeply attached to the Abbey. Within fifty years another judicious marriage temporarily replenished their coffers and enabled the eighth baronet to buy it back to great national and local acclaim – not least because he defeated a rival American bid for it. His moment of triumph was, however, short-lived. Neither he nor his successors were able to live at the Abbey, which was let out and much of its land sold off. In spite of a succession of family tragedies, and much reduced circumstances, they managed to hang on as owners for another fifty years – long after many other families had been forced to sell their country estates. The later Websters put on a brave face and continued to behave as if to the manor born. But by now they were living in a world of fantasy, to which the family trustees put an abrupt end by their decision to sell the Abbey in 1976.

While the eight Webster baronets hold centre stage in this family saga, their wives also play significant parts in it. Most of them were chosen for their wealth and youth – three of them were more than twenty years younger than their husbands – but some brought trouble too. The second baronet made the mistake of marrying a tough young Scots girl, Martha Nairn, late in life: her lengthy widowhood proved very inconvenient for all concerned. The fourth baronet fared even worse. The serial infidelities of his teenage bride, Elizabeth Vassall, brought in their train scandal, disgrace, divorce and his early death.

Among other Webster men were three soldiers who experienced very varying fortunes. The most prominent was Sir Henry Webster who saved his brother, the fifth baronet, from a disastrous liaison just before his marriage and later distinguished himself on the eve of the battle of Waterloo. His youngest grandson, Guy Webster, was a very different character, a dissolute Guardsman who drank himself to death; and the most unfortunate was Godfrey, the young son of the eighth baronet, who like so many others of his generation was killed in action during the first world war. It was his death which was the prelude to the extinction of the Webster baronetcy and the family's eventual departure from the Abbey.

While they were there the Websters were on the whole well regarded locally. They were of course an important source of employment and regular custom for tradespeople and shopkeepers in Battle. Members of the family also benefited for a long time from the deference habitually accorded to the gentry. The tardiness of some of them in paying their bills was a frequent source of irritation but several of the Websters were regarded with genuine affection and the town shut down in respect when they died. By the time of their final departure deference had given way to a more critical set of attitudes. But while some resented the air of superiority maintained by the last of the Websters others regretted the loss of their rather eccentric presence and panache – as well as a plentiful source of gossip.

As far as their stewardship of the Abbey itself was concerned, the Websters' record was not impressive. The first and fifth baronets poured money into those parts which they used as their country house, but there were long periods when impecunious widows lived there without the means to keep it in good repair. There were complaints, too, about the Websters' lack of taste in such changes as they did make, especially from the Duke and (more particularly) the Duchess of Cleveland who bought it from them in 1858 and lived there until the Websters returned in 1902.

When the Websters finally left it proved to be the end also of the long period of private ownership of the Abbey which had begun with Henry VIII's Dissolution of the monasteries in 1538. In spite of the family's erratic stewardship there were still a good many people in Battle at the time who would have preferred another private owner rather than its acquisition by the government. But, having by then become part of the national heritage, there was a certain logic about its transfer to public ownership.

The change in attitudes towards the Abbey, and levels of public interest in it, can be traced back to the work of 18th century antiquarians who laid the foundations for the idea of a national heritage based on the history, landscape and buildings of the country. This led in turn to a much wider public interest in places such as the Abbey. In the early 19th century, after the end of the Napoleonic wars, there was a steady rise in the numbers of those seeking to visit it. The Websters were responsible for the first response to this growing demand by instituting public days and guided tours for visitors. During their absence in the second half of the 19th century, after the arrival of the railway in 1852, visitor numbers increased dramatically. The Clevelands, who were then its owners, were taken aback by the hordes which descended on them. They had to take urgent steps to try to control the weekly invasion, the Duchess recounting with a mixture of alarm and amusement their encounters with the public.

After the return of the Websters in 1902 visitor numbers rose even further with the introduction of annual holidays, cheap railway excursions, the advent of the charabanc, and later the spread of car ownership. The arrangements to deal with them were far from satisfactory, and the decision of the 8th Webster baronet to rent out the Abbey rather than live in it himself meant that the problems created by large-scale tourism had to be shared, uneasily, between the family and its tenants. This posed particular difficulties for the school which arrived in 1922 and which remains embedded in the heart of the Abbey today.

If the configuration of the site has created problems for the exploitation of the Abbey as part of the national heritage, so too has its history. While there is no doubting the decisive importance of the battle which gave rise to the Abbey, both its ruins and the battlefield convey rather mixed messages. They stand on the site of a catastrophic national defeat when the last Saxon King was slain, his army defeated, and the country subjected to foreign conquest. That was not exactly a glorious moment in the nation's history. Nor was the destruction of the renowned medieval monastery by Henry VIII. Not surprisingly, some of the commemorative occasions that have been held at the Abbey have laboured to find the right note to strike. Turning history upside down, valiant efforts have been made to convert these into celebrations of Anglo-French friendship, or wider European unity. It has also been asserted, with rather more justification, that the battle marked a turning point in the history of the western world by providing the political and legal institutions for our former colonies as well as for our own country. This certainly accounts for the sustained interest in the Abbey in the United States – and for the crucial contribution made by American benefactors to its purchase for the nation in 1976 – an ironic outcome in the light of the earlier vocal opposition to the possibility of American ownership.

In the making of this national icon a very selective memory has also been at work. This rarely puts much emphasis either on the defeat sustained in 1066, or the vandalism which followed the Dissolution. What now resonates more than anything else is the Abbey as a symbol of national invulnerability – because it celebrates the last, and now very distant occasion, when there was a successful invasion of the country. It is this message, above all others, which ensures a special place for the Abbey in the pantheon of the national heritage. The Websters were right to be proud of their ownership of it.

2

AN AMBITIOUS ARRIVAL

At the time the Websters bought the Abbey in 1721 it had already been in private hands for almost two hundred years. Following its dissolution in 1538 it was given by Henry VIII to a Court favourite, Sir Anthony Browne. Many of its buildings including the minster, bell-tower, chapter house and cloisters were either razed to the ground or stripped of their roofs. The stone and other materials were used elsewhere or sold for cash.

It is not clear whether or to what extent Sir Anthony himself was responsible for this or any further demolition: most of it may well have been carried out before he took over. But, according to an oft-repeated legend, he did not escape the fury of the dispossessed monks. One of them appeared when he was celebrating taking over his new possession to threaten Divine retribution on the family which would be 'wiped out of the land by fire and by water'. It was to be no empty threat as far as Sir Anthony's successors were concerned, and was to be recalled when misfortune also struck the Websters.[1]

Country house conversion

This threat did not, however, dissuade Sir Anthony himself from seeking to make good use of his new prize. Extensive though the destruction was, the more domestic buildings of the Abbey were left intact, including the refectory, the kitchen, and – above all – the former abbot's residence forming the western side of the cloisters. It was this which Sir Anthony set about converting into a country house.

This change of use, which also occurred in many other former religious houses elsewhere in the country, was not difficult to achieve. The abbot had lived in considerable style in a range of buildings which included a magnificent hall built in the 15th century, a great chamber, a chapel, and a private kitchen. Relatively few changes, apart from extensive repairs, were needed to accommodate its secular owner: a new west front was built on to the hall, the old upper hall was

Monument to Sir Anthony Browne and his wife in Battle parish church

divided into bedrooms, and more rooms were created between the new hall and the monks' dining room. Outside, a double avenue of yews was planted along the line of the former nave and a flower garden created. Later, Sir Anthony also began to rebuild the abbey's guest range when the future Queen Elizabeth was put under his charge with the intention that she should live at the abbey. He died however before it was completed.[2]

Six years earlier an event had occurred which in any case significantly lessened the degree of his commitment to Battle Abbey. He inherited from his half-brother, the Earl of Southampton, extensive estates including the splendid mansion of Cowdray. It was there that he and his successors established their main country seat, though Sir Anthony who died in May 1548 was brought back and buried in Battle parish church after a magnificent funeral. He is commemorated there by a splendid monument in which his effigy lies alongside that of his first wife.

From this point on, Battle Abbey served only as a secondary, and occasional, residence for the family. His son, a staunch Catholic, was raised to the peerage as Viscount Montague by Queen Mary but the family subsequently sank heavily into debt, and during the Civil War all their estates were sequestered. Although these were returned at the Restoration, the family remained heavily indebted: to raise cash more buildings, including the former monastic kitchens, were pulled down and the materials sold off.[3]

By the early 18th century the Abbey had long ceased to be even an occasional residence for the family and was in a dilapidated and neglected state. According to local accounts it had become a favourite resort of the smugglers who then infested the county. The vaults in the Undercroft of the Guest Range by the Lower Terrace, which could be easily and silently reached from the park, are said to have been used as storerooms for their goods. Anyone who strayed that way at an inconvenient moment was scared away by strange noises – which became the source of many ghost stories.

Nevertheless, in spite of pillage and neglect, the Abbey was still an impressive monument on a site with a very special historical resonance. It was also part of an extensive estate, with the added allure of having been associated for almost two hundred years with a noble family of considerable renown. It had, in short, much to recommend it for a man of ambition, a sense of history – and substantial resources.

The Webster family

The change of ownership of the Abbey in 1721 replaced a debt-ridden Viscount by a cash-rich Baronet. Socially the new owner, Sir Thomas Webster, was several notches inferior to his predecessor, but he was a member of an ambitious family which was on a rapidly-rising curve both of wealth and status. That process had greatly accelerated during his own lifetime. His purchase of Battle Abbey marked a further stage in their ascent and was to mark the apogee of the family's fortunes – but also the beginning of their troubles.

According to tradition, the Webster family came over from Flanders towards the end of the 14th century during the reign of Richard II and established themselves at Lockington, north of Beverley, in Yorkshire. But the more immediate ancestors of Sir Thomas were to be found in Chesterfield, Derbyshire from the early 15th century. Several of them took an active part in municipal affairs in the 16th and early 17th centuries, and it was there that Thomas's father, Godfrey, was born in about 1650.[4]

Abigail Jordan

Thomas Jordan

Other members of the family had already made their way to London, and one in particular, Godfrey's uncle Peter Webster, had become a successful merchant and a prominent member of the Clothworkers Company. Godfrey was given a flying start in life by being apprenticed to him, and being admitted himself to the Company in 1670, eventually rising to become its Master in 1695. In the course of a long life – it spanned most of seventy years – he took full advantage of the more settled conditions which the ending of the Civil War and the Restoration brought with them. His was rather a typical story of an ambitious, energetic and successful entrepreneur, whose commercial activities carried out in the grubby docks and warehouses of the east end laid the foundations for his wealth and social advancement.

Having begun as a clothier, Godfrey, who was often described as a 'packer' later branched out into shipping and overseas trade. He acquired a house in Fenchurch Street in the heart of the City for his own use, and bought and developed property both there and in the docklands. He seems to have had a sure instinct for a good investment: on one site by the river, for instance, he built both a Victualling House and an adjoining coffee house called the Bear-Key. His affairs prospered, and he was elected a Freeman of the City in 1670. Two years later he further enhanced his position and prospects by marrying Abigail Jordan, the daughter and co-heir of Thomas Jordan, a successful merchant adventurer.

He was then able, like many successful City men before and after, to acquire a place in the country. This was Nelmes, a mile and half north-east of the village of Hornchurch, then in Essex, a residential area much favoured by the gentry. Originally a medieval manor house (one of twelve in the area) Nelmes had been rebuilt in the 16th century to become a fine building which had been occupied for some years by a previous Lord Mayor of London.[5]

Another crucial development followed after William III came to the throne in 1688. By then Godfrey Webster was one of those with sufficient wealth to provide loans for the monarch. In return he was rewarded with contracts to supply clothing to the army, and also hemp to the navy. Like many governmental suppliers before and since, he profited greatly from these privileged arrangements, which further substantially increased his wealth.

During the following reign royal favours continued: in 1708 he was knighted by Queen Anne. This was the culmination of a dazzling career, which was accompanied by the amassing of a great fortune. By 1710, for instance, he had sufficient stock in the Bank of England to qualify as one of its governors. But his material success was accompanied by a certain independence of mind, and a social conscience. He built a meeting place for religious dissenters at Havering Well near Romford and in his will left a legacy for the minister there, and £500 to be divided between other poor dissenting ministers in Essex. On his death in 1720 provision was also made for many charitable bequests including £1,000 for the poor of Chesterfield, £700 for twenty poor clothworkers of London, and £500 each to St Thomas's Hospital and Bishopsgate workhouse. Out of his substantial fortune which included £15,000 worth of South Sea stock and £8,000 in Bank of England shares he was also able to set aside £15,000 for the coming-of-age of his five grandchildren.[6]

Sir Thomas Webster

Godfrey's financial and social achievements provided a powerful springboard for the ambitions of his only child and heir, Thomas. Born in 1676 – he was baptised on 12th November that year – he advanced purposefully during his twenties through a series of moves which steadily promoted his career, his wealth, and his social standing. In 1697, like many other aspiring young men

Sir Thomas Webster as a young boy

of his generation, Thomas Webster entered the Middle Temple and acquired a grounding in the law, but he quickly found his true vocation as an entrepreneur, trader, and property speculator like his father, with whom he began his career. When he came of age in 1698 he was already a property owner, leasing out for instance a mansion house, farmhouse and land at Barking for £150 a year – but taking care to reserve for his own use in the mansion an upstairs room looking over the best garden, together with lodging for a servant in one of the garrets.[7]

Two years later in November 1700, at the age of 24, he was able to buy his own place in Essex, the estate of Copped Hall (or Copthall) at Waltham, which he purchased from the Earl of Dorset, Charles Sackville, for £13,500. This was a much grander place than his father's country seat. It had originally been a timber-framed manor house, but had been greatly enlarged and rebuilt in the 1560s in brick and stone. Arranged around a spacious square courtyard it consisted of three three-storied ranges, and an entrance loggia with a central porch flanked by imposing columns, and surmounted by a parapet. Four square towers stood guard at the corners of the building, embellished by cupolas (which may have been the source of the name of the Hall). The first floor of one wing was entirely occupied by a 174-foot Long Gallery. It was a most imposing pile, set off by extensive formal gardens including an elaborate parterre to the rear of the Hall.[8]

Thus equipped, Sir Thomas married the following year on 2nd October 1701 at St Mary Abchurch in the City. His bride, Jane Cheeke, was well chosen with an eye to the main chance. Her father was another successful and wealthy businessman, described as a citizen and soapmaker of London, with a country house and estate at Sandford Orcas in Somerset. On her mother's side, Jane was the grand-daughter of a fabulously wealthy man, Henry Whistler, a member of a distinguished family tracing its origins back to Berkshire in the late 13th century and a former Member of Parliament for Oxford. The connection thus established with the Whistler family proved not only very important in the short term for the very substantial additional resources which it brought to the Websters, but also the beginning of a close relationship between the two families which was to continue over the centuries and into recent times.

The next move in the social ascent of Sir Thomas was to ingratiate himself with the Queen and her ministers by contributing to the cost of keeping a garrison in Ulster. He provided £1,095 to pay for thirty soldiers there over a period of three years. His due reward came in 1703 when he acquired a baronetcy bestowed by Queen Anne. This significant move up the social ladder provided him and his heirs with an hereditary title, and elevation into a superior category of the gentry.

His new status also opened the way to further honours. In 1703 he was appointed sheriff of Essex, and the following year was elected Master of the Clothworkers at the age of 27. It also helped Thomas towards another objective – entry into the political elite of the country via a seat in Parliament. This he achieved in December 1705 when he was elected Member for Colchester in a by-election at the age of twenty-eight. This was 'an open, corrupt and expensive borough, usually represented by wealthy London merchants who had purchased Essex estates'. Its population included a large number of Dissenters, of whom over four hundred were eligible to vote. It was a place to which Sir Thomas, with his cloth-trading background and strong Nonconformist sympathies, was well suited – though his political views and his activities as a navy contractor also made him enemies.

Sir Thomas had three spells in Parliament, but did not have an easy passage. His initial entry in 1705 was greatly facilitated by the timely creation of a hundred extra freemen, most of whom voted for him. But some six years later, in late January 1711, the Tories had their revenge and mobilised a majority in the House of Commons to expel him. The same thing happened a second time when in the election of August 1713 the creation of another hundred freeman helped secure his re-election, only for him to be expelled in May the following year. It was only after an eight year gap that Webster and his friends re-established control over the constituency and in March 1722 he was elected for a third time. By then the Whigs were in a much stronger position, and on their way to establishing a monopoly of power which was to be consolidated by Robert Walpole's long spell as prime minister between 1722 and 1746. As a Member of

The 18th century House of Commons

the ruling party, Webster was part of a network of power and influence, as well as enjoying the social prestige attached to membership of the House of Commons. He retained his seat until 1727.[9]

In parallel with his political activities Sir Thomas continued to be an active wheeler and dealer. The contracts he and his father had to supply the navy with hemp were normally very lucrative though on occasion ships were lost, or losses sustained through unexpected falls in prices. There were also problems about extracting payment from the Navy: in 1711 Webster led a delegation of its creditors to complain about their treatment. Two years later, however, Webster cooperated with the Commissioners of the Navy to break a rival syndicate which had forced prices up.

The Whistler inheritance

There was always need of more money to finance Webster's many business and property deals. Late in 1716 for instance he raised a mortgage of £2,000 from the Earl of Dorset on various properties and land in Derbyshire and Staffordshire and another of £2,025 on the security of Copthall. But Sir Thomas's financial prospects were radically transformed by three deaths which occurred in quick succession in 1719 and 1720. In the first of these years his wife inherited property from her father and also – after a contested will was settled in her favour – the vast estates of her maternal grandfather Henry Whistler. These included extensive property both in the commercial heart of London (in such places as Lombard Street, Cannon Street, and St Katharine's, Wapping) as well as elsewhere in the capital, a share in the waterworks in York, property in Londonderry, and a manor

in Hampshire. The sale of his stock alone realised over £30,000. The following
year Thomas inherited his own father's substantial estate, which brought more
properties in central London, including three houses in Bishopsgate (one of which
was the Great James Tavern), and another in Woolwich, as well as his parents'
home Nelmes and other property in Essex.[10]

This was a major upturn in the family's fortunes, which promptly led to an
extensive spending spree. The first stage was the purchase in 1720 of a fine house
in St James's Street from Charles Seymour, Duke of Somerset, for £6,000. The
choice of location was significant. Strategically placed close to St James's Palace
and other seats of power, it provided an excellent base for furthering his social
and political ambitions. (It was later to be occupied by Boodles). He promptly
spent another £2,000 on fitting it out to make it a worthy setting for a man of his
position. Two years later he also purchased from the Crown the lease of another
house close by in Jermyn Street which he proceeded to demolish and rebuild.[11]

A portrait of Sir Thomas painted at around this time (see colour section)
shows him as a typically 18th century figure, splendidly arrayed in wig and
sumptuous frock-coat with lace cuffs, his right hand thrusting forward holding
a gold-tipped cane, confidently looking out at the world against a background
suggestive of the countryside and classical antiquity. We know from the
personal papers he left, which included payments to his wig-maker, tailors and
'haberdashers in hats' that though he was economical in his costume, 'he wore
his velvet coat conformably with the fashion of his time, and his gold laceman's
bills evince that the Baronet could, and did, display a bedizened exterior at the
Smyrna Coffee House, and elsewhere, amongst the gayest of the gay.'[12]

Sir Thomas was not only a fashionable figure, he was also an avid collector
of books, paintings and prints. His papers record considerable payments to the
principal booksellers of the day as well as to a number of art dealers such as Mr
Kinsey to whom he paid five guineas in February 1726 for 'a whole–length picture
from Mr Murray' and Mr Bonnell 'one of the cognoscenti of the day' who advised
him on his purchases. When the latter had the misfortune to be imprisoned in
1728 Webster sent him a guinea. Like his father he was a regular contributor to
charitable causes, including five guineas to the poor of Hornchurch at Christmas
1720 and four guineas for galley slaves in April the following year.[13]

Purchase of the Abbey

Sir Thomas also had a keen interest in history and antiquities. It may well have been this which was a decisive factor in his otherwise surprising – and still unexplained – decision in 1721 to purchase Battle Abbey from Lord Montague and subsequently to buy up a number of neighbouring estates in Sussex.

This marked a striking and radical departure from the strategy he had so far pursued of maintaining and building up a social and political base in Essex. His country house and estates were there: so too was the constituency he had represented for many years. It is true that he had not sat for Colchester since 1714, but he must have been aware of moves afoot which were to lead to his re-election in 1722 for a further five years. In other respects he had also apparently become well entrenched. He became sheriff of the county, and at the time of the Jacobite rising in 1715 he was commissioned by the Lord Lieutenant, the Earl of Suffolk, as a lieutenant-colonel of the Red Regiment of Foot, the trained bands raised by the earl. In 1718 he became a Verderer of Waltham Forest for life – and after his father's death there was the prospect of being appointed a Deputy Lieutenant of the county (which in fact happened in July 1722).[14]

Sir Thomas perhaps thought that he could both maintain his Essex connections and cope with his new commitments in Sussex. Had he merely bought Battle Abbey that might well have been the case. Although much of it was in a ruined state and clearly required substantial investment to make it habitable again, the level of expenditure required would not have been insupportable. But how should one explain the purchase of over 10,000 acres at a cost not far short of £100,000? That was another matter entirely.

In the absence of any documentary evidence, we can only speculate about Webster's motives. What is not in doubt is that in the 18th century ownership of land was a crucial element in social status as well as a major source of income. Its virtues were all the more apparent in the wake of the catastrophic failure of the South Sea Company which imploded in 1720 and ruined many who had borrowed heavily to speculate in its shares. We do not know whether Webster himself invested in it, and profited or lost as a consequence – though he inherited from his father some of its stock nominally worth £15,000 in trust for his children. The collapse of the Company may well have encouraged him to seek greater security

by further investment in
land, the price of which fell
in its aftermath. He may also
have believed that there was
money still to be made in the
Wealden iron industry. But
there was, almost certainly,
another and perhaps more
powerful motive. Battle
Abbey commemorated a
momentous event in the
country's history. Its ruins
held a special fascination for

The South-Sea House: headquarters of the ill–fated Company

those interested in the past, and it was a recognised place of pilgrimage for the
select but growing number of antiquarians. For Sir Thomas this was no ordinary
purchase: he was also buying a stake in history.[15]

This consideration must have overcome whatever doubts he may have had
about Sussex itself. It was a part of the country which at the time had a reputation
for being an impoverished backwater notorious for its vile roads, miserable
hostelries, and lawlessness. Horace Walpole was a more jaundiced and choleric
traveller than some, but many would have echoed his famous tirade, penned some
twenty-five years after the Websters arrived there:[16]

> 'If you love good roads, conveniences, good inns, plenty of postillions
> and horses, be so kind as never to go into Sussex. We thought ourselves in
> the northest part of England; the whole country has a Saxon air, and the
> inhabitants are savage as if King George the Second was the first monarch of
> the East Angles. Coaches grow there no more than balm and spices. We were
> forced to drop our post-chaise…Sussex is a great damper of curiosity'.

The roads were certainly bad in winter: Sir Thomas, for instance, was to
find that he had to pay for oxen to assist in getting his carriage from Robertsbridge
to Battle. There was also a good deal of poverty. It was hard for smallholders to
make a living from the marginal agricultural land of the Weald, and smuggling
– accompanied by a good deal of violence – was rife. On the other hand, the

Wealden iron industry though past its peak had experienced a partial revival since 1689 during the wars with the French and was still attracting investors and entrepreneurs. The ranks of the gentry were also being swollen by those (like the Websters) who had made money in the City and elsewhere, some of whom were building splendid new country houses or refurbishing older timber-framed ones.[17]

There was rebuilding going on in Battle itself, too. The town had grown up as an appendage of the Abbey, and must have suffered from the disruption caused by the Dissolution – though some were able to profit from the building materials, and especially the stone, thus 'liberated'. It was still much the same size as in the 12th century, most of its 115 dwellings lining the road leading to and beyond the Abbey. But the town, which was on the coach route between London and the coast, had kept its functions as a legal and administrative centre, its weekly market and annual fair and specialist crafts such as leather-working, tanning, and shoe-making. Those involved in these varied activities were sufficiently well off to support the building of some new houses, as well as the refacing or rebuilding of others to contemporary standards. Local people were certainly also ready to welcome a new owner of the Abbey after its period of neglect, especially a Protestant with a good supply of cash.[18]

The Abbey and its estates

The Abbey and its 8000 acre estate which Sir Thomas bought in 1721 cost him £56,000. But this was only the beginning of his acquisitions in Sussex. Two years later he purchased the Ewhurst estate from Sir Christopher Powell which included Bodiam castle and over 800 acres at a cost of £8,500. In 1726 he bought Robertsbridge Abbey and its estate of some 1,100 acres from Lord De Lisle and Dudley for around £30,000, and in 1733 neighbouring land, amounting to some 486 acres at Fairlight. In the space of a few years, and at a huge cost, with funds mainly provided by his wife's inherited Whistler money, Sir Thomas became a major landowner in east Sussex.[19]

By the time Sir Thomas arrived at the Abbey he and his wife had a growing family. There were six children in all. The succession had been assured by the birth of two sons, Whistler in 1709, and Godfrey nine years later. There were also four daughters, Mary (who died in 1722, shortly after their arrival in Sussex), Jane, Elizabeth and Abigail. In 1721 Abigail was married to Edward, son and heir of Sir Edward Northey, the Attorney General, of Compton Bassett near Calne. For this, Sir Thomas had to provide a dowry of £20,000: another drain on his resources at a time of very heavy expenditure in all directions.

There can be little doubt that Webster also had to spend a good deal of money to refurbish the Abbot's House, which was in a decayed condition, and to make it into an acceptable residence. Curiously, however, he does not appear to have been able to deploy his good taste in other matters to the fabric and decoration of his newly-acquired country house. In 1743 the Reverend Jeremiah Milles, who was later to become President of the Society of Antiquaries, visited Battle ('a pretty little town') and recorded that Sir Thomas ' has made a habitable, though not a handsome, house out of some of the apartments of the old abbey.' Webster was nevertheless clearly very proud of it and the estate which he now owned. He became a subscriber to Richard Budgen's new survey and map of Sussex published in 1724, which offered him an early opportunity to take his place among the other notable landowners of the county by having his coat of arms displayed alongside theirs. He also commissioned Budgen to survey and record in a series of maps the extent of his huge estates in Sussex.[20]

At the time he bought the Battle Abbey estate, the residence itself seems to have been generally known as Battle Place or Battle House – it appears under the former name in Budgen's map and both names are used in contemporary legal documents. But by the 1730s both disappear in favour of Battle Abbey, a reversion to its historic name which Webster himself may well have favoured and promoted. He was certainly deeply conscious of its historical importance, and proud to be its owner. He subscribed, for instance, to a volume of Samuel Buck's 'Perspective views of remains of antiquity' published in 1737, a collection of prints including Battle Abbey and Bodiam Castle – both duly dedicated to Sir Thomas. He also pursued his interest in its history by asking the King's librarian, David Casley, in 1727 to transcribe for him not only the Abbey cartularies which came with the estate, but also the Battle Abbey Chronicle in the Cottonian library. When the Rev Milles visited the Abbey he saw these two folio books in Sir Thomas's study, 'but they were locked up so I could not get sight of them.'[21]

To his estates Sir Thomas applied the same entrepreneurial vigour as

Battle Abbey in 1737 by Samuel Buck

he had to his other commercial enterprises. He encouraged improvements in agriculture, and in 1731 purchased for almost £100 new implements from the celebrated innovator Jethro Tull including a plough costing eight guineas. Day-to-day management was entrusted to his stewards, initially James Ashenden, and from 1729 George Worge, a local solicitor who was the son-in-law of John Collier, a Hastings solicitor who did a great deal of work for the Pelham family. Much of the land was rented out to provide a steady income from the Sussex estates which in 1744 amounted to over £4,000 a year. An average of 7-8 shillings an acre was charged, though some rents were in the range 13-14 shillings. Over the period of his ownership some rentals were increased: in the case of Barkham Farm at Bexhill, for instance, a rate of 8 shillings an acre was specified in leases granted in 1723 and 1738, but rose to 9s 6d in 1748.[22]

Webster's solicitors were kept busy drawing up and negotiating the terms of the leases, which contained the usual balance of rights and duties for owner and tenant. These included restrictions on the conversion of pasture to arable land and the imposition of penalties (usually £5 an acre) if this occurred, as well as fines if more than three arable crops were grown without marling and liming. In some cases limits were also placed on the acreage of hops that was permitted. Normally Webster reserved the rights to hunting, hawking and fowling – and sometimes fishing too. But he also assumed obligations: for instance, to maintain property in habitable condition, and to reduce the rent if an extension of ponds submerged part of the land.[23]

A significant feature of many leases was the great detail with which the rights and obligations of both landlord and tenant with regard to timber and underwood were specified. These included the quantities and price of the wood to be made available by the owner, as well as his rights to fell and cut. The degree of detail reflected the fact that timber and wood were a valuable resource, needed not only for a wide variety of uses by individual tenants, but also – and above all – for the iron industry which had been a major activity in the Weald for many centuries. Although by the middle of the 18th century local production was on a much reduced scale compared with its peak in the previous two centuries because of domestic and foreign competition, it was still a significant activity – and Sir Thomas, in common with many other landowners, had a stake in it.

Within three years of arriving in Sussex Sir Thomas joined with its established landowners in an attempt to revive the industry. He went into partnership with Lord Ashburnham to rent Beech Furnace in Battle and in 1731 he assumed sole responsibility for it, and contracted with its owner, Richard Hay – a descendant of one of the great Sussex iron entrepreneurs – to buy all the timber felled on the latter's Battle estate over a period of two years. In 1727 he began to exploit the Robertsbridge furnace and forge which he had acquired as part of that estate, and in 1733 he took a seven year lease on a forge and mill at Etchingham. But from 1737 the Robertsbridge plant at Salehurst was leased out to two founders and ironmongers of London, William and George Jukes. Nine years later they renewed their lease for a further seven years at a slightly increased rent of £100 a year.[24]

We do not have the evidence to judge how profitable or otherwise these ventures proved to be. But Beech Furnace seems to have run into difficulties. As part of his 1737 agreement with the Jukes brothers Sir Thomas undertook, for a modest £12 annual payment, not to compete with them by continuing to use it as a furnace, even though by then he had it on a lease for the life of Richard Hay. This suggests that it had not proved to be a good investment. In all probability Sir Thomas, in common with others who entered the industry too late, lost rather than made money out of Wealden iron.[25]

It is not clear how he fared with another local venture – joint ownership

Bodiam Castle

with two others of a gunpowder works at Sedlescombe – but by the end of the 1720s the cost of the money he had borrowed to make such extensive capital investments (which included some distant ventures such as a share in the Toledo waterworks in Spain) and his heavy regular outgoings put his finances under strain. A period of consolidation was needed to reduce the volume of debt he had accumulated and to ease his cash flow problems.[26]

In 1728 Sir Thomas mortgaged the Robertsbridge estate and a number of London properties, and three years later he began to do the same with parts of his Essex estates. In 1731, for instance, he pledged the manor of Bretons near Romford and other property to a notorious usurer, John ('Vulture') Hopkins, the object of satire in Alexander Pope's 'Moral Essays'. The following year he mortgaged much more including Copthall itself, the manor of Ongar, and lands in Waltham and Epping. Even so, by 1733 his personal debts had risen to £54,000 – including £20,000 still owed to Viscount Montague for his purchase of the Abbey – and in addition he owed his children large sums which he had borrowed from the South Sea stock fund left them by their grandfather.[27]

The only way this mountain of debt could be reduced was by selling off a number of properties and rationalising, as far as possible, the remaining estates. As a first step a settlement was drawn up in 1731 which involved the exchange of extensive Whistler properties in London inherited by his eldest son for land of equal value in Sussex. This was followed in 1738 and 1739 by the disposal of the Sandford Orcas estate, and the Essex part of the Webster domains, including Copthall itself which was exchanged for land and properties in East Grinstead. By such means the volume of debt was substantially reduced by 1744, though the balance due to Whistler and his other children was still £39,899.[28]

A Christmas accident

In spite of these problems the family continued to enjoy life at the Abbey, especially at Christmas which was usually a time of intensive social activity for its younger members. Two of the daughters of the Hastings solicitor John Collier (who fathered no fewer than eighteen children) were regular visitors on these occasions. In January 1740 Cordelia Collier reported 'My sister and I was at the Abbey where there was a great Deal of Company, and we had a Private ball, which lasted five hours, and I had the Honour of opening it with Mr Webster.' In a separate letter her married sister Mary added that it had gone on until five and six in the morning, that both of them had stayed at the Abbey ('much more comfortable than mounting the hill after Dancing'), and that Lady Webster had been 'prodigious civil to us'.[29]

Two years later, however, there was a serious accident at the abbey to the same Mr Webster – Godfrey, the younger son of Sir Thomas, then in his twenties – which put a damper on the festivities that Christmas. Mary wrote to her mother:[30]

> 'I suppose my Papa told you of the great pleasure we proposed in our Ball on Monday and other things that were to have been next week which all are prevented by a Shocking accident which I imagine you may by this time have heard Something of […]
>
> Mr Godfrey Webster got up yesterday morning with an Intent to go a Shooting, and put half a Pound of Powder over a chaffing dish of Coals to dry while he wrote 2 pretty long letters to go by the Post, which when he had done [and] went to stir the Powder, at the instant the Plate melted and immediately it Blew up, threw him Senseless on the floor, burst open the Door and went out of another room's window.
>
> He is miserably burnt in face, neck and hands so that his Clothes were obliged to be cut off by bits, but the greatest Danger is his eyes which they are very

much afraid that he will lose though Dr Young gives great hopes of them when the inflamation is over, but at present they are intirely gone. This melancholy accident has put us all in a great Consternation that we hardly know what we do … I think I shall never bear the sight of powder or a gun again.'

Towards the end of January 1742 Cordelia herself wrote from Battle to report that 'We have had but a Dull Xmas this year. I have not supt out at one house since we have been here but at the abbey and that I don't reckoned any thing'. She added 'The Family goes all away next week, but Mr Godfrey who must stay till he has got some eye brows and Lashes which come as fast as possible.' A week later Mary Collier told their mother 'Mr Godfrey is not gone yet but Stays in the Country till his eye lashes begin to grow, though I Think he looks Just the same as he did before the accident.' She added that all their friends had now set off for London 'and left us all Dolorous…We shall live pretty much retired.'[31]

Later life

By now Sir Thomas was in his sixties, and beginning to feel his age. In September 1744 he wrote:[32]

'Taking into my view the fatigue of managing so extended an Estate requires, which my Age makes uneasy to me, and the necessary attendance upon it impossible, of course the estate must suffer from want of the necessary attendance and application to it and that must with years be a growing disadvantage as indolences etc, with every year go on increasing.'

To deal with the outstanding debts towards his children, he proposed that his eldest son Whistler should take over the East Grinstead estate which Sir Thomas had acquired in 1739 in exchange for Copthall, the income from which would cover his remaining debts to his son; that his younger son should have Nelmes; and that the income from other properties be used to liquidate his debts towards his daughters. He also proposed further measures to dispose of outlying parts of the estate that gave trouble and 'don't add to the figure and weight of a family.'

In the midst of these financial preoccupations, Sir Thomas still found time, characteristically, to be concerned about helping others in difficulties. On 27 January 1745 he wrote to John Collier[33]:

SUSSEX ARCH SOC

Battle parish church

'This morning I had a message from an honest and very unfortunate man, Mark Taught, to let me know one of your boatmen at Hastings died last night, and begging me to recommend him to your favour to succeed in the place. If it is in your power and no previous agreements it would be a generous act of charity in you, and a pleasing one to me.'

He added a comment on the current Jacobite incursion: 'Our unaccountable miscarriage in Scotland causes great consternation. These repeated pannicks, and ill behaviour of so many of our troops, becomes serious and big with just apprehensions of bad consequences.'

Six years later, on 30 May 1751, Sir Thomas died and was buried 'in linnen' in a new family vault in Battle parish church. His had been a remarkable life. Building on the foundations laid by earlier members of the family, and in particular his father, he had not only achieved great wealth but also had risen socially in a spectacular fashion, and consolidated his position among the more affluent gentry by the acquisition of Battle Abbey and its extensive related estates. It was an impressive legacy which he left to his successors, but it was one which was to prove impossible to match, and difficult to sustain.

His wife survived him by almost nine years, until 30 January 1760, leaving instructions in her will that her funeral should be as quiet as possible and attended only by her servants. Its financial provisions, however, were to lead to much dispute within the family, and prolonged litigation.[34] (see below, p31-32)

In the meantime, it was their eldest son Whistler Webster who inherited his father's title and became the second Webster baronet.

3

BORN WITH A SILVER SPOON

Sir Whistler is in many ways a tantalising figure. We do not know enough about him to reach a definitive judgment on many aspects of his life. We know what he looked like from contemporary portraits, both as a boy and in his prime. But there are substantial gaps in the information that has survived about several periods in his life, and not much direct evidence about his character and personality. What emerges from the little that is known is that he was a victim as well as a beneficiary of the circumstances of his birth. Although he began life with many advantages, Sir Whistler displayed little of the entrepreneurial spirit or determination of his father. Great wealth may have induced a certain indolence. His early confidence may also have been sapped by

a disappointment in his private life imposed on him by his main benefactor. He sat for a long time in Parliament, displaying a degree of independence from party, but to no great effect.

As the owner of the Abbey he has been accused both of vandalism and neglect. Some of this criticism is exaggerated, but it is true that some further demolition took place during his tenure and that the deterioration in the condition of what remained continued. It was subsequently aggravated by a well-meaning provision in his will which had unforseen and very unfortunate consequences both for the Abbey itself and for one of his successors: an early example of the Websters' capacity for self-inflicted misfortune.

ENGLISH HERITAGE

Whistler Webster as a young man

A confident young man

Whistler's arrival as his parents' first child, some eight years after their marriage, must have occasioned much rejoicing. Baptised on 2 September 1709 at St Mary Abchurch in the City, his early life coincided with the period of the family's rising prosperity which culminated in his father's purchase of Battle Abbey and extensive estates in Sussex. A portrait of Whistler, painted when he was fifteen, shows him as a confident young man, very fashionably dressed in a sumptuous red outfit, set against a romantic landscape. At that point he had much to be confident about. Both his parents had recently inherited extensive estates and property as well as money: as their eldest son he could look forward to a substantial part of these considerable resources, as well as the baronetcy, in due course. On his coming of age in 1729 he was already a wealthy man inheriting a portfolio of property in London and elsewhere. Four years later his assets were increased still further when his mother passed on to him a number of properties in the City and Wapping which she had inherited from her grandfather, Henry Whistler.[1]

The Whistler money, however, did not come without strings. As a young man Webster fell in love with his cousin Elizabeth Byde and sought to marry her. But Henry Whistler disapproved of marriage with so close a relative, and was determined to prevent it happening. In his will he bequeathed the lady £1,000 worth of East India Company stock, and a farm at Ware in Hertfordshire, subject to her having come of age and 'was not married to Whistler Webster.' Miss Byde, we are told, 'obediently took another husband.' Webster, for his part, remained a bachelor until late in life, and childless.[2]

With his financial fortunes apparently secure, he decided to follow in his father's footsteps and seek a political career. His first attempt at Hastings in 1734 proved unsuccessful, but five years later Sir Thomas came to his son's rescue. As part of the strategy of moving his base from Essex and concentrating his land holdings in Sussex, he exchanged Copthall for the East Grinstead property of Edward Conyers, the sitting Member of Parliament for that borough. It was one of twenty-nine constituencies where the franchise was attached to property rather than to persons. There were 36 burgage tenements in all, of which 29 belonged to the Sackville family: the Websters had six (one of them the Crown Inn). With the agreement of the Sackvilles, Whistler at the age of thirty-three was returned to Parliament unopposed in 1741, and retained the seat for the next twenty years. The arrangement with the senior member of the Sackville family, the Duke of Dorset, was strong enough to allow Sir Thomas Webster to repulse very firmly an approach in 1750 by the Prince of Wales (the future George III) on behalf of Dorset's son who opposed his father's choice of candidate for the family's seat at a by-election in the constituency.[3]

A portrait of Whistler Webster painted during this period *(see colour section)* shows him in a sumptuous embroidered coat and breeches standing in a classical pose by a tree in a river landscape. Like his father, he appears to have been content with the social prestige and connections that membership of Parliament conferred rather than using it as a springboard for a political career. He was elected as a Whig, but for most of the time he consistently voted with the Opposition. This meant conflict with the powerful Pelham family – a brave but rather foolhardy thing to do as it excluded him from political preferment both nationally and in Sussex. However, at around the time that he inherited the baronetcy and Battle Abbey, he appears to have changed tack, and made his peace with the Pelhams and the Administration. In 1751, for instance, he asked the Duke of Newcastle for a place in Prince George's establishment for his brother in law, Sir Edmund Thomas. Sir Whistler did not stand for Parliament in 1761, and although in 1768 he was invited by the Pelhams to become a candidate again, by then ill health led him to decline what was no doubt a welcome sign of political favour.[4]

Neglect at the Abbey

Whistler remained a Member of Parliament for ten years after inheriting Battle Abbey and its estates in 1751 at the age of forty-one but there can be little doubt that from that point onwards it was his role as a country gentleman and landowner which predominated.

As far as his stewardship of the Abbey itself is concerned, he has had a rather bad press. In her history of the Abbey, the Duchess of Cleveland accused Sir Whistler of "a passion for demolition" and of having pulled down a considerable part of it and greatly neglected the rest. To support her contention she quoted at some length from comments made by Horace Walpole when he visited the Abbey in August 1752. A later article in the *Country Gentleman* of 7 December 1901 was even more damning, accusing Webster of being 'a thorough vandal' who 'dismantled a great part of the Abbey, to the disgust of Horace Walpole.'[5]

In fact, however, Walpole's visit took place when Sir Whistler had been in occupation of the Abbey for only about a year, and he made no criticism at all of its new owner. His comments applied to the changes Sir Thomas had made, and the criticism was directed at his taste and the neglected state in which he had left the Abbey, rather than to anything that his successor had done:

> 'Battel Abbey stands at the end of the town, exactly as Warwick Castle does of Warwick; but the house of Webster have taken good care that it should not resemble it in anything else. A vast building, which they call the old refectory, but which, I believe, was the original church, is now barn, coach-house etc. The situation is noble, above the level of abbeys; what does remain of gateways and towers is beautiful, particularly the flat side of a cloister, which is now the front of the mansion house. A Miss of the family has clothed a fragment of a portico with cockle-shells ! The grounds, and what has been the park, lie in a vile condition.'

It was Lady Cleveland rather than Horace Walpole who asserted that Whistler Webster was responsible for pulling down a 'considerable part of the abbey'. This is certainly an exaggeration, given the extent of the destruction carried out at the time of the Dissolution, and subsequently by members of the Montague family. Her own account mentions just two further acts of demolition. The lesser of the two was to have 'raised to the ground' the section of the western precinct wall which ran from the Gateway for about four hundred yards before it turned eastwards along the Lower Terrace. Much more important was the destruction of the guest range initiated by Sir Anthony Browne, a prominent part of the complex of which only its twin towers were left standing. Lady Cleveland observed however in mitigation of Sir Whistler's action that 'probably the house was much out of repair, and its restoration would have cost more money than he cared to lay out upon it: or he may not have thought it a desirable residence.'[6]

While the evidence does not support the view that Sir Whistler was a vandal, it does lend weight to the alternative charge of neglect. Contemporary drawings and prints – including Paul Sandby's view 'from Mr Wyndhams' – make it clear that he failed to keep the fabric of what remained of the Abbey in good

SUSSEX ARCH SOC

The Abbey from Mr Wyndhams by Paul Sandby, 1780

order. One result of this was the collapse of the roof of the Court House during the great storm of 28 September 1764.

A visitor to the Abbey towards the end of the second Baronet's life advanced a different, but familiar, criticism of the Webster treatment of the Abbey buildings – though here again it may have been directed at the changes made by his father rather than by Whistler himself. The Reverend William Gilpin, an experienced traveller and author, called there in 1774 and wrote 'This abbey is converted into a modern dwelling which has been the cause of a second Dissolution. The mixture of old building, and new, is something like the barbarous cruelty we read of uniting living bodies to the dead.' His aesthetic judgment was clearly unfavourable, but the criticism is of bad taste rather than vandalism.[7]

Three years later, in 1777, the illustrator Francis Grose and his patron Sir William Burrell visited the Abbey. The comments which Grose made in his diary are much less judgmental. He recounts that Mr [Godfrey] Webster showed them the Dorter, the place where Harold is reputed to have fallen, divers vaulted rooms, the stable ('a very handsome building') and the great hall, where he noticed 'a kind of chest used for repainting it remains drawn up by ropes; this is occasionally lowered to receive workmen.' After dinner they went to the Abbey 'in pursuance of an invitation to drink tea there. Lady Webster showed us the house. Most of the lodging rooms were originally used as an infirmary and this is sufficiently evinced by the passage which is extremely long and narrow, the rooms all opening into it. The present library was the infirmary chapel.[...]On the south side there are remains of some beautiful arcades...In the Abbey are some tolerable pictures.'[8]

Managing the estate

As far as Sir Whistler's management of the estate as a whole is concerned, the available evidence points to a continuation of the careful practices which had characterised his father's period of ownership. George Worge stayed on as his Steward for a number of years, and was succeeded around 1757 by John Turner, whose account books give comprehensive details of the expenditure involved in running the estate including the purchase of oats, hay and straw; maintenance work such as hedging and ditching, tiling and glazing; and seasonal activities including shearing, mowing, reaping and threshing. Turner was paid a salary of £45 a year: his accounts were punctilious, though often settled rather belatedly by his master.[9]

Whistler maintained a stake in the local iron industry, though continuing to lease out rather than himself work the Robertsbridge furnace, which in 1754 was taken on by a Staffordshire ironmaster, John Churchill. For a number of years this apparently flourished, an extension being built to the forgeman's house for which in January 1760 Whistler agreed to pay half the cost. Eight years later both furnace and forge were still in operation, the lease then being taken on by two local men – though only for a year – at the same rent of £100 p.a. Whistler, for his part, built a lock at great expense to maintain access by the river Rother to the plant – a move which prompted a petition by a group of local residents to ask if he could extend access as far as Robertsbridge itself ' to the general advantage' given the high cost of transport by road. They added that the recent improvements in the roads – in which Sir Whistler had been involved as a Turnpike trustee – made

HASTINGS MUSEUM

The Abbey from the west by Francis Grose, 1761/62

this all the more desirable, and that the expense would be repaid by the increase of business for his own barges.[10]

Whistler inititially retained most of the land and property he inherited from his father, which was now concentrated in three main areas. The first, centred on Battle, included land at Salehurst, Mountfield, Ewhurst and Bodiam; the second was in and around Bexhill and Hastings, while the third was some way to the north-west around East Grinstead. After he ceased to sit in Parliament for that town, however, Whistler began in 1761 gradually to dispose of properties there, as they had now served their purpose and were in any case distant from the main Webster estate and more difficult to administer.

On 30 January 1760 Whistler's mother, the Dowager Lady Jane Webster, died and was buried on 8 February in Battle parish church. In her will she left £500 to her younger son Godfrey, and a similar sum to two of her daughters, Jane and Elizabeth, but only £100 to her other daughter Abigail. She had married a wealthy baronet, Edmund Thomas, who was also a Member of Parliament. Whistler, as the eldest son, was due to receive the remainder of the estate amounting to the substantial sum of £68,000. But Abigail refused her meagre legacy, and went to court arguing that her mother had no right to overturn what she asserted had been the intention of her great-grandfather, Henry Whistler, to divide his estate in roughly equal portions. She asked that the will be set aside as unequal, illusory and fraudulent. This war between the Webster siblings involved high stakes, and proved to be a very protracted affair. Although Sir Whistler's legal advisers assured him that there was not the least fear that he would lose, it was not until 1770 that the Court of Chancery decided in his favour. The ten-year-long wait must have weighed heavily on him.[11]

A late marriage

Perhaps emboldened by this decision, on 20 November 1766, Whistler at the age of 58 married Martha, the daughter of Dr Nairn, the Dean of Battle who was twenty-one years younger than him. They had thirteen years together at the Abbey, of which unfortunately little record has survived. There were no children, and Whistler's health began to fail, though he survived until 22 September 1779 when he died at the Abbey aged 71. He was buried in the parish church on 7 October.

In his will, Whistler left the Abbey to his widow for her lifetime. It was a well-meaning decision but one that was to have unforseen and seriously detrimental consequences both for later members of the family, and for the Abbey itself. A tough

ENGLISH HERITAGE

Lady Martha Webster as a young woman

and determined Scot, his widow lived on for another thirty-one years and firmly resisted all attempts to dislodge her as the fabric crumbled around her. No doubt it was this part of his legacy which was to weigh heavily in the negative judgments later passed on Sir Whistler's tenure of the Abbey. It was a final, and posthumous, misfortune for a man whose life had initially promised so much.[12]

The 3rd Baronet

After his death, the baronetcy passed briefly to Whistler's younger brother Godfrey. Born in 1718, when his parents were still living at Copt Hall in Essex, he later moved with them to Sussex after their purchase of Battle Abbey. There he was educated privately – as were the sons of other gentry – with a Mr Bear, the vicar of Shermanbury, north of Henfield in West Sussex. In 1737, at the age of eighteen, he went to Oriel College Oxford where he was admitted as a 'Commensalis', a student who enjoyed special privileges including eating at the Fellows' table.[13]

He may still have been an undergraduate there when he nearly lost his sight in the gunpowder accident at the Abbey in December 1741 recorded earlier (see pp.21-22) A few years later, in November 1748, he married Elizabeth, daughter of John Gilbert Cooper of Lockington in Derbyshire – an interesting link with the area from which the Websters originated. They then went to live at Crofton, a few miles south-east of Wakefield, in Yorkshire. A visit they paid to the Abbey early in their married life in November 1751 is briefly recorded in a letter from Elizabeth Worge to her father John Collier:[14]

> 'Mr Godfrey Webster, his Lady, and Child were come to the Abbey. Since which the Child has had a Violent fevour and was given over by the Doctor but has happily recovered to the great Joy of the Family who were under great afflicken – Mrs Webster is a good pretty woman – Very Gay and Merry and about my Size as to height.'

The child in question must have been their first, Godfrey born in 1749. Five other children followed, who grew up at Nelmes, the original Webster country seat, which their father inherited after the death of Sir Thomas Webster in 1751. Like other members of the family, he also had a house in London, in Newman Street, Marylebone.

In September 1779 he inherited the baronetcy on the death of his elder brother, but Sir Godfrey survived only another six months, and died in March 1780 still in his early sixties. In his will made two months after his assumption of the title, he left his widow £1,000 a year, £6,000 in trust for the marriage of his daughter Elizabeth, and £1,000 for each of his younger sons. The bulk of the estate, together with the title, then passed to his eldest son, another Godfrey.[15]

4

AN UNFORTUNATE RAKE

The fourth Webster baronet has the melancholy distinction of being the best known, but also one of the most unfortunate of his line. His was a turbulent, and ultimately tragic, life brought about by a combination of circumstances in which his abrasive character played a major part. The easy affluence of his early life meant that he rapidly became an idle spendthrift. When subsequently he took action to shore up the family's finances, his life was ruined by a single decision which proved to be a catastrophic mistake. It was another, and striking, example of the Websters' capacity for self-inflicted misfortune.

Sir Godfrey was baptised on 14 December 1749 at Crofton in Yorkshire where his parents had their country seat, but two years later his father inherited Nelmes in Essex, and it was probably there that he spent most of his early years. The family also had a house in town, and in his late teens London became the centre of his professional and – above all – his social life. He entered Lincoln's Inn in 1768 when he was eighteen and was called to the Bar in 1773 but the reputation he established was not there but in the salons and gaming houses of the capital. The wealth to which he had access offered temptations which he was unable to resist. He became a notorious rake and one of the most reckless gamblers of his day. He was also known for his uncertain and harsh temperament and bouts of violent and ill-controlled temper when he seemed at times to verge on insanity. His nickname 'Sir Wedfrey Gobster' reflects his unpopularity even among the other young aristocratic profligates whose company he kept.[1]

Like many others in his group, he was accustomed to spend time in the country as well as in town, and in spite of the fraught nature of the occasion when he was taken to Battle Abbey by his parents before he was two he later became a frequent visitor there. In 1777 for instance he is recorded at the age of twenty-seven as showing two distinguished visitors round it, Dr William Burrell the antiquarian and the artist Francis Grose. He subsequently breakfasted with them, and arranged to meet them at Winchelsea where he was found 'fully occupied in drawing the fine monuments.'[2]

The following year his involvement in Sussex was strengthened when he took a commission as a Captain with the Sussex militia. This was at a time when the country, confronted by the revolt of the American colonies and embroiled in a war with both France and Spain, was threatened with invasion. Godfrey Webster served with the militia throughout the period of hostilities, which ended with a truce in January 1783, and subsequently maintained his commission during the next conflict with France which arose as a result of the French revolution, becoming a major in 1793.

Inherited problems

In the meantime his father's death in 1780 meant that at the age of thirty-one he inherited the bulk of the Webster lands, including the Battle Abbey estate. This was an important turning point in his life. Up to that time he had been able to live without family responsibilities or much regard for the future. This was no longer the case. He was now the senior member of the family, entrusted with the welfare of its members and the administration of its estates, including the care and maintenance of Battle Abbey.

This was a heavy and frustrating burden to assume. The deaths in rapid succession of two Webster baronets had serious consequences for their successor. Sir Godfrey was faced not only with substantial financial commitments which they had made to their widows and other children, but also the inconvenience of the longevity of his aunt, Dame Martha Webster. She was still in occupation of the Abbey, and made clear her

ENGLISH HERITAGE

Dame Martha, in old age by Ozias Humphrey

determination to exercise her right to remain there for the rest of her life. So, having inherited the title, the fourth baronet was not only saddled with heavy financial obligations imposed on him by his predecessors but deprived of the family home in which he had hoped to live.

At first Sir Godfrey does not appear to have made any significant changes to his lifestyle. He became, said a contemporary, immensely popular in the county – 'perhaps partly on account of his liberality and extravagance.' But this 'combined with his gambling propensity, greatly helped to dissipate the large sum of ready money to which he had succeeded.' The failure of a bank in which he had invested added to his financial problems. So to maintain his lifestyle Sir Godfrey was obliged to continue the policy of progressively selling off outlying parts of the family's estates, which included Nelmes in 1781, and land and properties at East Grinstead. This was a process which was to continue throughout the rest of his lifetime[3]

The management of the Webster estates was entrusted to the capable hands of stewards, John Furner during the first four years of his ownership (1780-1784) – who was paid £50 a year – and James Inskipp for the remaining sixteen (1784-1800). His basic salary remained the same but he also enjoyed free fuel for his kitchen fire and 'bark from timber felled for repairs' which he estimated were worth an extra £100 a year. When in 1792 Inskipp complained about the cost of entertaining visitors on estate business Sir Godfrey immediately put £20 on his annual salary and also made him an allowance for a horse of £16 p.a.[4]

During this period there was a steady rental income of over £2,000 a year, and a substantial additional revenue from the sale of timber and underwood which on occasion brought in another £4,000 over the year. More modest sums were raised from the sale of cereals and hops. The stewards carried out a wide range of functions, including the collection of rents, the payment of bills and taxes – sometimes also the debts of Sir Godfrey – as well as the organisation of work and labour on the estate. In addition they reported to him, during his frequent and prolonged absences, on a variety of topics. ('Your hops are thriving and will be a middle crop.' wrote Inskipp on 27 August 1796. 'Your wheat is not so good as I could wish but the oats and peas and potatoes are very good and great crops').

While Webster was abroad, Inskipp also kept him in touch with the political scene at home during the turbulent years of the French Revolution. One of his most difficult tasks was to act as a buffer between Sir Godfrey and the Dowager Lady Martha. Their relations were always strained. In January 1796, for instance, she objected to his plan to plant a holly hedge and firs by a particular wall: she wanted it to remain as it was. On this occasion, it appears, Sir Godfrey insisted and Inskipp was instructed to 'forward the whole as fast as possible.' But, as we shall see, he was not always the winner in their constant conflicts.

In Parliament, but silent

While others looked after the estate, Sir Godfrey like previous members of the family, plunged into politics. Continuing in their tradition of Whig opposition, he became a prominent member of the reform movement in Sussex, introducing a petition for parliamentary reform at a meeting in Lewes on 18 January 1783. Subsequently, he became a supporter of Charles James Fox, who had substantial local support including backing by members of the Pelham family who had previously supported the Tory government of Lord North. It took several attempts, however, for Webster to get into Parliament. He tried unsuccessfully for a seat at Hastings in 1784, and the following year stood at Seaford, supported by Baron Pelham of Stanmer Park who was trying to wrest control of the seat from the Treasury. He and a colleague were defeated, but the election was declared void, and although Webster again lost at the re-run in March 1786, this time he was seated after a successful petition.[5]

At Westminster he duly supported the Whig opposition, but apparently never spoke during the four years he was there as Member for Seaford, and made no mark in the House. And although he stood again with the support of Pelham at the next election in 1790, the family temporarily lost control of the seat which was won by a Treasury candidate. Once again there was a petition against the result, which was partially successful, but his sponsor failed to honour a promise to give preference to Webster. Instead the seat went to another candidate. In spite of a renewed commitment by Pelham to find him another either at Seaford or elsewhere, Webster came to the conclusion that there was not 'any prospect of advantage from the present state of politics' and decided to devote himself to other pursuits.

A fateful marriage

Chief among those at that time was the very young wife he had married four years earlier. Sir Godfrey was in urgent need of shoring up the family's finances, and he had turned to what appeared to be the best available option – to which those in his position frequently had recourse – of marrying into money.

His bride was Elizabeth Vassall, the daughter and sole heiress of Richard Vassall whose family had acquired in the 17th century extensive estates in the West Indies as well as property in New England. The family was very wealthy, and as an only child Elizabeth had already at the age of eight become a lady of means. Not suprisingly, she soon attracted suitors and when Webster wrote to her parents formally asking for her hand, he acknowledged that they 'wld not be v. ready to part with Her.' They must have been aware of his reputation, but nevertheless and perhaps surprisingly, they gave their assent in spite of the huge age gap between them. Sir Godfrey was thirty-eight, she only fifteen.[6]

No doubt Webster, like many men before and after, thought he could handle this, and that he would be gaining in a single stroke both a compliant wife and great riches. It seemed to be a sure bet, and was heralded as one of the major events of the season:[7]

> 'We are going to have a great many marriages this Spring; it is pairing time and therefore not very extraordinary. Lord Fairford is going to be married to Miss Sandys; Lord Malden to a rich East India widow; and Sir Godfrey Webster to a West India heiress.'

The wedding took place on 26 June 1786. Because she was still a minor, a special licence from the Archbishop of Canterbury was needed. Three days earlier, a marriage settlement was agreed under which the usual provisions were made to ensure the succession to the Webster estate of the eldest male child, as well as £10,000 for each other child of the marriage, and for Elizabeth a jointure of £1,000 on the death of her husband, as well as £300 annually for 'pin money'.[8]

Decay at the Abbey

The new couple quickly made it clear that they had their eyes on Battle Abbey, though it was still occupied by its life-tenant, the Dowager Dame Martha

Webster. By then considerable parts of the former abbot's residence as well as other buildings were suffering from neglect. A watercolour drawing of the Dorter (then believed to be of the former Refectory) by Hieronymous Grimm during his visit in 1783 shows its walls covered in ivy and other vegetation hanging down from gaping holes in its roof.

Another contemporary observer, the Honorable John Byng (later the fifth Viscount Torrington), who visited it five years later in August 1788 commented on the general state of neglect and – like others before him – also criticized some of the changes made to the fabric by the Websters. The Abbey, he wrote, had a 'grand approach' by 'a noble gateway' but this showed 'a sad want of taste as in the centre are two mean modern sash windows with white shutters'. The interior was all in ruins, as was the adjoining almonry (then called the armoury). His account went on:[9]

> 'The abbey commands pleasing views but there is no care, no taste, no cleanliness! All the habitable part of the building is meanly and modernly glazed; the stables are under old arches, and above them is a prodigious grand hall in shameful rubbish, with a ruinous modern roof, falling down; and the sooner that happens the better.'

The visitor and his companion were shown around by one of Lady Webster's servants, 'a forward ignorant fellow who talked the old folly about Queen Elizabeth's apartments' but who briefly showed them the hall and one old chamber, as well as 'yet a greater curiosity the family butler, Mr Ingall, 103 years of age who had been a post-boy in Queen Anne's reign; and now, frequently, in a passion, gives warning and threatens to quit his place. He was very deaf, else I would have spoken to him, but we both bowed to him, and his age bowed him to us!'

Continuing the visit, Byng reported: 'The southern side of the building is in fine ruins, and in fine dirty neglect too! The two remaining towers are of great height and beauty. The walls from, and betwixt them, have not long been pulled down. Our guide said 'That Sir Godfrey Webster longs to succeed the old lady that he may entirely pull it all down', and then there will be an end of Battle Abbey!!!'

Although, to judge from visual evidence provided by Grimm, the condition of Battle Abbey was not very different from that of some other gentry properties in Sussex, Sir Godfrey may have been encouraged to think of pulling it down by the example of his near neighbour, Mr Hare Naylor, who in 1777 had completely gutted the interior of Herstmonceux Castle. At all events, Sir Godfrey did nothing to arrest its decay, and in at least one instance sought to profit from it. Rather than repair the roof of the Court house which had collapsed as a result of the great storm of September 1764 he removed what remained and used the materials for his own purposes. The Dowager Lady Martha successfully sued him for that and was awarded £105 in damages, subject to a determination of how much, if anything, should be used for repairing the roof. It appears, however, that Sir Godfrey died before the final adjudication.[10]

It was not only Sir Godfrey who was frustrated at not being able to take possession of the Abbey. His young wife was furious that they were obliged to live in a smaller (though still substantial) rented house, Rose Green, in Battle rather than in the Abbey itself. The new Lady Webster was hardly more than a child-bride, but soon showed her considerable mettle when confronted with this disagreeable situation. She began to send across to the Abbey in the mornings to

NICK WHISTLER

ISAAC INGALL

This portrait is from a miniature commissioned by Sir Godfrey Webster in 1795 'as a memorial of this venerable man' who was then reputedly aged 113 and had been in the service of the Webster family for near ninety years. But in later life, as John Byng reported (see previous page) his relations with the family, and particularly Dame Martha, were rather stormy.

According to one account, she visited him in his room in one of the Gateway towers when he was 110 years old, and told him that she thought he might keep it cleaner – 'whereupon he said "If your Ladyship considers that I do not give satisfaction, I will find another place", and he walked off to Hastings with that intention, but was brought back, and ended his days at the Abbey'. He died on 2 April 1798, when it was claimed - almost certainly with some exaggeration - that he was 120 years old.

Dorter Roof by S H Grimm, 1783

enquire 'If the old hag was dead'. Then she resorted to stronger tactics 'devising ghostly apparitions, rattling of chains and other eerie noises' calculated to scare Dame Martha:[11]

> 'Horrible groans and noises echoed through the building and gather in a weird circle round the Dowager's bedroom; chains rattled along the gallery, furniture was thrown about; and goblin voices seemed to speak at her very elbow.'

But her intended victim was more than equal to her wiles:

> 'The stout-hearted Scotchwoman refused to be frightened. She used to listen with perfect unconcern, and then, turning round to the invisible dramatis personae, say quietly, 'Come, that will do. I hear you well enough, and I know well enough what you want. But I tell you, once for all, I won't go.'

According to another account, she was also more wily than Elizabeth and her allies:

> 'On one occasion, a dozen or more people were introduced into the Abbey after dark and distributed about the house. At a given time each commenced a kind of drumming noise in turn increasing in intensity. After the din had gone on for some time, and no notice was taken, the jokers came out of their hiding places only to find that Lady Webster had left the house with

her servants and taken the keys with her. There they had to remain till morning!'

On another occasion a crowd of panic-stricken country people invaded the Abbey with their carts and horses saying that they were fleeing from French invaders. 'They were in reality led by friends of Elizabeth, many of them in disguise. The old lady gave them as much food and drink as they wanted, and sent them away to tell the French that she would treat them in like fashion when they came, and that there she would be found until the day of her death.'[12]

Off on the Grand Tour

In the face of such determined resistance, Webster's young bride grew more and more miserable, especially as he was frequently absent. Battle became, as she later wrote 'that detested spot where I had languished in solitude and discontent the best years of my life.' Having done her duty and provided her husband with an heir – another Godfrey, born in 1789 – and the following year given birth again, to a second son who only survived briefly, she began to agitate to get away to the Continent. That was where so many of their aristocratic friends were accustomed to travel around, to visit the sights on the Grand Tour, absorb the culture, seek amorous and other adventures, and enjoy themselves, especially in the warm embrace of the Mediterranean. For the young Lady Webster this was a far more agreeable prospect, in every way, than being confined in Battle.

Although Webster himself much preferred to stay in England, once he had failed to regain his seat in Parliament he gave in to his wife's entreaties, and they set off in June 1791. Lady Webster kept a journal for both this and subsequent continental visits up to 1796 and this remains the prime source for an account of their marriage. It is a very one-sided picture. Sir Godfrey is mentioned only rarely, and always as a source of irritation and complaint. But it is abundantly clear from her own account as well of that of others that he had at least as much, if not more, to complain about in her own behaviour. It was during this period that she made the transition from a young and innocent girl to a highly-attractive, flirtatious and assertive young woman well versed in the ways of the sophisticated and licentious world of the 18th century upper class. It was a transition which spelled trouble for both of them as well as their marriage.

Paris, the Palais Royal

As the mother of one of the young men who paid court to Lady Webster observed, having met her early on in their travels: 'I have seen Lady Webster, she was a very pretty, innocent-looking woman, but I saw her in bad Company, with bad Connections – I mean bad for domestic Happiness – and her Husband never near her, and I then fear'd they would not long continue happy.' It was an acute and prescient judgment.[13]

The Websters went first to Paris, the habitual first stop for those on the Grand Tour. At that time it had a special fascination. France was in revolutionary turmoil. During their stay in the capital Louis XVI and Marie Antoinette tried to escape from their virtual imprisonment there. On the night of 20 June 1791 they fled in secret, the queen dressed as a Russian and the king as her valet. But they were caught at Varennes, a village close to the Swiss border, and ignominiously brought back to Paris. There the National Constituent Assembly was in session: Lady Webster attended a number of its debates, and heard Robespierre speak.

The party then moved off to Switzerland, where they were joined in Lausanne by the Hon Thomas Pelham, the eldest son of Webster's political patron. He was to play a significant part in the coming drama. Already on the eve of a visit to the glaciers at Chamonix, Maria Holroyd, daughter of Lord and Lady Sheffield reported that:[14]

'It will be a true Party of Pleasure, in other words, the most unpleasant thing in the world. The Party consists of Sir G. and Lady Webster, Severy and us. Sir G. is more cross than you can imagine, in short, he has just discovered that he is married, and that Mr P. has a great regard for his Lady.'

She added that Elizabeth Webster's behaviour was also a source of irritation:[15]

'If anyone ever offends you so grievously that you do not recollect any punishment bad enough for them, only wish them on a party of pleasure with Lady Webster! The ceremony began with irresolution in the extreme whether they should or should not go! How and which way they should go? And everything that was proposed she decidedly determined on a contrary scheme, and as regularly altered her mind in a few hours.'

A relationship under stress

Already at this stage serious tensions between Webster and his wife were clearly evident. Sir Godfrey (whom she later described as 'a pompous coxcomb') was no doubt rather relieved to be summoned back to London by his patron Baron Pelham to deal with the outcome of the Seaford constituency petition. His wife, for her part, was both angry – and relieved. As she set off from Switzerland after a stay of three months in late September for the south of France she recorded in her Journal 'I was left alone at twenty years old in a foreign country without a relation or any real friend, yet some of the least miserable, I might add, the most happy hours of my life were passed there.[16]

By then she had also come to the conclusion that if her husband was to rejoin her, there was safety only in numbers. 'As I had experienced such very cruel usage from the unequal and oft times frantic temper of the man to whom I had the calamity to be united, it was the wish of my mother, Lady Pelham, Ly. Shelburne, and those I most respected, that I should never venture myself in a journey alone with him.'[17]

Later that year the Websters were nevertheless reunited at Nice, where according to the misleading report of Thomas Pelham – who in the meantime had established an amorous relationship with Lady Webster – they were 'established very much to their satisfaction' in November. They spent the winter there and in the Spring they were joined by a raffish group of itinerant aristocrats including Georgiana, Duchess of Devonshire, Lady Elizabeth Foster – both accompanied by their illegitimate offspring – and Lord and Lady Duncannon, another unhappy couple. While Webster slipped away for a while to spend time back in England, his wife (who had been joined by their three-year old son Godfrey) quickly made friends with the ladies, Elizabeth Foster reporting to her father on 8 April 1792 that they saw a great deal of her and liked her very much: 'She is clever, good humoured, and very original.' Sir Godfrey, she added, was expected 'very soon.'

On 6 May the Websters left Nice and headed north to Turin, and thence to Verona, Milan, and on towards Germany. On the way they encountered a violent thunderstorm at Pizzighetonne where Elizabeth, who by then was pregnant again, had another of her tantrums. 'I stopped and notwithstanding abuse and threats I was resolved to stay and not risk my life and my child's with hot horses near a deep river during a heavy storm.'[18]

The bickering pair reached Dresden on 20 July where further trials of a different nature awaited them. There they met up with 'a numerous society of English', including Lord Henry Spenser, second son of the 3rd Duke of Marlborough. 'He was very witty and possessed a superabundant stock of irony' wrote Lady Webster. 'In short, he became ardently in love with me, and he was the first man who ever produced the slightest emotion in my heart.' Their passion for each other was such that one evening at court Prince Antony mistook them for husband and wife. Complimenting Lord Henry on her beauty he added 'I see by your admiration and love for her you are worthy to possess her.' Lady Webster blushed, her embarrassment 'too painful to bear'.

The relationship nevertheless continued when in early August the Websters moved to Vienna, and from there she made an excursion with Spenser to Budapest. They were only separated towards the end of September, when the Websters returned to Italy, making their way south to Naples where they arrived in mid October for a stay which lasted until late May the following year.[19]

By then, rumours were rife about the Websters – rumours which Thomas Pelham was anxious to dispel when, having caught up with them again, he wrote in reassuring terms to Lord Sheffield on 18 December 1792:[20]

> *'I found the Websters most delightfully lodged [...] both looking remarkably well, in very good spirits and what gave me most pleasure was to see the*

easy and pleasant manner towards each other with which they seem to live,
and which we have not only seen very different but I believe have greatly
lamented; and I think I can venture to assure you that there is not the
slightest Idea existing with either of them of verifying the unpleasant reports
of their separation which I found very generally believed in different places
I have been in. He complained at times of his being out of England but the
next minute he proposes plans for staying longer abroad and seems to enjoy
the Continent in his way as much [as] any man I ever saw.'

The news which Webster received from his steward James Inskipp early in
1793 was also on the whole reassuring:[21]

'You ask me of politics. England hath been a little noisy about Revolution
and Equality. But meetings have been called in the principal towns to
take the sense of the people. One was called for the Rape of Hastings and
held in the Court Hall of Battle on 24 December last and well attended
by a very great number of the principle (sic) inhabitants who showed the
greatest loyalty to the King and Constitution by Loyal Toast, Ring Bell and
Firing Guns, Burning Tom Paine and his Rights of Man. The Methodists are
numerous but I do not see but that all are well attached to the King and
Constitution.'

By then Lady Webster was in the final stages of her latest pregnancy: on 10
February 1793 she gave birth to another son, Henry. She was soon up and about
again, visiting Paestum, Salerno and other local sights, dining with the King of
Naples, and taking a full part in the hectic social life of the itinerant English
community. But in February revolutionary France had declared war on Britain
and this created some uncertainty. 'The Websters are not decided about their
summer plans', wrote Thomas Pelham on 6 April, 'Sir Godfrey I believe will at
any rate come to England for a short time, for he does not seem disposed to resign
his Commission which I think he might very honourably having served the whole
of the last War and having now two Children.'[22]

Early in May Inskipp reported that a meeting had been held in Lewes to
raise money 'for the Internal defence of the Kingdom'. It had been well attended
and had raised £5,000, a sum shortly expected to be doubled. He added: 'There
are to be several camps in Sussex. One I understand will be at Fairlight. Many
people in England are afraid of an invasion but in Sussex we do not entertain such

NPG 15364

Elizabeth Vassall (Lady Webster) by Robert Fagan, 1793

notions. If an invasion should take place on our coast which I have no notion of shall be glad if your Honour [would] next say what I should do or where send your Booke'.

A slow return to England

Later in the month the Websters left Naples on a leisurely journey northwards: Sir Godfrey was perhaps at that stage not wholly decided about a return visit to England. But there was no doubting Lady Elizabeth's sadness at their departure:

> 'I quitted those scenes of tranquil pleasure and harmless gratification with unfeigned regret. But ah me! What can please or cheer one who has no hope of happiness in life. Solitude and amusement from external objects is all I hope for: home is an abyss of misery! I am but as a zero in society, attached to none, belonging to none I esteem.'

In Rome, their next stop, her misery increased as Sir Godfrey grew bored with sightseeing. 'In all the collections much escapes me,' she complained, 'as I am always accompanied by one whose impetuosity compels me to hasten from objects I would willingly contemplate, and whose violence of temper throws me into agitations that prevent me distinguishing the objects when they are before me.'[23]

Soon they were off again, going north through Assisi, Perugia, Cortona and Arezzo to reach Florence on 20 June. There her misery deepened still further as, a week later, she reflected on her wedding anniversary: 'This fatal day seven years ago gave me, in the bloom and innocence of fifteen, to the power of a being who has made me execrate my life since it has belonged to him. Despair often prompts me to a remedy within my reach.' Another piece of bad news however prompted her into action. Learning that her father was seriously ill, she decided that she as well as Webster himself had to return to England. But she was determined that it would be only a short visit: as a guarantee of that she left their two children in Florence 'comfortable, established in a good house with proper attendants.'[24]

As they set off in July she complained in her Journal: 'How much I detest the prospect of a residence in England, even though it be but for a few weeks; country, climate, manners, everything is odious to me.' She was carried backwards over the Alps, her eyes fixed on her beloved Italy. Because of the continuing conflict she and Webster had to skirt around France, and go through Germany

Rome, the Vatican Museum

and the Low Countries. Even so on their way to Ostend they passed within two miles of the French lines, and also saw the opposing British army encampment. They arrived at Dover on 1 September 1793.[25]

Once back in England, the Websters went their separate ways. His wife complained bitterly about 'this odious country' where she was determined to spend as little time as possible. She paid duty calls to her father at Windsor (where she found him 'better, tolerably cheerful, but very weak') and Battle where she lodged at the Deanery but 'felt restless until I got out of the place for I felt half afraid of being detained by some accident.' But elsewhere there were consolations. One was at Stanmer Park. 'Mr Pelham was there, and of course enchanted at seeing me' she wrote. But of that encounter she told only part of the story: the rest became increasingly visible in the course of the following nine months. The other pleasurable time was during a visit to Brighthelmstone where she met up with the Prince Regent who 'chose to *combler* me with every attention and civility.'[26]

Webster in the meantime had been about his own business, which included a visit to London in November, when he obtained the King's permission to leave the country in spite of his commitment with the Sussex militia. Reunited with his wife, they set off together on 2 December from Dover. But they encountered very rough seas and it took them an horrendous fifteen hours to sail across to Ostend. It was a turbulent start to what was to be an equally turbulent – and decisive – period back on the Continent.[27]

SUSSEX ARCH SOC

Stanmer Park

A Florentine liaison

The Websters first made their way to Florence where they arrived on 8 January 1794. Having been reunited with their two children, they plunged once more into the usual intensive social round. It was while they were there that Sir Godfrey was painted by Louis Gauffier, a fashionable expatriate French artist who specialised in portraiture. Webster is shown in a confident pose in a neo-classical setting against a Florentine background: the painting (*see colour section*) gives no hint of his turbulent private life.[28]

Lady Webster, for her part, was soon the object of much amorous attention, some of it from unexpected quarters like Sir Gilbert Elliot, an old acquaintance, who one night tried to seduce her in a carriage from which she 'was compelled to get out…to avoid his pressing importunities.' But it was two twenty-year olds who arrived together in Florence in mid January who succeeded in capturing her affections, first Lord Granville Leveson-Gower, and then – more decisively and permanently – Henry Richard Fox, the 3rd Lord Holland, nephew of Charles James Fox.

Her first impressions of the latter, recorded in her Journal for Sunday 19 January, were only moderately complimentary: 'Lord Holland is not in the least handsome; he has, on the contrary, many personal defects, but his pleasingness of manner and liveliness of conversation get over them speedily.' According to one account, his first impression of her was even less flattering: he was reported to have declared that he was unable to understand how anyone could think her attractive. The story, as recounted by Lady Cleveland – a rather hostile source – goes on:

> 'Unhappily, this adverse opinion came to her ears. It was more than she could bear; for in addition to irritable vanity that could not rest under the smart of defeat, she had in the highest degree the strong will that delights in conflict, and welcomes any obstacle it may find to overcome. She resolved that, cost what it might, Lord Holland should be brought to her feet, the captive of beauty he had held so cheap.'[29]

Whether or not this was the case, Lady Webster certainly became far more enthusiastic about Holland after seeing more of him on a day's expedition: 'Lord Holland quite delightful: his gaiety beyond anything I ever knew; full of good stories. He seems bent upon politics, and, with his eagerness, I think it is lucky he is out of the way of saying foolish, violent things.'[30]

They met up again in Naples where the Websters arrived on 26 February, to find Lady Bessborough and Lady Spenser, together with 'a numerous band of young Englishmen from college; gambling and gallantry filled up the evenings and mornings.' At this stage Lady Webster still preferred his companion while becoming steadily more attracted to Holland:[31]

> 'My favourite, Ld G Leveson-Gower, used often to come to me in the evening, as I sat at home a good deal on account of my grossesse and disliking the card parties. His companion, Lord Holland, is quite delightful. He is eager without rashness, well bred without ceremony. His disposition and turn of mind are rekoned very like his uncle, Mr Fox; his manner resembles his maternal uncle, Colonel Fitzpatrick. His politics are warm in favour of the Revolution, and his principles are strongly tinctured with democracy – Though so zealous, he is totally without any party rancour; in short, he is exactly what all must like, esteem, and admire.'

From this it was but a short step to deciding to switch her affections to Lord Holland, Lady Bessborough having in the meantime conveniently fallen in

Henry Fox, 3rd Baron Holland by Louis Gauffier, 1796

love with Leveson-Gower. Both appear to have 'pulled off their covert affairs with great aplomb.'[32]

Their pleasures in the Spring of 1794, however, were somewhat overshadowed by the rapid advance of the French revolutionary armies across Belgium and fears of invasion at home. Many of the menfolk with commissions decided to return to England, and as a first step there was a general movement to Rome in mid April. 'Almost the whole of our Neapolitan set was there', wrote Lady Webster, including her favourite, who was in a party she took to Tivoli: 'Lord Holland's delightful spirits cheered us so much that we called him sal volatile and used to spare him to one another for half an hour to enliven when either were melancholy.' From there the Websters moved on to Florence, where Holland and companions also called in for a few days on their way to Venice – he assuring her (according to Lady Webster's account) that 'he came merely to make me a visit.'

On 12 June Lady Webster gave birth to a girl, Harriet. Somehow she managed to conceal from her husband that it was Henry Pelham's child rather than his. ('Thank God that all has ended so well in Florence,' Pelham wrote from Stanmer).[33]

The following months 'were passed very pleasantly', and in September Lady Webster resumed her perambulations, going on her own to Lucca, Massa and on to Pisa 'where to my surprise I found Lords Wycombe and Holland.' They reappeared again in November after she had returned to Florence where she moved house as the winter cold descended. In the meantime Webster had taken himself off for a visit lasting some months to Turin and Milan. He returned around Christmas, but they can hardly have had a festive time together. By now Sir Godfrey must have realised that his wife was in thrall to Lord Holland, and that she was determined to stay in Florence.

Early in 1795 the situation became even more complicated when Lady Webster's father died. This meant that she now became a very wealthy woman in her own right, with an income of upwards of £10,000 a year. ('Detestable Gold', she wrote, 'What a lure for a villain, and too dearly have I become the victim to him.') Webster himself was also due to benefit by obtaining a West Indian estate worth over £7,000 a year – but on condition that he changed his name to Vassall. This combination of circumstances clearly posed a huge dilemma for Sir Godfrey, and it is not surprising that he decided that he had to return home to seek advice. 'In May', Lady Webster wrote in her journal, 'Sir GW set off to England, as he affixed an importance to his own appearance there that I own I did not strive to convince him against.'[34]

Webster's departure left the lovers free to enjoy each other's company without inhibitions. Florence remained their base but they travelled around Tuscany and the Ligurian coast as Lady Webster, once again, grew large with child. Whose it was is not clear: she gave birth to a boy in October 1795 but he died soon afterwards. She quickly recovered and passed 'a delightful winter' in Florence: 'the evenings I generally spent at home. Lord Holland used to read aloud.'[35]

Webster's dilemma

Back in England, Webster no doubt consulted both friends and his legal advisers about what he should do. One thing was clear. If he was to secure his Vassall inheritance he had to observe the terms of his father-in-law's will and change his name, however repugnant this was, given the circumstances. This he did by obtaining a royal licence on 3 October 1795 by which he dropped the name of Webster and became Sir Godfrey Vassall. A financial imperative at this stage took precedence over the social embarrassment of apparently identifying himself even more closely with the family of his serially-unfaithful wife. There was an escape route, but it was not one to be undertaken lightly. A divorce could be obtained only through the annulment of the marriage by an Act of Parliament, and would also entail an action in the civil courts to obtain financial reparation. Both would generate much unwelcome publicity and ridicule. It is not surprising that Sir Godfrey hesitated to embark on such a course. It was apparently only in July 1796 that he began seriously to consider it.[36]

In the meantime, in Florence, Lady Webster had problems of her own. In February she had discovered that she was pregnant again – and this time there could be no doubt that the father was Holland rather than her husband. She realised that this would lead to divorce proceedings, and the loss of custody of her children:[37]

'My situation was such that a final separation with Sir Godfrey Webster was

Lord Holland by F Y Fabre

inevitable as soon as I returned to England. The certainty of losing all my children was agonising, and I resolved to keep one in my possession, and I chose the one who from her age and sex required the tenderness of a mother'.

She decided on a desperate stratagem. On the way to Modena with her children, she called out to her servants that her daughter Harriet, then two years old, had been taken ill and was developing measles – which was then prevalent in Italy. The fear was confirmed when the nursery maid saw a glimpse of red spots on the child's arm. Lady Webster ordered her servants to take her two sons on to Modena, leaving her behind with Harriet. Later she reported that Harriet had died, and that the coffin had been dispatched to the British consul at Leghorn for burial. In due course this news was conveyed to her husband in England.

The truth, however, was that Harriet had been spirited away, disguised as a boy, to Hamburg accompanied by a maid with instructions to await further orders. In the meantime Lady Webster had transformed her guitar case into a small coffin, filling it with rocks and pillows, together with a mask which customarily indicated the death of a diseased child – and sent it with a footman to Leghorn, where it was duly and officially interred. Harriet was later taken to England where she was secretly housed.

This extraordinary and daring charade was entirely successful, and for several years Sir Godfrey remained in ignorance of the truth. But when Lady Webster herself returned to England, accompanied by Lord Holland, in June 1796 there was no disguising her adultery and pregnancy. It must have been an extremely stormy encounter when they met in London at Sir Godfrey's house in Albermarle Street. Shortly afterwards she and Lord Holland rented part of Brompton Park House – where the Victoria and Albert Museum now stands – and it was there, in November, that she gave birth to Holland's child, a son who was christened Charles Richard Fox.

The end game

That same month Sir Godfrey was able to re-enter Parliament, this time as a Member for Wareham in Dorset, thanks again to his patron Pelham. But this was a small consolation in the midst of his personal preoccupations. Although the birth must have strengthened the pressure on him to proceed with the divorce, he nevertheless remained uncertain about his best course of action. He showed, it is said:[38]

> 'An indecision of purpose, almost verging at times upon insanity. At one moment he would refuse to go on with the proceedings, at the next he would state that he still adored Lady Webster, and for her sake would only be too ready to expedite matters, and would not even sue for damages. At another he wished to fight a duel with Lord Holland, not for running away with his wife, but because he had offered to buy a picture of her, by Romney, which belonged to Sir Godfrey.'

In the event, it was Sir Godfrey's harsher intentions which prevailed. His claim for damages was heard in the Civil Court at the end of February 1797 when he was awarded the whole of his wife's fortune, about £10,000 a year, during their joint lives leaving her only an allowance of £800 each year. Sir Godfrey also obtained £6,000 from Lord Holland (the jury having reduced his original demand for £10,000) and was made sole guardian of his children. The judge described the settlement as iniquitous, but the errant wife had to submit to it, and it was subsequently incorporated in the formal annulment of the marriage by an Act of Parliament which was passed on 4 July that year. The former Lady Webster later recorded in her Journal: 'On the fifth I signed a deed by which I made over my whole fortune to Sir G W for our joint lives, for the insignificant sum of £800. Every mean device, every paltry chicane that could extort money from us was had recourse to.'[39]

It was indeed an extraordinarily punitive settlement, even taking into account the outrageous behaviour of Lady Webster and the prevailing (if hypocritical) attitudes to women who flouted their marriage vows. But for his former wife it meant liberation and the start of a new life. Two days after Parliament granted the divorce she married Lord Holland and although she was for a time shunned by polite London society, and was never received at Court, she later established a major role for herself as a political hostess. At Holland House she presided regally over the most important salon of the day, frequented not only by the most prominent Whig politicians, but also foreign ministers and their ambassadors, as well as luminaries from other walks of life. There she was in her element, until the death of her husband in 1840.[40]

By contrast, Sir Godfrey, for all his financial gain, emerged as the real loser from his wrecked marriage. He promptly dropped his Vassall surname in favour of his original name, but nothing could erase the unwelcome and hostile publicity that his own behaviour had attracted and the indignity of having become a notorious cuckold. He made little mark in Parliament, and though he still had a considerable income from his Sussex estates, his aunt was still in occupation of Battle Abbey, which made it impossible for him either to sell or occupy it. He sought refuge at the gaming tables – but this only increased his miseries as he met with 'ill luck at play.' His immediate financial situation became so acute that in May he wrote to his Steward James Inskipp asking for a loan. The latter replied in sympathetic but embarrassed terms:[41]

> 'As to the money your Honour wishes to have it is out of my power to lend.
> The money I have is principally in my family's hands, your Honour knows I
> have eight children and all of them of age.'

A son 'gone to sea' had cost him £150; one of his daughters was thought to be about to marry. He hoped he might be able to find £400-500 by Christmas. He added: 'I will raise all the money I can from the estate…and will do everything I can by savings to get your Honour out of difficulties.'

But it was too late. By this time Sir Godfrey was suffering not only from debt but also the advanced symptoms of syphilis. His mental state deteriorated; he suffered from bouts of acute depression; and twice tried to end his life by taking laudanum. He finally succeeded in doing so when he shot himself at his home in Tenterden Street, off Hanover Square on 3 June 1800. The verdict at the inquest was 'lunacy'. He was only 52.[42]

5

A DISASTROUS PROFLIGATE

The first fleeting but sharp impression we have of the young man who became the fifth Webster baronet is provided by an entry in the journal of Lady Holland, his mother, for 12 April 1799. Godfrey, her eldest son, was then nine years old and at Harrow. She wrote:[1]

> *'I had the happiness of seeing Webby three times, but by stealth, at my mother's; she insisted upon my hazarding an interview. He was very affectionate. He seems clever but is not handsome. He is cold in his disposition, and taught by his father to be a boaster'.*

The reservations expressed by his mother about his character and the influence on him of his father were to prove all too accurate. They boded ill for the future of the family's fortunes.

The turbulence surrounding his early years undoubtedly played their part in shaping his personality and outlook. Born on 6 October 1789, and baptised the following day at St Marylebone in London, he was less than two years old when his parents set off with him on their continental travels and not yet three when in July 1793 they left him and his baby brother Henry with Dr John Stewart in Florence for six months while they returned to England. Neither parent had much time to devote to their increasing number of children as their estrangement – and Lady Webster's infatuation with Lord Holland – grew. Godfrey was seven when divorce followed in July 1797, and ten when his father shot himself. Both must have been deeply traumatic experiences, depriving him of the security of a settled childhood, and increasing his propensity to live for immediate excitement and pleasure.[2]

It is doubtful if either of the guardians appointed to look after him – his grandmother, the Dowager Elizabeth Webster and his aunt, Elizabeth Chaplin – were able to exercise much control over him. He spent two years at Harrow, and in 1806 when he was seventeen went up to St John's Cambridge. But as for so many young men of his background the university at the time was a social rather

Sir Godfrey Webster, 5th Baronet

than intellectual experience. London soon beckoned where he was caught up in the dissolute society of the capital, becoming a drinking companion of Byron whose lifestyle was typical of the group around him. 'I am buried in an abysss of Sensuality', Byron wrote to a friend in February 1808.' 'I have renounced hazard, however, I am given to Harlots, and live in a state of Concubinage.' In April that year he added: 'I form one of a very sad set, consisting of Capt Wallace, Sir Godfrey, Sir B Graham, and other sensual Sinners, we have kept it up, with the most laudable systematic profligacy.'[3]

Among the young women with whom Webster dallied was Caroline Bessborough, only daughter of the 3rd Earl, who later became Lady Caroline Lamb. The affair, described as 'a violent flirtation' prompted Godfrey's mother to intervene and persuade Caroline to break it off. But it later came back to haunt him when early in 1816 she published a fictionalised version of her amorous relationship with Byron and his circle in the novel *Glenarvon*. Webster appeared in this thinly disguised as Buchanan, an arrogant, selfish and cold man, preoccupied with horses and gambling.[4]

Physically Godfrey, like his father, was a tall and good-looking man, but shortly before he came of age in October 1810, one of those who knew him well described him in far from flattering terms:[5]

'One of the greatest blackguards in London. He is young, indeed, well-born and well-looking, but...I never remember to have heard of anybody more generally disliked, or more completely excluded from the pale of good company. He is quite confiscated to habits of low profligacy, and not deemed a sufficiently respectable associate even by the members of the Whig club. At

The Abbey in disrepair: 'a drawing taken on the spot by Miss Augusta Hawkins'

The Abbey from the Park by G Rowe

*the Argyll Street rooms...he acquainted us that for the last fifteen mornings
he had breakfasted punctually at 9 o'clock before going to bed.'*

Like his father, Sir Godfrey had become an inveterate gambler. Typical of
his passion for outrageous bets, and his capacity to lose money on them, is a story
told of a wager at Whites:[6]

*'He noticed two wood-lice crawling along the arm of his armchair;
whereupon he and a friend had a bet of £6,000 as to which one would win.
Sir Godfrey, wishing to hurry his along, pricked it with a pin. This proved
his undoing, as the wood-louse promptly curled itself into a ball, and his
money was gone.'*

Horse-racing was another sport in which he indulged on a considerable
scale. In April 1809, for instance, in a single deal he bought half shares in five
horses – Bacchanal (for £750), Saragossa (£250), Timeloser (£650), Laida (£600)
and Hippomines (£250) – and undertook to pay out another £120 for training
them, and £100 for a jockey to ride them. No doubt he also bet heavily at the
races and it would be surprising if that also did not prove a substantial drain
on his resources. Sailing was another expensive pastime: he commissioned
the building of a luxury yacht, the Scorpion, but was unable to pay for it, and
eventually it had to be sold.[7]

Webster gravitated into the orbit of the Prince of Wales 'an apt school
for learning how to spend money.' It was through this connection that he took
a commission in the 10th Hussars, the Prince Regent's regiment. Although this
was a fashionable pursuit, there was also a more serious side to it as the country
was at war with Napoleonic France . In April 1808 Byron reported that Webster's
army duties had temporarily removed him from the London scene, and later
when he became a Lieutenant in the 14th and 18th Light Dragoons he served with
them for a while in the Peninsular war. In 1812, however, Webster resigned his
commission to devote himself to new and challenging responsibilities.[8]

Renovating the Abbey

When he came of age in October 1810, Webster had become the owner of Battle
Abbey and its associated estates. On Christmas Day that year the death at the age
of eighty-one of his great aunt, the Dowager Lady Martha (widow of Sir Whistler

Webster) at last liberated the Abbey. But it was in a dreadful state. According to Lady Cleveland's account, 'He found it in a most ruinous and dilapidated condition, for during her tenancy of thirty-one years, the old lady had apparently spent little or nothing in repairs'. The roof of the Courthouse, adjoining the Gateway, had fallen in sixteen years before and that of the monks' Dormitory 'though entire, was literally dropping to pieces, while the dwelling house itself admitted the rain in such torrents that during wet weather the Dowager Lady Webster had to proceed along the gallery to her bedroom in pattens.' The area to the side of the house was rough neglected pasture, strewn with great heaps of rubbish. 'There was no flower garden, and the whole place must have presented a forlorn aspect of decay and desolation.'[9]

Greatly to his credit, Sir Godfrey set about its renovation. He loved spending money, and he lavished a fortune on a major refurbishment of the Abbey. He put in a new timber roof to the abbot's hall, clad its lower walls with carved oak wainscotting, added a music gallery and large chimney piece, and filled four of its windows with coloured glass. He also converted a vault under the abbot's great chamber into a drawing room, and created a new large room at the south end of the abbot's hall to replace a two-storied building which was pulled down. In addition he built a new kitchen and scullery, as well as some other rooms and outhouses, and three small rooms and a staircase in the west wing. He also refitted the house from top to bottom. All this cost a great deal of money. According to Lady Cleveland the bill for woodwork alone amounted to £13,000. The subsequent maintenance costs were also very substantial; in the three years between 1819 and 1821, for example, over £2,000 was paid out to two contractors for work in and around the Abbey.[10]

Sir Godfrey set out to embellish the Abbey in other ways. He commissioned a gigantic painting of the Battle of Hastings from a noted artist of the day, Frank W Wilkin, with himself as the model for William the Conqueror shown discovering Harold's body on the battlefield. The artist lived at the Abbey for some months during 1820 while he was working on it, and was subjected to a number of practical jokes by his host. According to Lady Cleveland's account, Wilkin was 'a vain, boastful but exceedingly timid man, and Sir Godfrey's mischievous delight was to put his often-vaunted courage to the proof.' One night a coloured lamp was let down from the roof to the level of his bedroom window.

'The unlucky painter, startled out of his sleep by the sudden glare, fairly lost his wits, and jumping out of bed, snatched up a sword kept by his bedside and rushed wildly about the house, flourishing it round his head.' On another occasion 'Sir Godfrey and his madcap friends masqueraded as highwaymen, waylaid him and stripped him to his shirt.'[11]

Nevertheless, the painting – thirty-one feet long and seventeen feet high – was eventually finished and hung up in the great hall, occupying the whole of the width of the southern wall, blocking out part of the window above. Painted very much in the style of the times, it was later to prove rather an embarrassment to the Websters when they left the Abbey, and to Hastings Corporation to whom they donated it.[12]

Sir Godfrey also commissioned the cabinet maker George Bullock to redecorate and furnish the drawing room, dining room and Great Hall. More controversially, he embellished the Hall with a stuffed black horse which he displayed above the main fireplace. It had been a favourite and much admired regimental charger, which he had ridden on ceremonial occasions – though visitors were solemnly told that it was identical to the animal ridden by the Conqueror at the Battle of Hastings.[13]

Extensive works were also carried out on other buildings and in the grounds of the Abbey, including the creation of a large pond in the park 'on which a number of workmen were employed for a great many months.' Lady Cleveland did not approve of some of the changes Sir Godfrey made, which included the demolition of an old wishing well which had been a place of pilgrimage for young girls in search of a husband. Her main criticism, however, was directed at his 'nefarious design' of converting the Dorter into stables. A new low-pitched slate roof was substituted for the original shingle roof, and the north end banked up with soil to make an entrance for the horses. Providing an access to it involved cutting down large swathes of the avenues of yew trees created by Sir Anthony Browne, as well as making 'a sad havoc' of his garden. The arrangement, however, did not persist for very long. It proved impractical when in about 1818 an entrance carriage-way was constructed from the Gate House to a double porch opening into the great hall. New stables and a coach house were then built.[14]

In the course of these very extensive works, carried out over a number of years, part of the nave of the old Abbey church was uncovered, and with it

HASTINGS MUSEUM

A contemporary view of the interior of the Great Hall by William Brooke, showing the Battle of Hastings painting commissioned by the 5th Baronet

BATTLE ABBEY AND THE WEBSTERS

various relics included a quantity of bones: 'enough,' said an old mason who had been there, 'to fill two sugar barrels, for no one thought anything of 'em in those days.' They were left lying around in a heap, he reported, until they gradually disappeared in the pockets of visitors.[15]

Growing public interest

The number of these visitors increased steadily during the Regency period (1811-1820) and particularly after the end of the Napoleonic wars. Greater affluence had created a much wider public with time and money to travel, take holidays, and visit places of interest. In Sussex, hitherto regarded as an unruly and inhospitable backwater, the discovery of the health-giving properties of sea water and sea bathing had already made Brighton into a fashionable resort before the arrival of the Prince of Wales in 1783 and the conversion of his residence into the exotic Royal Pavilion. Between 1760 and 1821 visitors to the town increased from four hundred to around eleven thousand a year.[16]

No doubt some of the visitors to Brighton also made their way to Battle Abbey, though its appeal was of a different nature. The ruins of the Abbey and the famous battlefield were now in any case of increasing interest in their own right to a much wider public than the handful of antiquarians who had visited them in the early days of the Websters' ownership. There were a number of reasons for this. One was the prevailing Romantic delight in ruins and the sensations and reflections which they evoked. But these particular ruins, and the site on which they stood, were very special. They were a reminder of a decisive moment in the country's history which was viewed, paradoxically, less as a catastrophic defeat than as a turning point in its development as a nation. They spoke to the growing sense of national identity and patriotic pride which had developed during the 18th century, and which had been reinforced during the long years of struggle with the French. Now the wheel had come full circle: the threat of invasion had been repulsed, and the French defeated. Britons could lift up their heads and view the place of Harold's defeat with equanimity, and indeed with satisfaction.

Closely associated with the growth of pride in the nation was not only a greater interest in its history, but also the emergence of the notion of a national

Romantic ruins: The Refectory by James Rouse, 1807.
(The building is now more correctly named the Dorter)

heritage. As a recent study has shown, by the end of the 18th century 'the foundations for the construction of the idea of national heritage – manifested in the history, landscape and buildings of the country – had been laid.' This was largely the work of antiquarians whose interest in ancient artifacts led them to argue both for their preservation and – in the case of important monuments – that they should be regarded as the property of the nation at large. Once their interest in the past had been harnessed to the idea of national identity the objects of their study became more relevant to a much wider public. In this context Battle Abbey occupied a special and indeed unique position.[17]

'Public days' introduced

It was in response to the growing demand to visit the Abbey and its ruins that 'public days' were introduced at some point during the first or second decade of the 19th century. By the middle of the 1820s it was open to visitors each Monday, as attested by a passage in the entry about Battle in Pigot and Co's Commercial Directory for 1826/27:

Visitors in the grounds of the Abbey. A popular print by F Arundale.

'*The town itself is made interesting by the perfect state of the Abbey gatehouse, which has a grand effect; the mutilated state of the remains of the other part of this once extensive and magnificent building presents a rich treat to the antiquary; which, with all the other parts of it, are open every Monday for the inspection of the public.*'

Artists and publishers hastened to meet the needs of this new public. Battle Abbey was included, for instance, in a volume of prints of Sussex by JMW Turner published in 1820, and also in another set of prints issued the same year by Longmans & Co under the title Excursions through Sussex. Both prints and watercolour drawings of the Abbey were produced in ever greater numbers. Its gateway was the most popular theme of an outpouring of visual material which itself stimulated interest in it and no doubt contributed also to increase the flow of visitors.

Before long, Battle had its own publisher to meet the needs of the visiting public. In 1833 Francis William Ticehurst, a member of a long-established and distinguished local family, moved to 76/77 High Street and set up as a printer and publisher. He was to be responsible over the coming years for publishing an early history of Battle in 1841 and the first guide book to the town ten years later, as well as a steady output of prints and other visual material about the Abbey. His long and busy life (1811-1902) also included being Postmaster (in succession to his father), Deputy Superintendant Registrar, and Clerk to the Battle Board of Guardians for forty-four years.[18]

An independent MP

Once he had established himself at the Abbey Sir Godfrey set out to emulate those of his predecessors who had been Members of Parliament. This was still seen as a highly desirable objective for an ambitious country gentleman, in spite of the increasing cost of electioneering, which was to prove ruinously expensive.

Webster had an early slice of luck when John ('Mad Jack') Fuller of Brightling, the sitting Member for the eastern part of Sussex, decided in advance of the 1812 election not to stand again having lost credit after a tempestuous incident in the Commons two years earlier. There was no obvious successor. Grandees like Lord Ashburnham, Lord Sheffield and the Earl of Chichester were uncertain what to do. Fuller himself resisted pressure from the Prime Minister, Lord Liverpool, to support a candidate the premier favoured, as well as a suggestion that he should either stand again or support a nephew's candidature. Instead he gave his support to Webster when he emerged as the front runner. There were long-standing business and sporting connections between the two families and they knew each other well through their shared passion for fox hunting. But Fuller was a Tory, whereas the Websters were traditionally Whigs. It seems that in order to get into Parliament Sir Godfrey put expediency before principle. Standing as a Tory and a supporter of the government, he was elected unopposed.[19]

Several of the grandees had serious doubts about the new Member. The Duke of Richmond wrote on 1 March 1813: 'I always thought Sir Godfrey Webster against us till he wrote to the ministers to say he meant to support. He had better take care what he is about or he has no chance of coming in again for Sussex.' Lord Sheffield was equally critical. Arguing that Webster had 'not a single well wisher or friend in Sussex' he added that he had 'most stupidly squandered between £2,000 and £3,000 on the precious mobbility of Brighton and Lewes.' Although he had comported himself well so as to attain 'a degree of character' he feared that 'episodes in his career will not be creditable to us.'[20]

These reservations proved amply justified. Webster immediately upset his supporters by voting with their opponents. Like his predecessors, he proved to be a sturdily independent Member who sometimes supported the government, and sometimes opposed it. In 1815, for instance, he voted with ministers to approve the Prince Regent's extraordinary expenditure (a gesture which was rewarded by the latter's support for Webster's desire to command the Sussex militia) but two years later opposed the suspension of habeas corpus, describing it in his only reported speech on 27 June 1817 as unnecessary and a prelude to arbitrary government.

Not surprisingly, in view of his wayward and erratic behaviour, his former sponsors sought to unseat him at the next general election in 1818. Webster stood down and another Tory candidate was chosen. But Webster was persuaded by a friend of liberal opinions to change his mind, and his opponent then withdrew. Sir Godfrey took his seat with the Opposition and continued to vote against the repressive measures being applied by Lord Liverpool's government in the face of mounting social and political unrest. He also increasingly identified himself with the cause of electoral reform. In terms of his parliamentary career he was living on borrowed time, and his opponents were to have their revenge at the next general election in 1820.

A mistress and a child

In the meantime, Sir Godfrey's private life had been equally reckless. One embarrassing problem arose from a liaison with a young Hastings woman, Ann Robinson, who became pregnant with his child. He continued the relationship even when he was about to acquire a wife, and in a manner that threatened disaster. Incapable of dealing with the crisis, he sought the help of his brother Henry when they dined together on a July evening in 1814 at Long's Hotel in Bond Street. 'You know, Henry' he said 'how soon I am to be married, but Ann is at the Abbey and I don't know what to do about her.' His brother rose to the challenge immediately. 'If you will give me full powers to inform her of what your intentions are regarding a provision for her I promise you that within four and twenty hours neither she nor anything belonging to her shall be in the Abbey.' He went down to Battle early the following morning, saw Ann, and told her about Sir Godfrey's impending marriage and of his intention to make her an allowance of £200 per year for the rest of her life. A few hours later she quit the Abbey.[21]

In early August that year, two weeks before Sir Godfrey's impending marriage, Ann Robinson gave birth to a son, baptised Henry. The following month Webster undertook to pay for the maintenance and education of his illegitimate son until he reached the age of twenty-one, and charged his trustees with making a further payment of £5,000 when he attained his majority. But if the immediate problems were dealt with, this was far from the end of the affair, the commitment to a life-long allowance for Ann Robinson becoming the subject of a prolonged case in Chancery after Sir Godfrey's death (see pp.85-86).[22]

Sir Henry Webster

The brother who saved him from the immediate consequences of his folly went on to a distinguished military career. Henry Vassall Webster, who was four years younger, had been briefly to the University of Edinburgh thanks to the intercession of his mother who continued to be concerned about him long after her divorce from his father. He had been sent there in the hope that ' the society and air of Edinburgh may communicate to him some taste for information and reading.' His tutor in mathematics was reported to be well pleased with him, but he stayed only over the winter of 1809/10 and then entered the army.[23]

He was an immensely tall man, a towering six foot-eight. *(see colour section)* After serving in the Peninsular war, where a fellow officer described him as 'a very fine young fellow', he found himself three years later at the centre of events immediately preceding the battle of Waterloo. As a Lieutenant in the 9th Light Dragoons he was aide-de-camp to the Prince of Orange. On the morning of 15 June 1815 he was with him and the Prince of Saxe Weimar who were defending the farmhouse at Quatre Bras south of Waterloo. During the day the Prince left for Brussels to consult with Wellington, telling Webster to bring him any urgent despatches.

At ten o'clock that night news arrived that the forward troops of the

The gardens by J P Neale, 1824

Prussian ally advancing from the east had been driven back at Ligny. Webster was ordered to leave without a moment's delay with a despatch for the Prince. He was told 'A horse ready-saddled awaits you at the door and another has been sent on, half an hour ago, to a half-way house to help you on the faster. Gallop every yard! You will find your chief at the Duchess of Richmond's ball. Stand on no ceremony; but insist on seeing the Prince at once.'

Webster's account continues, 'I was in my saddle without a second's delay; and thanks to a fine moon and two capital horses, had covered the ten miles I had to go within the hour!' He arrived at his destination in Brussels to find it 'all ablaze with light; and such was the crowd of carriages that I could not well make my way through them on horseback; so I abandoned my steed to the first man I could get hold of, and made my way to the porter's lodge.' Having delivered his message, Webster hid in a recess 'for fear of being asked awkward questions.'

The news was indeed serious. Not only had the French repulsed the Prussian forces, they had also pushed up the road leading north directly towards Brussels. At first Wellington was reluctant to believe it, having earlier expected their main thrust to come further to the west. But the dispatch finally convinced him about Napoleon's real intentions, and he told the Prince that he should miss supper and return immediately to his headquarters. 'Webster!' he called out. 'Four horses instantly to the Prince of Orange's carriage for Waterloo!'

Wellington then went into supper, characteristically maintaining an air of great calm. But having announced after a decent interval that he was retiring, he revealed his true state of mind to the Duke of Richmond. 'Napoleon has humbugged me, by God! He has gained twenty-four hours' march on me'. He promptly gave orders for his army to concentrate on Quatre Bras before finally going to bed late into the night.[24]

As Wellington suspected, the bloody but indecisive engagement which was fought there was only the prelude to the more critical battle, and narrow victory, at Waterloo. Henry Webster managed to survive the bloodshed, and his astonishing feat of horsemanship (which it is said others have tried to emulate, but without success) was rewarded with several Dutch honours including being made a Knight of the Order of William of the Netherlands. He rose to the rank of colonel in 1831, and was knighted in 1843. Four years later however, on 19 April 1847, like his father (and perhaps as a result of the same medical condition) he committed suicide in a fit of insanity. He was buried in a lead coffin in the family crypt in Battle.[25]

Sir Godfrey's marriage and family

The marriage which Henry helped to save took place on 22 August 1814 at St George's, Hanover Square when Sir Godfrey, then aged twenty-four, married Charlotte, daughter of Robert Adamson of Westmeath in Ireland, and 25 Hill Street, Berkeley Square. She was twenty-two years old and a well-known beauty. For once, a Webster baronet married for looks – and maybe love – rather than money. Perhaps his father's disastrous experience had something to do with this; at all events the marriage settlement gave Sir Godfrey little financial gain. His wife brought with her a modest portion £250 a year and the prospect of £5,000 after her father's death against substantial future commitments of £20,000 for each child of the marriage and a £1,000 per annum jointure for his widow.[26]

The couple proceeded to have six children in quick succession in the seven years between July 1815 and September 1822. Exceptionally, all of them were

Lady Charlotte Webster by Scott-Pierre-Nicholas Legrand

boys. The arrival of the first was celebrated by the planting of three cedar trees at the Abbey (one for the father, one for the mother, and the other for their infant heir), but the next two died in successive years when only five and six months old so the arrival in July 1819 of a fourth son – destined to become the seventh baronet – was the occasion for much rejoicing. The Duke of Sussex agreed to become one of his godparents, came to the christening, and stayed for a visit to the Abbey. As the Earl of Albermarle, another of the guests reported, the townsfolk also joined in the celebrations: 'At the bottom of the hill on which the town of Battle is built the horses were taken out of the carriage and were dragged up to the Abbey by the population amidst cries of "The Queen and Sussex for ever!" We were welcomed within the gates of the Abbey by a military band and a salvo of artillery.'

Webster was a lavish host: the occasion was one of exceptional magnificence. Those present 'often afterwards spoke of this entertainment, and especially of the number of keepers – I think there were twelve – who, dressed for the occasion in green and gold, attended HRH when he went out shooting.'[27]

This event, the high point of the fifth baronet's tenure of the Abbey, may well be the origin of the reputation the Websters acquired for lavish entertainment, and of a story related to that which could refer to an earlier moment in Sir Godfrey's tenure of the Abbey. On one occasion, it is said, at a great banquet an enormous pie was placed upon the board and when it was opened a beautiful naked woman emerged.[28]

Gambling and debt

Although this may be an apocryphal story, Sir Godfrey certainly enjoyed pranks, games, and gambling for high stakes:[29]

> 'He was passionately fond of play, no form of gambling came amiss to him, and it is said that he would go into a rickyard and offer a friend an even thousand as to which of them should pull the longest straw out of the rick. Then, if he lost, the land-agent would be sent into his woods to cut down the requisite amount of timber. It need scarcely be added that he was, in all other respects, a profuse and extravagant man, and lived expensively.'

The accumulation of debts had long been a way of life for Webster, accompanied by a constant and sustained barrage of court cases as his creditors sought to recover the sums he owed them. Between 1811 and 1820 there were only two years when new cases were not introduced against him, and he was often confronted by multiple demands in several courts at the same time – before the Court of Common Pleas, the King's Bench and the Exchequer. A new avalanche of cases began in 1826 and continued with few intermissions until his death. His creditors were numerous, the sums usually considerable and in some cases huge. In 1814, for instance, he was being sued for a total of £46,000 in three cases (one brought by the Earl of Yarmouth) before the Court of Common Pleas, while facing demands by another three creditors in the King's Bench for a further £5,000.[30]

Soon after Sir Godfrey became the owner of the Abbey his steward James Inskipp began to experience cash flow problems. On 24 February 1803, for instance, he reported 'I do as little repair as I can. I am now paying the tradesmens' bills due Christmas last', and in late May he had to go and see the redoubtable Dowager Lady Webster to ask if she could wait until Christmas for the £500 she was due. Not surprisingly, he was firmly rebuffed. 'Her answer,' he reported, 'was that she could not wait but must have it at Midsummer.'[31]

Initially, however, Sir Godfrey was able to profit from the knock-on effects of the rapid rise in food prices during the twenty or so years from the beginning of the French Revolution to the defeat of Napoleon. Land values almost doubled, and rents rose significantly. Webster took steps to increase revenue from the estate, commissioning a survey of it in 1811 which led to the negotiation of higher rents, and another with a similar purpose in 1824 when good farms were fetching between sixteen and forty shillings an acre.[32]

A variety of other measures was also taken in an attempt to meet Sir Godfrey's voracious appetite for income. More of the estate was sold off, including Fairlight in 1811-12, and Ewhurst and Robertsbridge between 1816 and 1822. A brisk trade in the sale of advowsons (the right to nominate to vacant church benefices) was developed, a number of creditors agreed to accept annuities in settlement of their claims, and his brother and sister were persuaded to relinquish the annuities granted under their parents' marriage settlement.[33]

In spite of these and other measures, a day of reckoning loomed soon after the great celebration. To avoid his clamorous creditors Webster took the route frequented by many others in his situation, and fled across the Channel. In November 1820 parts of the estate were put in the hands of trustees. Messrs Adamson Cullen and Capron were given authority to reduce his load of debt by selling, leasing and mortgaging land and property, by enfranchising copyholds, and cutting timber. Even the great old oaks on the estate – 'the finest in this part of the country' wrote Lady Cleveland – came under the axe. Only one growing below the south terrace of the Abbey was spared after intercession by Lady Webster, 'but being left isolated and stripped of all its surroundings, it was blown down in the first heavy gale that followed.' Out of the proceeds the trustees were to make an allowance of £1,500 to Sir Godfrey, a meagre sum for a man of his position and spendthrift habits.[34]

In the course of 1821 the decision was taken to embark on even more drastic action. For the first time since the Websters had owned the Abbey it was rented out. It was put on the market, fully furnished, at a proposed rental of £800 a year. The first tenant, Henry Alexander, the father of Lady Stratford de Redcliffe, moved in at the end of the year, having agreed to keep on the head gamekeeper, gardener and housemaid. He was followed in April 1825 by Sir George Prescott of Theobalds Park, Hertfordshire who took it on a five-year lease at a rent of £472 10s a year. But he stayed for barely two years, being followed by a Colonel Fitzgibbon in August 1827. He seems to have been a rather peppery man, berating Mr Cox who was acting for the trustees ('Mr Fitzgibbon was so exceeding angry at my not going to Battle today that to appease him I consented to leave here tomorrow'), and getting into an argument about shooting rights over the estate. Very soon, at the end of the year, he was asked to terminate his lease, and was replaced early in 1828 by Thomas Barton, a wine merchant from Bordeaux.[35]

Shortage of money had forced Sir Godfrey not only to abandon his ancestral home, but also his parliamentary seat when a general election loomed in 1820. He initially offered himself for re-election for his county seat, and was greeted rapturously at Hastings where he was very popular. He and his wife were met by a large crowd which insisted on taking the horses out of his carriage and drawing it in triumphal procession through the streets. But his support for parliamentary reform had enraged the county grandees who were determined to keep him out. Webster withdrew in the face of their opposition and financial

The Particulars

OF

BATTEL ABBEY, IN SUSSEX.

THE GOTHIC LODGE,

At the Entrance from the TOWN of BATTEL,

WITH THE PORTER'S APARTMENTS, AND OTHER BUILDINGS.

THE MANSION,

CALLED

BATTEL ABBEY,

Contains Eleven Bed Rooms for Servants, Five other Rooms and Chambers appropriated to the Nursery.

Nine principal elegantly-finished Bed Chambers and Two Dressing Rooms on the Principal Floor, together with an Anti-Room, spacious Drawing Room and Boudoir which opens to the Gallery at the East End of the Great Hall.

A Principal Staircase, and a Secondary Staircase descends to the Ground Floor, on which are a handsome Eating Room, Breakfast Room, Libraries, The Great Hall, Entrance Halls from both Fronts, and a beautiful arched Saloon.

Domestic Offices of every Description for the Accommodation of a large Family.

A detached enclosed Stable Yard with Three Stables containing Eleven Stalls, with Harness Rooms and a Coach House for Four Carriages.

A Dairy and Ice House, Cow House, and Dog Kennels, Lawns, Pleasure Grounds, and Kitchen Gardens, walled round, containing altogether

A.	R.	P.
10 :	1 :	20.

The HOUSE is well supplied with very excellent Water, and will be let with its elegant FURNITURE, subject to the Tenant's paying all Taxes, at - - - - - £.800 *per Annum.*

	A.	R.	P.		
And if with the Upper Park, containing - - - - - - -	44	1	30	— 875	*per Annum.*
And if with both Parks, then more, - - - - - - - - -	43	2	25	— 945	,, ,,
And if with the George Meadow, then more, - - - - -	10	3	13	— 975	,, ,,
And if with the Seven Cow Fields } then more, - - - adjoining the Park, - - - - - - - }	42	2	38	— 1060	,, ,,

The Lands will be shewn by Mr. SPRAY, the Bailiff.

There is a Farm contiguous to the Abbey Lands, containing 130 Acres, which is now in Hand, and which the Tenant of the Abbey may also have, at a Nett Rent of Two Hundred Pounds per Annum.

The Abbey to let, 1821

clout. In a message to the electors, he wrote:[36]

> ' *I candidly confess that the pecuniary array brought against me far exceeds that which I can alone oppose to it, the sum of money which the coalition is prepared to expend for the openly avowed purpose of fulfilling the threat held out at the last election, namely, that Sir Godfrey Webster should never sit again for Sussex, is so enormous, that even a successful issue would prevent my serving you with that independence which the distinguished situation of your Representative demands.'*

This was the end of Sir Godfrey's parliamentary career, though not of his political ambitions. Having returned to the country in 1823 (and revoked the powers given to his trustees) he promptly tried to get back to Westminster, this time for the Chichester borough seat when it was vacated by the sitting Member, William Huskisson, on his appointment as President of the Board of Trade. Webster tempted supporters with a bowl of punch, constantly refilled and open to all comers, which he kept at the Old Swan Inn in East Street. But the election, held in June, proved to be a doubly unfortunate experience. Having made up his mind to stand only at a late stage Webster took even his friends by surprise, found the odds stacked against him and after a few days campaigning gave up the contest, leaving the field clear for his opponent, who was duly elected by 292 votes to Webster's 194.[37]

An alleged abduction

But that was not the end of the affair. The following month Sir Godfrey was accused of seducing and abducting a young girl he had met in the course of the election. On Saturday 26 July, the Brighton Herald – quoting The Times – reported that 'a very respectable-looking woman', Mrs Anne Saunders, of Chichester had appeared at Bow Street magistrates court 'in a state of great mental distress' to allege that her only daughter Maria, aged nineteen, had become 'violently attached' to the baronet who had contested the seat – 'a circumstance which she would have reason to lament as long as she lived'. Maria had corresponded with him, and then on 23 June had suddenly left Chichester for London with a friend, Mary Gilbert. She was subsequently reported by Miss Gilbert to be 'living in London under the protection of Sir ---', but she did not

WSRO FULLER PD 478

Chichester in the early 19th century: East Street Market by J F Gilbert

know where. Mrs Saunders said she had been advised to apply to the Court for assistance in locating her daughter. Told by the magistrate that he could not help, she left in tears.

The following day Sir Godfrey appeared before the Court to deny the allegation. He said that he did not even know the girl by sight, accused her of being a prostitute, and his political opponents of circulating the story. But that evening Webster returned to the Court accompanied by his solicitor and Mrs Saunders – who he said 'was prepared to admit that she had no other ground than mere surmise for charging him.' He offered a reward of ten guineas to any officer who could find and return her daughter. The presiding magistrate now offered the assistance of the Court, without charge. 'God Bless you Sir!' exclaimed Mrs Saunders, bursting into tears.

On 9 August it was reported that Maria had written to her mother to explain her motive for leaving home, and had subsequently been seen by her mother in the presence of an officer of the Court. A considerable mystery still surrounded the affair, however, not least because one of Sir Godfrey's friends had taken the letter and 'Mrs Saunders could not afterwards regain possession of it, although she parted with it under a promise that it should be returned to her.' A week later the Herald said that Sir Godfrey had left for the Continent, though promising to return. But the matter had clearly troubled his political friends who later that month were said to be 'staggered' by his mysterious absence. The correspondent added that 'a considerable secession will most certainly take place if something satisfactory does not shortly proceed from Sir Godfrey.'[38]

When Webster finally turned up on Monday 15 August at the Anchor in Chichester to meet members of his political club, the Pink and Purple, nearly two hundred people were present. 'Violent applause' greeted his assertion of innocence, but when Sir Godfrey was challenged to produce the documents which he said would completely exculpate him from the charge of having seduced Maria Saunders and having seen her in London, he told the meeting that 'he had left Portsmouth in such a hurry as to leave his writing desk behind.' He added that as he intended to bring those responsible for the allegations before the King's Bench 'he might, by thus reading his evidence put them too much on their guard.'[39]

Webster duly consulted Counsel about the possibility of a libel action but was dissuaded from proceeding. It was no doubt wise, but in spite of the accusations made about his conduct, Sir Godfrey retained enough political support to have two more attempts in 1826 and 1831 at the Chichester seat, as well as a seeking to regain his former county seat. During these years he aligned himself with the radicals who sought electoral and parliamentary reform and in 1830 he took a leading part in the activities of the Hastings Reform Association. Opponents in Chichester accused him of seeking re-election as a way of fending off his creditors, but if that was part of his motivation it was another unsuccessful gamble. He failed in each of his attempts, at a further heavy cost to his increasingly empty pocket. His electoral expenses in 1826, for instance, were nearly £2,000.[40]

Webster's political and financial woes were not the only problems he faced. His philandering, forced-flight from his creditors, and temporary loss of the family home at the Abbey had, not surprisingly, put a great strain on his marriage. In 1824 his wife was left stranded in Switzerland. On 21 December that year she wrote from Bern to her father about her financial problems, saying that she was no longer able to draw on money 'as before.' Two years later relations with Sir Godfrey had deteriorated to the point at which a formal separation was negotiated. She and a group of trustees (including her father) were given custody of the four surviving children, and Sir Godfrey was obliged to convey various properties to the trustees to provide income for Lady Charlotte and to meet interest charges on a number of mortgages. Something of the relationship must, however, have survived. In 1830 the Websters were reunited at the Abbey, and after a gap of nine years, conceived a seventh child – another son – before they separated again in 1832. Born on 5 November 1831 and appropriately named Guy, he was to be a source of much concern to the family: a real chip off the old block.[41]

Defending law and order

In Battle Webster found himself in the midst of another difficult situation. It was a time of serious and widespread agricultural poverty and discontent. The Weald was a tinder box of unrest, and Battle one of the centres of the agitation. Political demonstrations took place there after a visit by William Cobbett in mid October 1830, and the following month there was a series of attacks on local overseers of the poor, including the licensee of the George Inn, where a fire was started on 3 November. Troops were sent in to quell the unrest, but their arrival triggered more protest meetings both in the town and surrounding villages.

In spite of his debts, absences and troubled private life, Webster was still a magistrate, with authority to quell riots and disperse mobs. His relatively liberal political views did not extend to condoning threats to law and order, of which he became a forceful and physical defender. He had twenty men arrested in Battle, and was involved in a fracas at Herstmonceux when a demonstration against local tithes attracted a large assembly which occupied Gardner Street. The Riot Act was read and Sir Godfrey went into the Woolpack Inn to order all present to quit and return home. A confrontation followed. 'The magistrate, as all the world then knew, was no craven, threatened, and soon proceeded to force, when in a moment, he found himself sprawling on the floor of the room.' Webster had to be rescued from further violence by a police officer and three soldiers.[42]

Times were rough, and Webster was prepared to be rough too. As a fellow magistrate later recalled:[43]

> 'During the riots of 1830 I dined with the late Sir Godfrey Webster (of Battle Abbey) at Lewes. At a not very early hour the Baronet prepared for his

homeward journey. "You are a marked man", said I. "How are you armed?
Barkers?" "Pooh," said he, pulling from the right and left pockets of his great
coat a couple of hog knives. "These are the tools – they never miss fire."'

Final years

These events did not, however, diminish Sir Godfrey's enthusiasm for
parliamentary reform. On receiving news of the passage of the Reform Bill in
June 1832 he drove down in his private carriage, flying two royal standards, to
Hastings where he 'was received with ringing of bells, firing of cannon, lighting
of tar barrels, feasting and general rejoicing.'[44]

But this was the last occasion when he had good news to celebrate. In the
few remaining years of his life Sir Godfrey sank deeper and deeper into debt.
The estate melted away as more and more properties and land, as well as timber,
were sold off. In 1828, Bodiam Castle, which had been neglected by successive
Websters and was in a very ruined state, was put on the market and sold to Jack
Fuller of Brightling for three thousand guineas. In 1835 a third of the Vassall
estates in Jamaica was also sold.[45]

In that year the same fate befell even the muniments of the Battle Abbey
estate. Their sale was a true measure of the desperate straits in which its besieged
owner now found himself. The collection of documents was huge, consisting
of ninety-seven folio volumes: the catalogue itself filled two hundred and
twenty pages. It was a priceless source for future historians of a major national
monument, but it was sold for a mere £300 to a London bookseller, Thomas
Thorpe, who resold it for £1,200. It was a very bad bargain for Sir Godfrey,
and for the nation at large. Fortunately the collection was kept together as it
passed through various hands, and eventually to its present resting place at the
Henry E Huntington Library in Los Angeles.[46]

While Lady Charlotte remained at the Abbey – and was visited in 1834
by the future Queen Victoria three years before her accession to the throne
– Webster himself lived an itinerant life, hounded by creditors, sailing back and
forth between ports on the south coast and the Channel Islands. It was more
than flesh and blood could stand. Eventually, in failing health, he came to rest in
November 1835 at the York Hotel in Albermarle Street. He died there on 17 July

1836, at the age of forty-six. His remains were taken back to Battle Abbey and placed in the great hall 'which was lighted up and some hundreds of persons were permitted to pass through.' His funeral took place in the parish church on 23 July, attended by 'upwards of sixty of the most respectable inhabitants of Battle and the neighbourhood', his body being placed in the family vault there.[47]

When Webster died his personal effects and the portion of his remaining annuity then due were insufficient to meet his hotel bill, the charge for medical attention and his servants' wages. His other outstanding debts, amounting to some £3,000, included more than £600 due to his solicitor R H Capron, nearly £300 for his saddler, over £200 for a firm of coachmakers, £198 for his tailor, £103 for his bankers, and £46 2s 9d for his Oxford Street tobacconist. Far worse, by the time of his death he had disposed of the whole of his personal estates, all his landed estates not under settlement, and his life interest in the estates in Sussex – with which he had bought an annuity. So involved were his circumstances that shortly before his death he had sold part of that to an insurance company to provide some much-needed ready cash. In the course of his short lifetime the fifth Webster baronet's profligacy had made huge inroads into the remaining family resources. It was a miserable and depleted legacy that he left to his successors.[48]

6

TWO WEBSTERS AT SEA: A RELUCTANT SALE

The consequences of Sir Godfrey's financial and personal recklessness were very serious for the Webster family. He died both intestate and insolvent, leaving his widow and successors to grapple with a mountain of problems, some of which proved insurmountable. For the Abbey it meant another prolonged period of neglect before a reluctant decision to sell.

The days when the next generation of Websters could simply live off income from the estate were now over. Sir Godfrey's two eldest sons had already seen the need to earn their own living. Neither of them, however had the entrepreneurial zest of those who had founded the fortunes of the family. The young Websters preferred service in the Navy. This was now the most powerful in the world, and offered the prospect of travel to far places, adventure – and eventually a pension. Both joined at an early age as midshipmen, and Godfrey who became the 6th Baronet on the death of his father decided to remain in the service. His mother, Dame Charlotte,

Godfrey, the 6th Baronet as a young boy

stayed on at the Abbey. But she was left with only a modest income, her jointure of £1,000 a year together with some 'rents and profits.'[1]

In July 1838 she was confronted with a demand from Ann Robinson for payment not only of the arrears of her annuity, but also its continuation for the rest of her life – as had been promised by the 5th Baronet, her former lover. The dispute over these demands led to a prolonged Chancery court case. Dame Charlotte was obliged to provide extremely detailed information about the family's finances, and to appear on several occasions before the Master of the Court to answer questions about them. Initially she and her lawyers argued that the bond entered into by her late husband was 'void against all persons save the said Sir Godfrey Webster dead', that in any case he had 'left no personal estate whatsoever', and the rest of the estate was already earmarked for other payments (like her own jointure and those for her younger children). But eventually, in 1857 – after almost twenty years of argument – her son Augustus, who by then had inherited the baronetcy, came to the rescue with a meagre compromise. In return for the surrender of the original bond, Ann Robinson accepted a greatly reduced annual payment of £52 (rather than the original £200) together with expenses of £100. It was a sorry end to a miserable affair.[2]

The 6th Baronet, Sir Godfrey

In the meantime the new baronet had continued his career in the Navy. This had changed little since the days of Nelson. But though still reliant on sail, it commanded the oceans of the world and was deployed by successive prime ministers to assert British influence. Palmerston used it, for instance, in the pursuit of his policy of shoring up Turkey when its army was attacked and defeated by the Egyptian Mehemet Ali. Against opposition in the cabinet he employed it to help recapture Acre (now Akko) in 1840. HMS Thunderer, in which Sir Godfrey was serving as a Lieutenant, took part in the operation.[3]

He was still serving in the Mediterranean in November 1849 –'I suspect safe for another year,' wrote his anxious mother– but throughout this period the financial problems of the family continued to demand his attention. In 1843, for instance, he had been obliged, when his younger brothers started pressing for their portions as they came of age, to raise a mortgage of £2,000 on parts of his Sussex estates and on an insurance policy on his own life. At the same time Thomas Gamelen of Furnivals Inn, Middlesex, was appointed receiver for the whole estate, with authority to apply the proceeds to meet its liabilities which totalled no less than £48,700. More properties were leased, and timber sold but such was the pressure on the family's finances that his mother sought a tenant for the Abbey, even writing in 1849 to Louis Philippe, the French king deposed in the 1848 revolution who had fled to Sussex. He, however, showed no interest. Three years earlier, in 1846, she had been equally – and more woundingly – rebuffed when she had invited Louis Napoleon, nephew of the former Emperor, and a future French Emperor himself, to dinner. He eventually replied with a brief apology, saying he had mislaid her address.[4]

During these years one of the few developments with positive financial possibilities for the estate, as for the area as a whole, was the proposal of the South Eastern Railway (SER) to construct a line south from Tunbridge Wells passing through Battle on its way to Hastings. For a long time there was considerable uncertainty about whether this would be realised, in part because of the fierce rivalry between the SER and the London, Brighton and South Coast company. Its proposed route was also contested, not least by Lady Webster, as it ran virtually through the middle of the estate, in a north-south direction, and not very far from the Abbey. She was, however, persuaded to drop her objections in return for £5,000 which would be paid within three months of the necessary parliamentary Bill receiving the Royal Assent 'as compensation for the annoyance, discomfort, anxiety, and pecuniary sacrifice to which she as Occupier of Battel Abbey had been, or might be subjected'. The same agreement also provided for a payment to Sir Godfrey (on whose behalf she was authorised to act) for the land required for the railway line itself.

Lady Webster duly received the £5,000, but the agreement was the cause of yet another internal family dispute, this time with her son. In June 1847 he sought Counsel's advice about how far his mother was entitled to this payment, and 'whether she is not liable to account for the whole or a portion of it to Sir Godfrey'. He also wanted to know whether, if the answer was in the affirmative, he personally would be entitled to the money, or if it should be paid into Court for the purposes of the family trust. The replies offered to these questions were far from conclusive, and the two contenders eventually decided to sink their differences and make common cause against the railway company. In 1849 they told the family solicitors that they were both 'extremely dissatisfied' with the agreement and instructed them to seek Counsel's advice on whether they could with propriety annul it. Lady Webster, they said, had acted 'in a very hasty

West view of the entrance to the Abbey by Mary de Humboldt

manner at the eleventh hour', having agreed to compensation at only £100 per acre when 'many properties in the neighbourhood have got £200'. On the other hand, she was determined to hang on to the £5,000 she had already received. It was a rather delicate and weak position from which to argue with the railway company. It is not clear how the negotiations progressed beyond this point, and whether Lady Webster was able to hold on to the money, but Sir Godfrey certainly eventually emerged with a much better deal.[5]

A brief marriage

In July 1851 Sir Godfrey, having left the navy, married at the age of thirty-six. His bride may not have been his first choice, but like several of the Websters he chose a rich heiress. Unlike some of them he opted for a lady of mature years. She was Sarah Joanna, the rather formidable forty-eight year old childless widow of the younger son of the 3rd Earl of Ashburnham. She came from stock familiar to the Webster family. She was the daughter of William Murray of Latium Plantation, Jamaica, and the granddaughter of Samuel Virgin who held vast property and plantations in the same island. Her share of his estate also included negroes and slaves, for whom she was paid £3,491 6s 8d in compensation when they were freed in 1835. Under the marriage settlement concluded on the eve of the wedding, Sarah Joanna – whose personal fortune amounted to £33,473 8s 4d – was to receive annuities from her mother, Elizabeth Murray who was living in Brunswick Terrace in Brighton, amounting to £2,600, while Sir Godfrey was committed only to a modest jointure of £500.[6]

Dame Charlotte then left the Abbey and went to live at Rose Green, which had been rented by the fourth baronet in the early days of his unfortunate marriage, and which she had bought in 1840 for £12,000 with a loan of £4,000 from her son, Sir Godfrey. Before she left, she made what was probably intended as a farewell gesture to local people by throwing open the Abbey and its grounds. On 9 August 1851 the Sussex Express reported:[7]

> 'Inhabitants were again indulged on Sunday last with an invitation from Lady Webster to pass the evening among the ruins and gardens as well as to view the great hall. Numerous parties derived much gratification from this courteous act of her ladyship.'

SUSSEX ARCH SOC

Battle Station in the mid 19th century

Dame Charlotte was no doubt happy at the prospect of much-needed new money for the Webster family – a prospect which received rapid confirmation when Mrs Murray bought from her £827 worth of furniture and fixtures at the Abbey for her daughter. For her part, the new Lady Webster seems to have lost no time in making her mark there. She appropriated the helmet from the tomb of Sir Anthony Browne in Battle church to decorate the fireplace in the great hall, created new flower beds in the grounds, and built a summer house which in practice – to the astonishment of a later owner – was used for her bees.[8]

The Webster family now appeared to be firmly re-established in Battle. In addition to the new baronet there were also his two younger brothers. Augustus, the next in line, had left the Navy too and become a regular member of the local Bench while his younger brother Frederick was the unanimous choice to chair an important meeting of local traders held in February 1853. This was called as a direct result of the arrival of the railway the previous year in January 1852.[9]

Built by the South Eastern Railway, who advertised it rather ambitiously as 'The Direct Continental Route' it provided a service of three passenger trains each weekday (and two on Sundays) in each direction to and from London Bridge, taking about three hours between Battle and the capital. Local traders were as much interested in the commercial opportunities it offered – an early indication of the impact this new means of communication was to have on the town. The proposal put forward at the meeting was to add a fortnightly stock market to the existing market for corn. Frederick Webster backed this enthusiastically. It would, he said, be 'peculiarly advantageous to farmers in Sussex and Kent, especially now that the railroad was open.' The meeting agreed, and Webster was elected to the committee set up to organise the new market.

This new lease of life for the family proved, however, to be very short lived. On 4 May 1853, after less than two years at the Abbey, and only two weeks after being appointed Deputy Lieutenant of the county, Sir Godfrey died. He was only thirty-seven. A week after his 'lamented death' he was buried 'unencumbered by any costly display' in the family vault in Battle parish church. Shops throughout the town closed as a mark of respect, and 'a very large concourse of persons assembled to watch the solemnities.' The coffin was carried by 'men belonging to the Abbey' who wore white smocks. They were accompanied by 'a walking procession of the principal inhabitants.' It was a striking expression of local esteem and sympathy for the unfortunate young baronet and his family. Few can then have thought that the Websters' ownership of it would shortly come to an end.[10]

The 7th Baronet, Sir Augustus

The baronetcy passed to Godfrey's younger brother, Augustus. Born in April 1819 at Portland Place in London – to great rejoicing after the early deaths of two intervening baby brothers – he had also joined the Navy in his mid 'teens as a midshipman. His career in it, which began in 1833, spanned almost twenty years and reflected its world-wide reach. One of his earliest postings, in the 428-ton sloop HMS Racehorse, took him in 1834 on a lengthy voyage from Falmouth via Newfoundland and Nova Scotia to Bermuda, where it had a refit, and then on into the Caribbean. The log kept by Augustus details the many places which the ship then visited as it criss-crossed the region performing a variety of tasks in a complex itinerary which included Jamaica, Columbia, Nicaragua, Grand Cayman, Barbados, Antigua and Martinique. He was a disciplined and precise observer, as well as a competent sketcher, and his pages contain information on a great variety of themes, including the occasional trenchant remark, especially about the persistent heavy rain. ('The only difference being that in the wet season it rains all day, and in the dry about six times a day.')[11]

In a scattered but important part of the empire, whose sugar islands had a virtual monopoly of the home market, flying the flag and being ready to protect British interests was central to the mission. In the summer of 1835 this took the Racehorse to Para (Belem) at the mouth of the Amazon in Brazil, to rescue a colony of British and other merchants who had been caught up in a prolonged struggle between local Indians and the Brazilian authorities. Augustus had little regard for the locals – 'The natives are lazy and indolent to an extreme, their principal occupations being to swing in their hammock, smoke, or play the guitar.' They were also 'proverbial for deceit of all description.' Nevertheless, it was quite dangerous work. As the ship was leaving, expecting a salute from the rebels in the town's fort, they were fired on – though 'as they were not the best marksmen in the world we received no further injury.'

Some five or six years later, after service on the Rainbow, Tribune, and Howe, Webster was in quite a different part of the world, serving as a Lieutenant and Mate on HMS Endymion in the Far East. This was a time when Palmerston claimed 'without any vainglorious boast, that we stand at the head of moral, social and political civilization.' But the so-called opium wars with China in which Webster and the Endymion were involved were fought with a less elevated objective, the opening up of a number of ports to British and other foreign traders. For his part in the operations Webster received the China medal.[12]

In search of gold

In 1849, after periods of service on two other ships as a Lieutenant on HMS Collingwood and HMS Sampson, Augustus Webster took time off from the navy to make a private visit to California. This was the time of the great gold rush, and both he and his mother were tempted by the thought that this might be the place where he could make his fortune. He obtained a post as Master of a passenger-carrying schooner, the Pera, and sailed off to San Francisco.

Family files for this period suggest that some careful research had been done before he set off. One item in them is a press cutting of early March 1849 asserting that 'Sober truth forces on the mind of the reluctant reader the incontrovertible fact that although there is much gold in California, yet it is by no means so abundant as had been represented.' It went on to report that 'all foreigners are warned

ENGLISH HERITAGE

Sir Augustus, the 7th Baronet, in naval uniform

off the lands of the gold region, as trespassers on the property of the United States,' adding that General Smith had been despatched from Washington 'with orders to enforce the laws of the Republic against trespassers.' Subsequently Lady Webster sought advice about the situation from George Bancroft in London. In his reply of 27 March 1849 he told her 'The harbours of California are open to the commercial adventurer[...] your son may safely sail to San Francisco and dispose of his cargo.' He went on however, to warn her that 'land can only be possessed by those who have a title to it,' and that if Augustus stayed in the Navy he could not own land. His only route to that would be to resign his commission and become a citizen of the United States.[13]

In spite of these warnings Augustus set off for California and, after a rather troubled voyage during which crew members and some of the passengers helped themselves to the provisions, arrived there during the summer. In a letter sent from Battle on 7 November by his mother it is clear that she was still tempted by the prospect of gold:[14]

'Thank God it is all right with you so far...We hear by the papers that there continues to be no end of gold in California...People who loved to laugh at the expedition begin to think it may answer, especially since a procession of *twenty-eight wagons with four horses each deposited about £1,000,000 in the Bank.'*

She added that she wished that Frederick had 'plucked up courage to have gone with you.' Sadly, however, it seems that Augustus did not find gold. The records are silent on what happened, but two years later he was back in the country and on 22 July was ordered to report at Portsmouth to join HM steamship Centaur as a Lieutenant. This appears to have been his last posting in the Navy, at a time when sail was beginning to give way in the face of a technological revolution brought about by the introduction of steam power and screw propellers.[15]

Dame Charlotte returns to the Abbey

On the death of his brother in May 1853, and his assumption of the title as the 7th Baronet, Augustus was asked by his mother, Dame Charlotte, what his intentions were about the possibility of her returning to the Abbey – to which she was greatly attached:[16]

> *'I must beg you to let me hear from you what your wishes are about my going there. Only be quite sincere...If you think you can rough it there without me and that being now weaned from the place I had better not go back...'*

She claimed that she had no desire to return, but added that she was 'ready to make the best of it if you desire I should.' Augustus accepted her offer and Dame Charlotte was soon in residence again. The move caused some friction with younger brother Frederick, who had jumped the gun by saying that he was going to set up a bachelor den there ('I doubt from past experience the respectability of his habits.'). He had sent up his furniture to the Abbey, and made it clear that 'evidently he neither expects or wishes for me.'[17]

Dame Charlotte's move also led to a row with the widow of the 6th Baronet, Dame Sarah Joanna Webster, who had moved out of the Abbey on the death of her husband and taken up residence not far away, at Court Lodge, Mountfield between Robertsbridge and Netherfield. The bone of contention was certain fixtures and fittings which she had left at the Abbey. These had originally belonged to Dame Charlotte and although they had been purchased from her she and her son seem to have assumed that they had been left as a present by Sarah Joanna. But the departing widow had certainly not intended this, as she indignantly informed their solicitor:[18]

> 'That I should have volunteered a promise to either of these persons to present Sir Augustus Webster (almost a Stranger to me) with the greater part of my Property would seem so extremely absurd and improbable that it appears needless to repeat that none of the Family have ever had the smallest grounds for such an imaginary arrangement – purely a Flight of Fancy.'

She went on to say that she had always assumed 'that Sir Augustus Webster would gladly take the Fixtures at the sum paid to the Dowager Lady Webster for them – viz. £600. I could not for an instant suppose that it would be agreeable to him to incur so great an obligation to me.' She added that as a consequence of Sir Augustus having declined to take the fixtures some of them had disappeared – but 'I think he has been wholly misinformed as to any injury having been done by Visitors.'

It is not clear how the matter was finally resolved, but Dame Sarah, who outlasted her husband by thirty-six years and lived into her late eighties, continued to be a significant, and rather irritating, presence in the Webster family for many years to come. One of the components of this irritation must have been the fact that, though bereaved, she was certainly not impecunious – unlike the new baronet and his mother. At Netherfield she funded the building of both a church and a school, of which she was 'sole Manager and Proprietor.' She provided much of its equipment, and was a powerful presence there for several years, teaching three or four days a week between 1864 and 1869, before eventually moving to Argyll Road, Kensington.[19]

Struggling with debt

Sir Augustus was confronted with a difficult financial situation. The details were spelled out to him in a letter from his solicitor R.C.Adams Beck on 2 June 1853. This showed that the estate was encumbered with debts consisting of mortgages and loans amounting to almost £43,000. Servicing these involved interest payments of over £1,600 a year, in addition to the jointures of £1,000 for his mother, and £500 for Sarah Joanna. There had been a windfall gain of almost

£8,000 from the South Eastern Railway Company, but all of this was earmarked for paying off some of the debt, and payments to his mother and his youngest brother. The conclusion at that stage was, nevertheless, relatively encouraging. Beck wrote 'I cannot but think that with good management and well looking after the local payments and expenses that you may still derive an income from the Estate.'[20]

Like his predecessors, Augustus sold off timber to improve cash flow; there was talk of selling off the Rose Green estate; and Frederick Webster was appointed to act as agent. He certainly sought to improve profitability, one of his schemes being a significant investment to re-equip and increase production of the estate brickyard. But the venture failed to attract customers, and the purchaser of the only sizeable order defaulted. Production ceased in 1855, and eventually the estate had to write off a debt of over £1,268.[21]

By the Spring of 1855 the overall financial situation too had clearly deteriorated. Like the 5th Baronet before him, Sir Augustus had to take refuge on the continent from his creditors. In a letter of 5 March his solicitor wrote to him complaining of a lack of information to deal with his affairs. 'Could you not safely come considerably nearer home but still out of jurisdiction?' he asked. 'If you were at Boulogne or Calais or even Brussels or Paris I would very quickly come over to you and something might be done.' It is not clear precisely what then happened, but in retrospect Augustus acknowledged 'I was...in a devil of a mess.' As the estate was already heavily mortgaged he had to do the same with his own life: the Law Benevolent Society lent him £3,000, but charged him a hefty 10% annual interest for the privilege.[22]

Meanwhile, at the Abbey, Dame Charlotte was also struggling. 'Her slender jointure', wrote Lady Cleveland, 'made it difficult to keep up the place'. A square three-storied tower in front of the south end of the Abbot's Hall threatened to become unsafe and had to be taken down. But its remains were left strewn around, and the terrace – according to the same source – was 'a woeful place enough, uneven, neglected, and surrounded by the jagged fragments of the destroyed.' No attempt was made to protect the old vaulting on which it stood from the weather, and in one place this gave way 'leaving a yawning rift through which one might peer down into the darkness below.'[23]

An American visitor

The Abbey nevertheless continued to be open both to private visitors on individual application, and also to the public one day a week, their numbers swelled by the easier access afforded by the railway. To meet their needs, the volume and range of prints and drawings of the Abbey also grew, not least through those published by Ticehurst in the High Street. In the 1840's, for instance, his output included a folder of 'Eight views of Battle Abbey, Church etc' which sold for sixpence. One of these *(see colour section)* was an updated version of Bucks' print 'South West View of Battle Abbey' bearing the inscription 'Dedicated by Permission to The Lady Charlotte Webster'. Originally published in 1736, and now reissued as a lithograph, it was embellished with two couples in the foreground as well as a typographical mistake which asserted, erroneously, that the view was 'As it was in 1637'. In anticipation of the arrival of the railway, and its expected bonus of still more visitors, Ticehurst also published in 1851 the first guide to the town and Abbey.[24]

HASTINGS MUSEUM

The Ruins of the Refectory by William Brooke.
One of a series of views published by Ticehurst of Battle.

What was on offer for visitors to the Abbey was vividly described by the American author Nathaniel Hawthorne in 1856. When he arrived, it happened not to be a public day, and he refused to send in a card requesting a visit. But his companion had no such scruples, and they were admitted and shown around by an old woman 'who lives, I believe, in the thickness of the Wall.' She was full of imaginative information. She told them that her room used to be the prison of the Abbey, and – pointing to a projecting beam under the great entrance arch – said that criminals used to be hanged on it. She then took them into ' a grand and noble hall...as stately a hall, I should imagine, as is anywhere to be found in a private mansion.' His account went on:[25]

> 'It was lighted at one end by a great window, beneath which, occupying the whole breadth of the hall, hung a vast picture of the Battle of Hastings, and whether a good picture or no, it was a rich adornment of the hall. The walls were wainscoted high upwards with oak: they were almost covered with noble pictures of ancestry, and of kings and great men, and beautiful women; there were trophies of armour hung aloft, and two armed figures, one in brass mail, the other in bright steel, stood on a raised dais underneath the great picture...Of all the domestic things that I have seen in England, it satisfied me the most.'

Having done a circuit of the ruins, on their way back they saw Lady Webster 'a tall and stately lady in black, trimming shrubs in the garden. She bowed to us very graciously; we raised our hats, and thus we met and parted, without more ado'.

The decision to sell

The following year the financial problems facing Sir Augustus became so severe that a desperate remedy was required. He came to the conclusion, no doubt with the utmost reluctance, that the Abbey had to be sold. It was at a point in his own life when, having ceased to be an itinerant sailor, and approaching forty, he was planning to marry and settle down. The obvious place to fulfil those ambitions was the Abbey which had by then been the family home for over 130 years. It was also a most prestigious address, their territorial and social base, and their most prized possession. His mother was especially attached to it, and his brother

Frederick was rapidly becoming a significant figure on the local scene. There was also the factor of the Abbey's historic importance, and the steadily increasing public interest in it. The pressures on Sir Augustus to find a way of holding on to the Abbey must have been very strong indeed. On the other hand there were the miseries which would accompany continued ownership – in particular the chronic problem of debt, from which there seemed no escape. Perhaps in the end, to tip the scales when making up his mind, the fact that he had spent so little time there over the past thirty years, and had been a man of the sea rather than the land, may have proved decisive.

Nevertheless, it was a decision which he must have taken with a heavy heart. 'What an old beast it is', he said, writing of these problems in April 1857. The outbreak of the Crimean War had exacerbated them by causing the failure of the brickworks for which he had to raise yet more money. He had made up his mind: 'I am desirous of selling the estate and intend doing so, and ask £200,000 for it.' If it had to be sold for less – between £175,000 and £190,000 – he calculated that, after paying off mortgages and funding jointures, this would still leave him with £100,000 for income. That would be acceptable, but somehow he also needed a capital sum of between £60,000 and £80,000 to buy another house – a substantial sum even if he was clearly thinking of a much more modest property than the Abbey.[26]

In August that year there was bad news from a Birmingham-based surveyor:[27]

> 'Giving full credit to the unique character of the Residence and to the historical associations which affect it, I am of the opinion that the sum of £140,000 is the extreme marketable value of the entire estate.
>
> While I know of no circumstance likely to raise this value there are many which may depreciate it, and to render it still less acceptable to the purchasing public. If, therefore, the offer you have received approaches that amount it should on no account be rejected.'

The agents to whom the sale was entrusted in 1857, Messrs Daniel Smith and Son, of Waterloo Place, Pall Mall, nevertheless did their best, garlanding the sale notice of the 'noble, highly distinguished and extensive domain of Battle Abbey', with a welter of enticing adjectives. 'This magnificent and peculiarly interesting Property', it read, 'comprising the venerable and splendid Abbey, the Residential portion...in the most perfect repair and enjoyable state in pleasing contrast with its contiguous splendid Ruins...associated with great historical interest standing amidst beautiful and varied Grounds, Gardens, Rosearies and Park-like Paddocks' was 'a complete and most desirable Territorial and Residential Property for a family of rank and fortune, and one of great influence and importance, capable also of great Improvement, being now by Railway within easy reach of the Metropolis, Dover and all parts of the Kingdom.'[28]

After the depredations caused by previous Webster baronets, the extent of the estate had been much reduced – a mere 2,000 acres compared with the 10,000 or so which the first baronet had acquired. Of these, the Abbey and its immediate surroundings, including parkland, occupied a relatively modest 155 acres. The bulk of the rest of the estate consisted of a number of farms, some of them substantial holdings like Marley Farm (305 acres) and Almory Farm (325 acres), others of more modest size such Course Barn Farm (174 acres), Beech Farm (149 acres), Down Barn Farm (130 acres), Little Park Farm (122 acres), and Park Farm in Battle and Catsfield (103 acres). The remainder included some 300 acres of land, woodland, several lodges, a corn windmill, a number of houses and cottages, the powdermill at Sedlescombe, and the Duke of Wellington pub in Battle.

The major attraction was certainly the Abbey itself, both as a country residence and a site of major historical and national renown. Sir Augustus and his advisers planned to go to auction if no private buyer appeared, but in fact one did so around the turn of the year. The negotiations , which were handled on behalf of Sir Augustus by the family's solicitors, Messrs Capron, Brabant, Capron and Dalton of Savile Place, New Burlington Street, proved extremely complicated and lengthy. This was due not only to the size of the transaction (which also included the purchase of the Hastings estate of the Websters), and the different status of its component parts – some of which was settled and in trust, while the remainder was the personal estate of Sir Augustus – but also the various encumbrances and obligations in the form of mortgages, portions and jointures.

On 23 February 1858 the prospective purchaser wrote to Sir Augustus complaining of the delay and absolving his side from any of the responsibility. On

30 March, evidently in response to some financial problems on the Webster side, he declared that he was 'not indisposed to make some arrangement of a loan', but announced a meeting to find out 'when there is a chance of the purchase being completed.' Two days later, on 1 April, he wrote again to Sir Augustus, telling him 'I'm of course a good deal annoyed at the delays and complications which are far more numerous than I could have dreamed of' – but it was not finally until 18 June 1858 that the conveyance of the Abbey and the remainder of the estate was signed.

The disengagement of the Websters from the Abbey proved not only lengthy and difficult, but also disappointing and distressing. The total proceeds of the sale, including fixtures, came to only £150,000 – far less than Sir Augustus had hoped for. In the meantime he had received a typically sharp letter from Dame Sarah:[29]

> 'You must recollect, and you will I feel sure forgive me from saying so
> – that your Brothers lose a good deal by the sale of the Abbey and Estate.
> They lose a House and Home – and Something attached to their name &
> position – and I hope you will bear that in Mind, and do what you can for
> them. I also hope you will not expect that I should relinquish my jointure.
> Of course, it is quite impossible to say how soon you may be relieved from
> it, but so long as I live it must be claimed.'

Some time later Dame Sarah briefly softened her attitude to Sir Augustus. They met ('I was quite delighted to see you looking so well') and she invited him to stay with her at Court Lodge, Robertsbridge ('The Place is very pleasant'). When he declined, she said she was extremely sorry. But even then she could not avoid offering some good advice. She was clearly concerned that Augustus was still a bachelor and without a direct heir. 'Ah! me', she wrote, 'why did you not make more of your advantages and please some one who might also have pleased you?' She went on to observe that 'though your Noble old home is fine, there are still fair scenes and broad acres to be had' and urged him to find a suitable companion and 'found a family on different principles – refresh and regenerate our name – in short dear Augustus – to do as your ancestors have not done!'[30]

In spite of the problems which accompanied him as he finally said farewell to the Abbey, Sir Augustus was undoubtedly glad to have got rid of it, and to be free to turn his mind to other and more pleasing prospects. But other members of the family were not so willing simply to put it behind them, as part of their past. The hope remained that some day, somehow, a Webster would return.

Sir Thomas Webster, 1st Baronet

Sir Whistler Webster, 2nd Baronet

Sir Godfrey Webster, 4th Baronet by Louis Gauffier

Lt.Col. Sir Henry Webster by Sir Martin Archer Shee

South West view of Battle Abbey

A version of Samuel Buck's print of 1737, 'Dedicated by Permission to The Lady Charlotte Webster'. This and the other prints which follow were published in the 1840s by F W Ticehurst, 'Bookseller &c', Battle.

The Gateway of Battle Abbey

'Dedicated by Permission to Sir Godfrey Webster Bart'

South East view of Battle Abbey

West view, Battle Abbey, Sussex

A PERIOD OF NOBILITY

In a striking reversal of the change of ownership in 1721, the sale in 1858 replaced a debt-ridden Baronet by a cash-rich nobleman. This ushered in a period of almost fifty years, coinciding with the high Victorian age and ending shortly after the Queen's own death, when the Abbey, refurbished and no longer starved of funds, was given a new lease of life. It flourished as a country house to which many of the great and good of the day came to dine and stay. At the same time its doors were open (if only once or twice a week) to the general public who came in ever increasing numbers to view what the Sussex Express called 'the famous historic pile'.[1]

The new owner of the Abbey was a man of impeccable pedigree and substantial resources. The Honourable George Harry Vane, generally known as Lord Harry Vane, was the third son of (and putative heir to) the Duke of Cleveland of Raby Castle in Durham. Born in 1803, he had first embarked on a diplomatic career and then turned to politics, entering parliament as a Liberal MP for South Durham in 1841. He was also a very substantial landowner. His new acquisition added significantly to his already extensive estates in Durham, putting him in an exclusive category among an elite group of twenty-eight noblemen who all possessed more than 100,000 acres of land in the United Kingdom.

NPG 5635

The 4th Duke of Cleveland by Frederick Sargent

He was described by a contemporary as 'a fine specimen of an English aristocrat' and 'a very striking personage' with his tall erect figure, piercing eyes and – in later life – his snow-white hair. He must have been a rather imposing figure, especially to workers on the estate. The story is told of a porter who was told to go and collect him and his luggage at Battle station. He was instructed how to address him, but forgot his lines when confronted with the Duke. When told what to do with the baggage he said 'Yes Sir, My Lord God Almighty!'[2]

Another story suggests that this deity could also act in a modest manner. One day when walking along North Trade Road he was accosted by a farm labourer who asked him if he was going into Battle. When the Duke replied that he was, the man asked if he would post some letters for him there. The Duke not only agreed but put them in the postbox himself.[3]

His wife, sixteen years his junior, was also an aristocrat, the daughter of the 4th Earl of Stanhope and the widow of Lord Dalmeny, the eldest son of the 4th Earl of Rosebery. Catherine Lucy Wilhelmina Vane was small in stature, but renowned for her beauty. In her youth she 'was declared to be without exception the loveliest girl of many a London season.' She had been a trainbearer at the coronation of Queen Victoria, and was also a bridesmaid at her wedding. According to Lady St Helier 'she had read widely, talked very well, and was a good artist.' Another contemporary, less fulsomely, described her as 'agreeable and on the whole kind, but could be intolerant and sarcastic.' What is certain is that she was a person of great energy, trenchant views, a fluent pen, and a ready wit. On one occasion an American millionaire, pointing to the palatial staircase in his house, remarked to her 'I venture to think, Your Grace, that even Battle Abbey cannot show a finer staircase than this.' 'Oh no', replied the Duchess, 'the Battle Abbey stairs are very shabby; you see, those old Crusaders wore them out so dreadfully.'[4]

Together they were a formidable pair. Lord Harry took an early opportunity, at the general election of 1859 to move his parliamentary base from the north to Sussex, being elected for Hastings. He retained the seat until 1864 when, on the death of his father, he succeeded to his title, and became the 4th Duke of Cleveland. Shortly afterwards he also changed his name from Vane to Powlett, the family name of his maternal grandmother, the Duchess of Bolton.

The future Duchess of Cleveland as a young woman

The Abbey refurbished

In the meantime, he and his wife had made their mark on the Abbey itself. In her *History of Battle Abbey*, published in 1877, Lady Cleveland is scathing about most of the changes which successive members of the Webster family had made to the Abbey, and the state in which they had left it. One of the buildings put up by the 5th Baronet, an extension to the old wing of the Abbey, was found to be 'damp, inconvenient and badly built, the lower floor being laid on bare earth, without substructure or ventilation.' In the Abbot's parlour, which she made into her sitting room, there were 'two ugly modern Gothic windows' for which he had also been responsible; and elsewhere 'a fine ancient window of great size was somewhat marred by the odious kaleidoscopic glass that seems to have been Sir Godfrey's special hobby.'

Nor was that all. He had also removed an ancient holy well and piped away the water from the spring which fed it; broken through the north wall, the only part of the church still standing, to make a gate; and had 'made a sad havoc of the pleasaunce created by Sir Anthony Browne on the site of the Minster.' He had cut down the whole of one side of an avenue of yews to make way for new stables, and most of another to provide access to them. In the process of excavation he had uncovered part of the nave and many relics – 'bones, broken coffins, shattered altar-tombs etc. But none of them were cared for or preserved.' Moreover, the crypt 'was choked with reeds, and more than half full of water. No attempt had ever been made to drain it.'[5]

The new owners must have been rather shocked with what they discovered, and they set to work with energy and determination to rehabilitate the Abbey within and without. With the assistance of Henry Clutton, a fashionable architect, extensive works were put in hand to embellish the Abbey's living quarters. Within three years, Sir Godfrey Webster's ramshackle building was pulled down, and in its place a dining room and a 76 feet-long library were built. An article in *Country Life* in November 1897 described both as 'very handsome'. Like their predecessors, however, the Clevelands were not to escape criticism of their taste from a later generation. In 1933 the architect Sir Harold Brakspear condemned the library as 'a very dull and incongruous erection' and the Gothic windows they had installed in the great hall as 'entirely incongruous with their surroundings.'[6]

The Drawing Room, sumptuously furnished by the Duchess

The new library built by Henry Clutton

Parquet flooring and bookcases were installed, and the main apartments were sumptuously furnished in the Victorian style, much of the furniture having been collected by the Duchess. The sofas and chair coverings were of flowered Genoese cotton and on one wall one of their most prized possessions, an Aubusson tapestry, was hung. A new balcony room was also built over the Duke's study, and a set of rooms which provided a dressing room for the Duke, a bedroom and dressing room for his wife, and another for the use of their sons.[7]

The Duchess had four children from her two marriages, two sons and two daughters. The eldest was Lord Rosebery, who was eleven when the family first arrived at the Abbey. He was to become a prominent and distinguished Liberal politician and, briefly, prime minister. He had a younger brother, the Hon. Everard Primrose, and two sisters, who later became Lady Leconfield and Lady Mary Hope. All of them grew up at the Abbey, the first young people there for some twenty years. It must suddenly have become a much more youthful and lively place. The Clevelands also had many guests. Both of them were very well connected and many of the most notable and distinguished people of the day came to visit and dine at the Abbey. Among them were the Duchess of Teck (mother of the future Queen Mary); politicans such as the Earl of Beaconsfield (Benjamin Disraeli), Joseph Chamberlain, and Lord Granville; the explorer H M Stanley; and military men including Lord Kitchener and General Sir Redvers Buller. The Duchess, it is said, was a charming hostess – though her neighbour, Lady Sybil Brassey, (probably a rather jealous observer) asserted that the Clevelands' parties were noted for being extremely dull, and that one of their guests had written 'From sudden death and Battle, good Lord deliver us.'[8]

A house and entertainment on this scale of course required a considerable staff. In April 1871 the Census recorded eleven of them resident at the Abbey – two ladies' maids, three housemaids, two kitchen maids, a still room maid, two footmen and a groom of the chambers. There must in addition have been a large non-resident staff, including gardeners. The estate provided employment for many others: during the Cleveland's tenure it was trebled in size to make a total of just over six thousand acres. Three farms were run directly by the estate – Little Park, Coarse Barn, and Marley. Hops were grown at all of them. During this period the estate was also noted for the fine cattle and horses which it bred.

Hay was mown by hand-held scythes: it was an impressive sight with eight men standing side by side, each a little behind the other.[9]

The gardens enhanced

Lady Cleveland herself was keenly interested in gardens and devoted a great deal of time and attention to them at the Abbey. She rarely returned from visits abroad without some unusual and beautiful plants. When she first arrived the only significant flower bed she found was the Fountain Garden, created by Sir Anthony Browne on the site of the abbey church. About two-thirds of it had, however, been lost as a result of Sir Godfrey Webster's alterations, and it 'was not very carefully tended.' Nevertheless, she kept it and contented herself with merely adding two vases to it. Another bed required much more work. This was 'an untidy flower bed straggling along the wall of the Lower Terrace, chiefly peopled with marigolds, which long defied all our efforts to extirpate them.' These were replaced with 'a variety of tender plants, mainly creepers.'

Elsewhere there were more radical changes. A line of Italian cypresses was planted, a bed of camellias established, and a new conservatory built to replace 'two very dilapidated vineries that, in the Webster's time, did duty both for flowers and fruit'. The area set aside for vegetables in the existing orchard was also deemed inadequate for their needs. A new kitchen garden was established further away from the house, on the far side of Powdermill Lane, on a much larger site of some two and half acres, and equipped with vineries, peach-houses and a cucumber house. Their solitary failure, Lady Cleveland boasted, was two successive crops of grapes which rotted.[10]

She was, quite rightly, very proud of what she had achieved in the gardens and devoted a section of her History to a description of them. Nor was she the only one to admire them. 'The surroundings of the abbey are very beautiful', wrote the author of an article in *Country Life* on 6 November 1897. 'The sloping ground opens out a fine prospect of the battlefield, and of the sea beyond, with Beachy Head in the distance. Magnificent trees grace the park, and the gardens are extremely choice.'

Two years later another article in the same publication also sang her praises:[11]

'To create the garden and adorn the park with new trees – mostly quick – growing Levantine oaks – to replace ancient giants that had been cut down, was a labour of love and pride. The Duchess of Cleveland takes a true delight in her beautiful garden. She values the crumbling walls of the old time, and loves to see them adorned with roses and clinging greenery. Very lovely they are under her care.'

Coping with visitors

In addition to these extensive improvements both to the interior and exterior environment of the Abbey, another striking change during the period of Cleveland ownership was the surge in the number of the general public visiting it. This inevitably brought problems in its wake, and led to the introduction of new ways of trying to deal with them, and to exercise some control over both the numbers and behaviour of the tourists. In her book Lady Cleveland devotes several pages to this theme, which provide an illuminating insider's view of the trials and tribulations involved.[12]

'No account of Battle Abbey could be considered complete', she wrote, 'without some mention of the visitors that hold a triumphal jubilee there on every Tuesday throughout the year.' They were most numerous in the summer months 'when the London shopkeepers take their annual holiday by the seaside and crowd the hotels and lodging-houses of Hastings and St Leonards. But they come in all seasons, and I may add, in all weathers. The local newspapers urge the excursion as an indispensable duty, and they are only too glad to have something to do and somewhere to go.'

The Clevelands first became aware of them soon after their arrival at the Abbey. During 'the tedious arrangements connected with its sale and transfer' it was closed to the public. But 'one of the first missives that greeted the Duke on his taking possession' was a formal request from the Mayor and Corporation of Hastings that it should be reopened. 'Battle Abbey had always been shown, time out of mind; Hastings considered that it had a prescriptive right to its 'lion' and could not bear to be shut out from the great attraction of the neighbourhood.' The Duke replied courteously, and agreed that the public should be admitted once a week to go over the ruins, and allowed to see the hall when the family was absent.

Formal flower beds by the East Front, re-modelled by the Duchess

The new owners were astonished at the response. 'We had no idea what the first public day would be like, and beyond appointing a directing guide, had made no arrangements. But never were two easy-going people more speedily put on their mettle.' Eight hundred people arrived. They congregated on the Upper Terrace ('at the time in a rough and ruinous state') and took a gate into a private area of the garden off its hinges, 'flooding the whole place like a sudden inundation and mocking the feeble efforts of the guide to show - it them.' Crowds peered into the study 'where the poor Duke sat writing his letters, till they fairly stared him out of countenance, and drove him from the room.' But the Countess herself was made of sterner stuff. 'Others glued their faces with equal persistence to the panes of my sitting room windows; but here they met with their match, for being aroused to great indignation, I resolved to try the power of human eye upon them in my turn.' She was wearing a large pair of spectacles. 'Armed with this powerful auxiliary, I stared steadfastly at my opponents, and rising very slowly from my chair, without averting my eyes, I moved gradually, step by step, across the room. Long before I reached the window, the whole party had fled.'

After that experience, she went on, 'we felt we had trifled with a serious subject, and that the admission of visitors must in future be regulated on strategical principles.' Everyone would have to have a ticket – 'distributed gratuitously by a bookseller in town' – and divided into groups of fifty. 'Patrols were placed on every side, and printed notices on large boards met their eyes whenever they strayed in forbidden directions.' Even so, it proved difficult to control the visitors. From time to time they penetrated deep into the house, on one occasion surprising the Duke who was using one of the upstairs bedrooms as a temporary sitting room. Outside, many attempts were made to get into the orchard where one day the Duchess found her hammock, placed in 'a secluded and unsuspected place', occupied by 'a joyous party.' Their favourite excursion was into the park – 'Not, I am sorry to say, with any idea of examining the field of battle, but simply to eat and drink'. A stop had to be put to this. 'We had so many complaints of the labour required to clear away the debris of these rural feasts that they were at last done away with.' In spite of this:

> 'The desire for a picnic remains as rampant as ever. Each Tuesday that the weather is fine, a great wave of humanity surges across the lawn, and breaks against the park gate; or sometimes, catching through the evergreens glimpses of a hidden path in that direction, break their way towards it through the bushes. The gardener put up a hurdle in the principal gap they had made, but they jumped it like so many deer.'

She nevertheless gave two good marks to the visitors: 'they never dream of picking any flowers, and it is only from Harold's chapel that they ever attempt to carry away a memento.' She also admitted that many were frustrated by not being able to visit the house, and that their complaints about guides were sometimes justified. One of them she judged to be too erudite for his listeners. Having told them that they were looking at the Calefactory, one group was heard to respond 'Ah yes, to be sure – the calico factory.'

Growing numbers but discordant voices

Criticism of the visiting arrangements was echoed in comments in some contemporary guide books. The 1868 edition of Murray's *Handbook for Travellers in Kent and Sussex*, for instance, noted that 'The pilgrimage to the remains of Battle Abbey must be made in the company of some dozens of visitors, congenial

Battle Abbey, from the Fish Ponds

or otherwise', while the 1875 edition of Black's *Picturesque Guide to the county of Sussex and its watering places* made the following acerbic comment:

'*On leaving this hallowed ground – this spot so sacred in the eyes of every intelligent Englishman – the visitor will join, we fancy, in the reprobation which has been pretty generally expressed of the mean and selfish restrictions here designed, as it would seem, to minister to his especial discomfort. Surely a place like this might be left for Englishmen to examine unshackled by half a score of absurd conditions and free from the constant supervision of a greedy janitor, whose cry, like the horse-leech's daughter is – "Give! Give!"*'

Twelve years later, another guide book voiced the same complaint:[13]

'*Battle Abbey should be avoided by quiet people between April and October because of the crowds who flock there: sometimes as many as 1,200 people are shown over in one day in the height of the summer, and in parties of from 50 to 100 – a system which, though unavoidable, is very unpleasant. Nothing is charged for the tickets, but in quitting the garden the guide stands ready to receive the free-will offering of his late flock as they disperse.*'

According to these sources, there was a period from around 1868 to 1875

– and possibly longer – when the Abbey was open twice a week, on Fridays as well as Tuesdays. But by 1887 the Clevelands had reverted to a single opening each week, on Tuesdays from midday to 4pm. This reduced the pressure on them, but increased it for visitors. There were other inconveniences too. One was that the visit did not include the battlefield. Part of it could be seen from the terrace of what was then known as the banqueting hall in the Abbey grounds, but a more general view could only be obtained if the visitor penetrated to high ground north of the town. The house itself, including the Great Hall, was also only to be seen when the family was not in residence.

Such considerations did not however deter the many who took advantage of special railway excursions from Hastings and elsewhere to visit the Abbey. August was always the busiest month: numbers taking advantage of the free visits to the Abbey regularly exceeded a thousand. On 15 August 1891 the *Sussex Express* reported that 'On Tuesday last we were favoured with a tremendous influx of visitors such as has not previously happened this year.' Both the Abbey and Normanhurst, Lord Brassey's place a short distance away, were open. 'By road and rail they crowded into the town, which was kept in a most lively state during the whole of the day.'

The demand for information about the Abbey prompted Lady Cleveland to write and publish (anonymously) a guide to it, and Ticehurst's, from whose shop on the Green tickets were issued, advertised sets of 'art photographs', mounted in a variety of sizes and sold at prices ranging from fourpence to two shillings each. 'These are very fine and entirely new, taken instantaneously on Dry Plates, and the sizes are much larger than those usually sold at the above prices.'[14]

On 29 August 1891, however, the *Sussex Express* recorded: 'On Tuesday last there was a tremendous influx of visitors to the Abbey, but great was their disappointment to find a notice posted on the doors that in consequence of the decease of the Duke of Cleveland they were closed until further notice.' His death at the age of eighty-eight was not unexpected for he had been ill for some time in his London home, Cleveland House, St James's Square from which daily bulletins on his condition had been issued. He was well respected in the town, many of whose activities and organisations both he and his wife had supported generously. The short comment published in the Sussex Express was, however, rather niggardly: 'His Grace was so very little amongst us that his decease will not create a very great void. General regret is expressed however that it will necessitate the closing of the Abbey to the Tuesday visitors for a lengthened period, and this means a corresponding loss for the tradesmen of the town.'

A busy widow

Fortunately for the shopkeepers of Battle the Duchess in due course reopened the Abbey and normal service was resumed. The Duchess survived her husband by ten years. She became a great traveller, visiting India, Egypt, Turkey, and Greece as well as Italy and Spain. But she also spent a good deal of time at the Abbey, took a keen interest in her tenants, and became a well-known character in the town. She drove around in a little carriage drawn by a magnificent Corsican donkey, and sometimes rode a snow-white Egyptian donkey given to her by Lord Kitchener. When they saw her coming local children used to shout 'Here comes the Duchess riding on her ass!'[15]

As is apparent from her books, her guide to the Abbey, and the articles she inspired, she was devoted to it and intensely interested in its history. Her husband left an estate valued at £1,440,889 and she was able to maintain a large staff and to entertain extensively. The 1901 Census reported that there were no less than eighteen servants resident at the Abbey – a butler, a chef, a groom of chamber, an under-butler, two footmen, a hall boy, a groom, a helper, a housekeeper, a ladies' maid, two still room servants, a kitchen maid, a scullery maid, and three housemaids. On that occasion there were also five additional visiting servants – 3 ladies' maids and 2 valets – accompanying six guests staying at the Abbey.

Lady Cleveland was then 81. On the Tuesday after Easter she left the Abbey to travel to Wiesbaden for an eye operation. That was carried out by an eminent German eye surgeon on 30 April – without a general anaesthetic, but some use of cocaine to deaden the pain – and was very successful. In the days which followed the Duchess went out daily either in a carriage or a bath chair, and wrote to her steward, Sir Anchitel Piers Ashburnham, that she intended to be back at the Abbey on 21 May. On the morning of Saturday 18 May she rose as usual and was served breakfast in her hotel room. But when her groom of the chambers, Russell, returned after a few minutes he found it untouched, 'a most unusual occurrence.' In the adjoining room the Duchess was sitting in a chair, 'life being extinct.' The news was later conveyed to the Abbey by her son in a brief telegram 'Sorry to say Mother died this morning of apoplexy – Rosebery.'[16]

The following Tuesday the Abbey was closed to visitors, and the town presented quite a deserted appearance. On the Friday morning a memorial service was held at Battle parish church at the same time as the burial took place at Staindrop, Durham. It was attended by a large congregation which included twelve Abbey servants and twenty-seven estate employees headed by Mr E Meppen, the bailiff. In the evening muffled bells rang out eighty-one times.[17]

An uncertain future

There was much speculation about what now might happen, and concern about its implications for the economy of the locality. The *Sussex Express* wrote: 'Whether the privilege of inspecting the famous historic pile which has contributed so much to the prosperity of the town will be continued must of course depend upon the new owner, but even a temporary closure during the summer months would mean a considerable loss to the town and also to the char-a-banc proprietors at Hastings and Eastbourne the visitors from which were very numerous.'

It was known that Sir Augustus Webster had been brought up to believe that one day his family would once again own the Abbey: since his nursery days he had been nurtured on the maxim 'When Gussie buys back Battel'. During the lifetime of the Duchess he had been a frequent visitor to the Abbey: on one occasion 'in the company of some 1,500 other people' he 'was hustled round in a party of seventy or eighty.' The Duchess 'is reported to have said tearfully that if Battle Abbey ever came to be sold she hoped Sir Augustus would buy it.'[18]

But the Abbey did not immediately come on to the market. In fact it was inherited by a nephew of the late Duke, Captain F W Forrester. On the last Tuesday of July he reopened the Abbey, reinstating the weekly public day – but introduced for the first time a small charge – part of the proceeds of which were later made over to local charities.[19]

The new owner, however, lived in northern England and did not wish to move. The Abbey was therefore put up for auction in December 1901. The question was: who would buy it? Might Sir Augustus still be interested – and in a position to make a bid for it?[20]

8

THE WEBSTERS DISPERSED

After the sale of the Abbey in 1858 Sir Augustus Webster, the 7th Baronet, moved to London to live in the Albany, Piccadilly. Until the proceeds reached him he was in considerable financial difficulties, and in 1859 sought a private loan of £6,000 to tide him over. The funds, once they were released, must have been very welcome both to him and his trustees, but the remaining estate was still heavily encumbered.[1]

Other members of the family also faced serious financial problems. This was particularly true of his two youngest brothers. On 19 September Arthur, the elder of them, wrote to him from Brussels, where he was training to be a singer, enquiring about 'the money due to him' (presumably in the light of the recent sale). He said that because he had moved into a new house, and 'now that the new bank has not succeeded', he had debts both in England and France. The youngest brother, Guy, also owed him more than £150 'and as the renewals cost me more than 15 per cent yearly, it is a constant drain on me and increase in debt'. He had been persuaded not to pursue his claim as 'the only result would be very likely to compel Guy to leave the army' – but his brother had behaved 'cruelly and ungratefully' towards him.[2]

Guy Webster: a troublesome brother

Guy had long been a great source of concern. A very late afterthought of an unhappy marriage, he had inherited many of his father's bad habits. In 1849, when he was in his late 'teens, he was 'turned away' (presumably expelled) from Brighton College. Two years later he joined the army, a commission in the Dragoon Guards having been purchased for him with £2,000 provided by the family trustees as an advance on his share of £20,000 he was due to receive on his twenty-first birthday under his parents' marriage settlement.[3]

He served in the Crimean war, reporting in December 1855 that the village in which they were stationed was 'an awful hole, like all Turkish villages, and so

The Crimean war: the Guards in action at the Battle of Inkermann, November 1854

dirty. For although it may be economical for the municipal authorities to make the main street act also as a main sewer, yet it has its disadvantages as you may imagine. Boots up to the thigh are the only things.' He added, 'I have been most awfully robbed.' Most of his clothes, including his laced jacket, together with his money, watch, dressing case and dispatch box had been taken: all that he had left for four or five days was a walking stick. He asked his brother Augustus to send replacements – but not through 'the usual channels. The system of robbery and plunder that goes on here is awful.'[4]

Most of Guy's problems were, however, self-inflicted. There is a suggestion that at some point he was in fact forced to leave the army, Sarah Joanna writing that he 'had been restored to his profession' and that she was going to make him an allowance of £200 a year. In 1859 he was serving in India with the Dragoon Guards, but seems to have returned (or been forced to return) to civilian life when he came back to Europe, and a way of life that scandalised his family. His mother wrote:[5]

'I hear dreadful accounts of Guy. He drinks three bottles of brandy a day, has constant fits of delirium tremens, swindles very badly, has no sense of shame and is over head and ears in debt. It would be a mercy to have him shut up'.

Dame Sarah – 'Saint Sarah' as she became for Arthur Webster – took a different view. She told Augustus 'I make sacrifices of my own personal tastes and habits in order to companionise with Guy, for the purposes of restraint... In short I have made it my mission to try to save Guy from low habits – which have been hinted at to me...I do not suppose any one can indulge in these habits with impunity – Guy less than anyone – and he will most assuredly kill himself if he does'.[6]

Marriage, a new home, but continued debt

In the midst of these family woes Augustus at last followed the advice of his widowed sister-in-law, Dame Sarah Joanna, and decided to get married. His bride on 31 May 1862 was Amelia Sophia, the second daughter of Charles Prosser Hastings of Taunton. As in several previous Webster marriages there was a huge disparity in ages: he was forty-three, but she only sixteen. The succession was secured when on 10 February 1864 they had a son, Augustus Frederick Walpole Edward and the following year the family trust purchased – with funds mainly provided by Lady Webster – the 64-acre Rosehill Estate at Stockbridge, Hampshire. The family now made their home there at Hildon House.[7]

This was a considerable move down-market, but in spite of the sale of the Abbey Sir Augustus was still in severe financial difficulties. The stark details were spelled out in a letter of 10 July 1865 from the family solicitors, Caprons, to the Legal and General Insurance Office. The Company had already lent Sir Augustus £23,000: this was an urgent request for a further loan. The letter explained that Sir Augustus was tenant for life of various funds producing an annual income of £3,765 10s 0d but had obligations amounting to £3,556 8s 6d, including a jointure of £1,000 a year for his mother, another of £500 for his brother's widow, and an annuity of £100 for his brother Frederick. That left him with an income of only £209 1s 6d.[8]

The letter went on to say that this might be increased to £369 if the land belonging to the Rosehill estate were let out, and that Sir Augustus had various other potential assets – including a reversionary interest in his Mother's jointure amounting to £6,000. (Caprons helpfully pointed out that she was now 70 and 'about a fortnight since had an attack of paralysis'). But he was in urgent need of £4,000. Half of this was needed immediately 'to pay off some pressing engagements', the rest 'to settle with Mr Robert Cook of Warwick Street, the notorious usurious money lender.' A friend of Sir Augustus, a London banker, was willing to guarantee any deficiency in income to meet the premiums and interest.

Confronted by these financial problems Sir Augustus was so desperate that he had already sought the help of Dame Sarah Joanna, in spite of her renewed hostility. ('I hear her abuse of you and me is as lively as ever', reported his brother Arthur). Not surprisingly, he was firmly rebuffed. Writing to Frederick Capron, the family solicitor, on 8 July 1865 Dame Joanna apologised for being unable to see him but went on 'As she has no intention (of which Sir Augustus Webster has been distinctly informed) of making any arrangement with reference to Sir Augustus's affairs, it would be needless.' Capron evidently tried again to see her, calling on her three times, but to no avail. In a further letter she reiterated in no uncertain terms her unwillingness to help:[9]

> 'Having in the most decided manner refused to have anything to do with
> the affairs of Sir Augustus Webster, and having expressed this several times
> to him, to Lady Webster, and to the latter's friend, Mr Thomas, I am greatly
> surprised that they should have so far misled you, as to induce you to make
> any further application to me.'

In spite of this setback, Sir Augustus somehow managed to survive financially. But two deaths in the family then followed in quick succession. That of his mother, Dame Charlotte who had moved to Warrior Square, St Leonards, occurred in 1867 at the age of seventy six. This relieved him of one of his financial burdens, but brought no new resources as she left all her property to a friend. The following year the family was shocked when Guy also died, at Ostend on 14 April, when he was still in his thirties, the result apparently of his dissolute life-style. Dame Joanna wrote, in typically censorious style.[10]

> 'Poor Guy's end has indeed been awful…I had hoped so much from this
> good quiet girl he was to have married… I can only hope and pray that this
> terrible event may not be without its lessons – Certainly the tenderest age is
> not too early to begin teaching self-control, self-denial and the Government

over the worst enemy – viz – Self. With the help of God this can be Done – without it – Nothing.'

Sir Augustus and his wife lived quietly at their Hampshire home. Eight years after the birth of their first child, a second son – Godfrey Vassall – was born in 1872, and five years later a daughter – Amelia Sophia Rous. She was not yet in her teens when Sir Augustus died suddenly of heart disease on 27 March 1886 at his home at the age of sixty-six. He left a modest estate of some £8,000, his horses, carriages, and household effects to his wife, sums of money to his daughter, and the residue to his eldest son, together with his gold flute, plate and personal estate.[11]

The 8th Baronet: a thespian soldier

The new Webster baronet, the eighth in line and another Augustus, was just twenty-two when he inherited the title. Somehow his parents – or the family trustees – had found the money to send both him and his younger brother Godfrey to Eton. This was a new departure for the Websters and an interesting sign of the times. In the case of Augustus it was followed by the Royal Military College at Sandhurst and in 1884 a commission as a lieutenant in the Grenadier Guards. He spent some time with the second battalion in Bermuda but otherwise was stationed in and around London – where he had a most agreeable time. He was a well-known figure in clubland, his membership encompassing the Guards, Bachelors, Whites, Arthurs, and Pratts.[12]

Early on, Sir Augustus – known to his friends as 'Gussie' – had shown some of the same love of devilry and gambling as his grandfather. One of the many wagers he won was when he was packed in a wooden case and sent to Windsor and back as a parcel. 'The journey took four days and nearly killed him; but he won his bet and is more proud of that feat than of any other.' On another occasion:[13]

> *'Having been locked into a box which was subsequently corded, he was supposed to emerge by means of a sliding panel. On one occasion, however, the charm did not work, and the victim was obliged to effect his escape by main force after a considerable period of time and in a severely damaged condition.'*

The Guards'

Burlesque

Company.

1889.

W. DAVIS, PRINTER AND STATIONER, 48 ROCHESTER ROW.

During his fifteen year spell in the Guards Augustus also displayed other impressive, but decidedly non-military, gifts. He became 'one of cleverest amateur banjoists in the Kingdom' as well as one of the stars of the Grenadier Guards Nigger Minstrel Troupe. 'He was regarded in the brigade', wrote *The Tatler*, 'as a "cert" for any kind of entertainment whether got up for the amusement of the officers' friends or the charitable and benevolent funds of the Guards in general.'[14]

He was a leading figure in the burlesques which the Guards

2

THIS EVENING, AT EIGHT O'CLOCK,

AN

ORIGINAL PLAY,

BY

SIDNEY GRUNDY, ESQ.,

ENTITLED :

In Honour Bound.

DRAMATIS PERSONÆ:

Sir George Carlyon, Q.C., M.P. · Capt. F. C. RICARDO

Phillip Graham · Sir AUGUSTUS F. WEBSTER, Bart.

Lady Carlyon · Miss SCARLETT

Rose DALRYMPLE · Miss St. MAUR

SCENE—

LIBRARY IN SIR GEORGE CARLYON'S HOUSE.

ESRO BAT4711

3

To be followed at Nine p.m. by a new and original

BURLESQUE DRAMA

BY

E. C. NUGENT, Esq., late Grenadier Guards.

Music by EDWARD SOLOMON, Esq.

ENTITLED :

THE REAL TRUTH ABOUT

IVANHOE

OR,

SCOTT SCOTCHED.

Cedric	Nick-named the Sack-son from his having disinherited his male offspring	Col. RICARDO, *Grenadier Guards.*
Ivanhoe	The offspring aforesaid, famed for never taking a denial, but always substituting Aye-for-no	Lieut. B. J. LIVETT, *Scots Guards.*
Sir Brian de Bois Guilbert	Ironically styled "the Good Templar," the secrets of whose life will not bear Brian into	Capt. F. C. RICARDO, *Grenadier Guards.*
Isaac	A Jew Pawnbroker, ugly enough to make your eyes-ache	Lieut. FRANCIS SANDFORD, *Grenadier Guards.*
Gurth	A Swine-herd to Sir Brian, formerly in Cedric's service, a Swine-herd remember! no cow-herd	Lieut. GEORGE MacDONALD, *Grenadier Guards.*
Wamba	Jest a Jester	Lieut. Sir HUBERT MILLER, Bart., *Coldstream Guards.*
Lieut.-Col. Robin Hood	Commanding the Merry Greenwood Volunteers	Lieut. GEORGE NUGENT, *Grenadier Guards.*
Capt. Little-John	His Adjutant	Lt. Sir AUGUSTUS WEBSTER, Bart., *Grenadier Guards.*

put on in the Theatre Royal at Chelsea Barracks attended by a fashionable audience. In February 1889 his portrayal of a romantic young lover received mixed but sympathetic notices. 'The funniest part of the comedy', wrote one critic, 'was the look of excruciating, unaccustomed misery depicted on Sir Augustus Webster's mobile countenance. Sentimental lovers are born, not made, and Sir Augustus had my deepest sympathy.'[15]

That same year, as a former lover in real life, Webster had other preoccupations. A lady with the somewhat improbable name of Ashton Yate Bunyan-Bunyan sued him for breach of promise. The case, brought in the Queen's Bench Division, also involved the child born of their illicit union. The matter was settled by a Deed

R.W. Bro. Sir AUGUSTUS F. WEBSTER, Bart.,
Provincial Grand Master, Grand Superintendent.
H. W. Salmon]   [Photo, Winchester.

Sir Augustus, the 8th Baronet

of Arrangement in April the following year, on the eve of the lady's marriage, when Sir Augustus agreed to pay £100 a year maintenance until the child was eighteen in return for the action being dropped, and silence maintained. Like his grandfather before him, Webster was able to buy his way out of an unfortunate entanglement.[16]

No doubt those in the circles which Sir Augustus frequented who knew about it regarded it as no more than a regrettable accident, which had been honourably settled. At all events, it proved no obstacle to his embarking on what became a long and distinguished membership of the Freemasons. In 1892 he was admitted into the United Grand Lodge of Ancient, Free and Accepted Masons of England (of which the Prince of Wales was Grand Master), and four years later was a founder member of the Household Brigade Lodge no 2614 – which other members of the royal family were later to join. These were important and influential networks, which combined social pleasure with good works – and also opportunities for role-playing and dressing up.[17]

Marriage and family

In 1895, at the age of thirty-one, Sir Augustus married. Like many of his Webster predecessors his choice fell on a rich heiress, and – like his father and great grandfather – on a very much younger woman. Mabel Crossley was nineteen, the only daughter of the carpet manufacturer, Henry Crossley, of Aldborough Hall, Bedale, Yorkshire. Her grandfather, Joseph Crossley of Halifax, who had started the business, left just under £1,000,000 when he died in 1868, and on her father's death in 1894 she inherited funds which provided an income of £16,000 a year. They nevertheless moved for the time being into the Webster's family home at Hildon House, and it was there that in 1897 a son, Godfrey, was born followed in 1900 by a daughter, Lucy, named after her maternal grandmother.[18]

After his marriage Sir Augustus left the Guards, having reached the rank of captain, to devote himself to domestic and rural pursuits. He was 'a keen collector of furniture, miniatures and objets d'art, an enthusiastic follower of hounds, an excellent shot and a capital dry-fly fisherman.' He exhibited regularly at the Romsey agricultural shows, and was also seriously interested in trees and shrubs, publishing a knowledgeable article about those on the estate, and their behaviour on chalky soil, in 1890. He is reported to have spent 'some years' (though it is not clear when) as a student of forestry in Austria, and to have become 'a walking student' of Veitch's Nursery in Chelsea.[19]

While Sir Augustus was enjoying his new Hampshire home, his younger brother Godfrey was following a different course. After Eton he had gone – unusually for a Webster – to university. He was an undergraduate at Christ Church, Oxford but seems to have spent a great deal of his time acting in both college productions and for the University Dramatic Society. He was like his brother in his love of the stage, and he also had some of the earlier Webster urge for adventure. He decided to seek his fortune in South Africa, setting off in

A Scene from the Boer War by Allan Stewart

August 1894. After 'a beastly bad voyage' he arrived there in mid September, and made for Johannesburg. This he soon found to be 'a beast of a place...the people in it are beasts and the weather is beastly.' Nor did his business ventures fare well. He set up as an advertising agent, and then with a partner as 'Advertising, theatrical and land agents', but the partnerships didn't work, business at the end of 1895 was 'awfully slack', and he fell ill with dysentery. Early the following year he tried farming, but soon abandoned it in the face of cattle disease, a two years' drought and '6,000 people doing the same thing.' At the end of the year he wrote home: 'I think I shall have to turn Barman as two other old Etonians here have, or become a bankrupt, the beginning of all millionaires up here.'[20]

He then tried speculating in land, but without success, and fell back on private tutoring. But in the autumn of 1899, faced with the outbreak of the Boer war, he joined up as a Lieutenant in Bethune's Mounted Infantry. He took part in a number of engagements in Natal, the Transvaal and Orange River Colony, was promoted to captain in charge of a squadron at the end of 1900 – but then was killed in a railway accident in February the following year when he was still only twenty-nine.[21]

This must have been a severe blow to Sir Augustus. But in the autumn of 1901 he had something else to think about. An announcement was made that Battle Abbey was coming on the market, and was to be sold at auction in London on Tuesday 26 November at two-o'clock precisely at the Auction Mart, Tokenhouse Yard, by Mr Joseph Stower of Chancery Lane.

9

RETURN TO BATTLE: TRIUMPH AND TRAGEDY

The announcement of the sale of the Abbey sought to strike a balance between the allure of 'its great antiquity and historic interest – not possessed to the same degree by any other property in the Kingdom' and its 'exceptional residential advantages.' It was 'situate in a most picturesque district, close to the South Coast, only 7 miles from Hastings, about an hour and a half's journey from London, in the neighbourhood of good society – the Estates of the Earl of Ashburnham and Lord Brassey adjoining and those of many county families contiguous – while the domain is of sufficient area, with the extensive woodlands, to provide considerable sporting.' The estate as enlarged by the Duke of Cleveland now extended to a little over 6,000 acres, with a rent roll of about £5,500 a year.

As for the Abbey itself, 'the east and west fronts present a grandly imposing exterior, while the additions on the north front, built by the late Duke of Cleveland, have a noble elevation entirely in character with the ancient battlemented structure.' The main reception rooms on the ground floor included the Abbot's Hall with its Minstrel Gallery, a vaulted Drawing Room, the Beggars' Hall, a Dining Room, a Morning Room (formerly the Abbot's Parlour), a Library and the Duke's Study. On the first floor were fourteen principal bedrooms, including one formerly used by the Duchess, with an adjacent boudoir having 'a magnificent view over the surrounding country extending to the sea.' Above this was a second floor with the servants' accommodation including a housemaid's sitting room, bedrooms for the valet, housekeeper, three ladies' maids, and visitors, and an attic with five more servants' bedrooms.

The servants' offices on the ground floor comprised a Butler's pantry, a still room, rooms for the Housekeeper, Steward, Chef, and Groom of the Chambers, a large Servants' Hall, the Under-Butler's bedroom, a kitchen (with gas stoves), a Cook's pantry and three large larders, a large Scullery, a small open Fernery, a beer cellar, wood shed, and coal and faggot houses. Outside was a large Coach

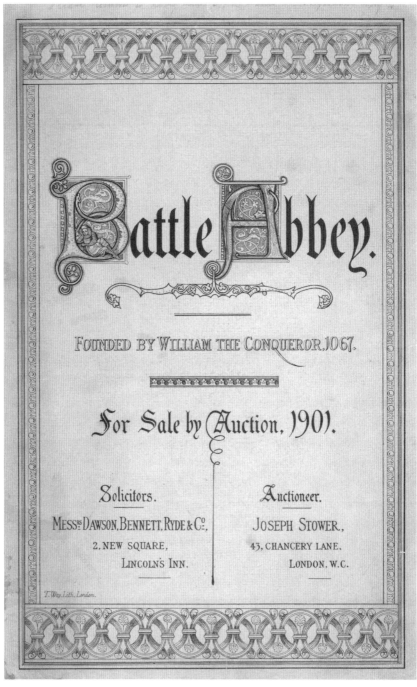

House with extensive stabling and two grooms' rooms.

The Abbey grounds extending to about eleven acres included a spacious lawn, shrubberies and wooded enclosures. On the Upper Terrace there was 'a beautifully laid-out Dutch-Italian garden' and a Conservatory Garden with 'tastefully laid-out flower beds', while on the Lower Terrace the two-hundred yard broad gravelled walk was flanked by 'a great variety of sub-tropical and greenhouse plants' growing against the wall. Beyond that was the Refectory Garden with magnificent magnolia trees, caenothus, and roses, including a 60-foot high Banksia rose; an orchard, a rose garden, a camellia walk, and a lily pond. The Park itself contained three ancient Stews ('being the Original Fishponds of the Monastery') as well as the New Pond, 'an ornamental lake of about three and a half acres, and a Pond in the Mountains, all well stocked with fish.'[1]

Over a thousand enquiries were received by the auctioneer, and an exceptionally large number of people turned up for the sale itself – so many indeed that shortly before the appointed hour the Auctioneer announced that 'to avoid discomfort' he had hired the large hall at Winchester House in Old Broad Street 'whither he asked those present to adjourn.'[2]

Once the company had been re-assembled Mr Stower opened the proceedings by briefly recalling the history of the Abbey from its foundation by William the Conqueror who, in a remarkable flight of fancy, he called 'probably the Dr Jameson of his day.' His rather jocular tone continued in a reply to a questioner who asked if it were true that the chancel of the parish church was included in the estate. 'Yes' he replied, ' but it was not to be taken away.' In a similar vein he brushed aside the first bid of £1,000 with the remark 'You must be trying to buy the wrong property!' But once the first serious bid of £50,000 had been made 'a fever of competition took hold.' The price was quickly doubled, and then went up by steps of £10,000 to £190,000. Beyond that it advanced more slowly by £1,000 bids to £200,000. At that point, 'after an ineffectual attempt by Mr Stower to obtain a further advance' it was knocked down to Mr Fox of Messrs Edwin Fox and Bonsfield.[3]

Everyone wanted to know who the successful bidder had been. Cries of 'Buyer?' rang out. But Mr Stower demurred. He said that 'as the matter was one of national importance, he was debarred for the moment from disclosing the name of the purchaser.' Rumours were rife that it was either Lord Rosebery or the American Mr William Waldorf Astor. It was some days before it was revealed that it was neither of these (though they had certainly been among the bidders) but Sir Augustus Webster.

A popular purchase

It was a very popular outcome, which attracted widespread comment in the national as well as provincial press. (The cuttings were assiduously collected at the time by Sir Augustus). There was a strongly patriotic note in much that was written. 'So the Yankees have not secured Battle Abbey after all' crowed the *Nottingham Guardian*. 'The abbey has gone back to the Websters ... Sir Augustus Webster, an ex-Guardsman and a popular sportsman, has always cherished the determination to regain the old property, and the public, which likes to see an old family keep its old estates, heartily congratulates him.'

This reaction did not pass unnoticed across the Atlantic. On 15 December the *New York Tribune* published a long article on 'South Coast relics. Battle Abbey and other famous sites near Hastings.' It commented: 'There has been much quiet satisfaction in England over the purchase of Battle Abbey by an English baronet whose ancestors were formerly in possession of the famous estate ...[Englishmen] would have shuddered if so historic a site had been auctioned off to a wealthy American.'[4]

The *County Gentleman* expressed similar sentiments: 'It is not often in these latter days, when Jack's as good as his master, that things call out right from a sentimental point of view in the case of any big purchase.[...] However, for once in the case of Battle Abbey and its glorious traditions things turned out satisfactorily.'[5]

In Battle, too, there was much satisfaction. On the eve of the sale the Dean of Battle, the Very Reverend Currie, had made a direct reference to local concerns at the end of his sermon:[6]

'The present time is a very anxious one for the parish. We know that possibly this week perhaps, or in a few days, may see the sale of the Abbey in this place. It cannot but have a great effect on the future welfare of this parish, and surely, if we believe in God's good providence, if we believe in

the efficacy of prayer, we shall, at this time, pray most earnestly to Him that this change of ownership may be for the honour and glory of His most holy name, for the good of His Church, and for the spiritual as well as the temporal good of all in the parish.'

Two days after the sale the *Sussex Daily News* reported that there had been much disappointment at the failure to reveal the name of the new squire. It added that in the meantime it had been officially denied that Mr W Astor was the purchaser. But, it went on: 'There is a rumour in the town that the new owner is Sir Augustus Webster, a relation of former owners…If this rumour is correct, Battle people will rejoice, for the Webster family was ever popular.' The following week the paper carried extracts from a speech by Lord Brassey, at the dinner following the annual Battle Stock Show, also welcoming the outcome of the sale. 'The new owner would come there', he said, 'with a warm feeling of interest in that district, and perhaps more desirous of promoting its prosperity than a stranger to the place.' In Sir Augustus Webster 'Battle will find a landlord who will undoubtedly keep up the old traditions of the Abbey.' The report concluded: 'The inhabitants are looking forward to a prosperous and happy time. It is to be hoped that the new owner will fulfil all their expectations.'[7]

The initial signs were encouraging. On 10 December Sir Augustus and Lady Webster paid a visit to Battle. They viewed the Abbey, lunched at the Deanery, visited the parish church, and had a drive round part of the estate on the outskirts of the town. They then left by the afternoon train. The *Evening News and Post* reported 'the great delight of the inhabitants' at the visit. 'Battle itself is bound up in the Abbey, and if there were no Abbey the reason for the town would almost cease to exist. It makes a vast difference to the townsfolk's pockets whether the Abbey is closed or open.'[8]

The *Sussex Daily News* added: 'The visit was intended to be a quiet one, but the fact that the Abbey's new owner was in town soon became known…Reminiscences of the Webster family were heard on all sides, and people began to wonder what the new "squire" would do. There is but little doubt that when the new landlord comes he will receive a right hearty old-English welcome.' In its issue of the following day *The Tatler* carried a full-page photograph of Lady Webster and her children under the heading 'The new hostess of Battle Abbey.' There was a general expectation that the Websters

No. 24, December 11 1901]   THE TATLER

SOCIETY IN TOWN AND COUNTRY

Week by Week.

Alice Hughes

THE NEW HOSTESS OF BATTLE ABBEY AND HER CHILDREN

Lady Webster, whose husband, Sir Augustus Webster, purchased Battle Abbey the other day for £200,000, is a daughter of
the late Mr. Henry Crossley of Aldborough Hall, Bedale. Sir Augustus Webster's ancestors formerly owned
the abbey for a period of 130 years

o   483   d

Lady Mabel Webster with Godfrey (standing) and baby Lucy

would take up residence once the purchase had been completed. This was scheduled for Lady's Day: press reports said they proposed to move in about the end of August.[9]

Another aspect of the return of the Websters also attracted a good deal of attention in the national press. Hastings Corporation was quick to offer the new owners the return of the vast painting of the Battle of Hastings which had been donated by the Dowager Lady Charlotte Webster in 1862 after the Clevelands had made it clear that they did not wish to keep it. For a great number of years it had been stowed away in the roof of the Market Hall, and then in the cellar of the Brassey Institute. No wall large enough to take it could be found for what was variously described as 'a gargantuan painting', 'an historic white elephant' and 'an unwieldy picture.' It was reported that the Corporation was asking £1,500 for it: the answer of Sir Augustus was awaited with interest.[10]

Disappointed hopes

But these hopes, like so many aroused in the immediate aftermath of the sale, were soon to be dashed. In mid February it was announced that a substantial volume of the contents of the Abbey was to be sold at auction, and in mid July that Sir Augustus was disposing of outlying parts of the estate, and had indeed already sold Northiam Place. Later that month there was the even more disturbing news that the Abbey had been let out, together with the shooting over the whole of the estate.[11]

In the absence of any documentary evidence, we can only speculate on the reasons why, having renewed his family's ownership of the Abbey, Sir Augustus and his wife decided not to live there. The purchase involved a substantial financial effort on his part: a first mortgage of £120,000 was negotiated with the London Life Association, and two further mortgages to make up the balance of the £200,000. Even with the greater security provided by his wife's financial resources, these constituted a considerable burden without providing the family with a home. Had the decision rested solely with Sir Augustus his choice would undoubtedly have been to resume occupation of the Abbey. No doubt his wife was willing to indulge her husband's desires up to a certain point. But perhaps once having seen the scale of the Abbey, considered the size and cost of the staff required to run it, and compared both with her experience of the much more modest Hildon House, she came to the conclusion that a line had to be drawn. At all events it was decided to seek an alternative base for the family in Battle, to rent out the Abbey itself, and also to sell off other parts of the estate. The dream which Sir Augustus had nurtured of a return to the Abbey was to be only very partially fulfilled.

He and his family took up residence in Powdermill House a short distance away on the estate, and it was there in 1904 that their third child, and second daughter, Evelyn was born. The Abbot's quarters continued to be used as a country house, but with new occupants.

The Grace family

A tenant was found quite speedily by Knight Frank and Rutley in July 1902. He was Mr Michael Grace, a sixty-year-old American citizen and millionaire of Irish descent who had spent a good deal of his life in Peru where he had attended Lima university, and subsequently resided and worked as a trader, becoming a judge of the commercial court and for a time diplomatic and consular representative of the Central American states.

For the Websters, with whom Grace and his wife Margarita enjoyed good relations, they were a fortunate and happy choice. They agreed to an initial lease of seven years, and advanced the money need to make the place habitable – some £7000 at a modest 4% interest – and provided an assured and regular source of income. They were to remain at the Abbey for a total of fourteen years.[12]

Grace had an extensive family and entourage, including four daughters and nine grandchildren. One of them, Peggie, later recorded her memories of her grandfather and their time at the Abbey. Known as 'Grandpoods' he was 'small and round, with pink cheeks, bright blue eyes, and a sparkling look. Without the slightest effort he charmed everyone.' He went to Florida for the winter, and took a shooting moor in Scotland every summer – but 'the place he really loved was Battle Abbey in Sussex. There he lived like a country squire, surrounded by his family, cousins, and friends, and it was from there that he gave in marriage his youngest daughter (my mother) and aunt Glad.'[13]

Unlike their aunt who found Battle 'a dull place, a countrified society, a rather poor hunt, and not much to do except go for long walks', Peggie and her brother found it enchanting. The Websters, Peggie recalled, were both friends and neighbours: 'one of their girls, Pickles (sic) was so pretty that even at that early age we all were under her spell.' Every Wednesday the Grace grandchildren trailed after the tourists who came to visit the Abbey (and who were at that time charged two shillings to visit the Abbot's Hall). They were not put off by the reputed presence of two ghosts, a white swan which sometimes visited one of the spare rooms, and 'the ghosts of the monks murdered by Cromwell' who on moonlight nights were seen slowly walking up and down the yew walk that led to the rose garden. They carried salt in their pockets to ward off these and other (equally unlikely) spirits.

Not everyone approved of the Graces. In a book published in 1906 Charles G Harper wrote disdainfully:[14]

> 'The wealthy American who resides there now and lords it over this historic spot and this beautiful park occupied by English gentlemen when the place whence he came was the primeval forest roamed by the North American redksins. It is a picturesque example of the newer conquering of England by the dollar, over eight hundred years after the famous battle that won it with the sword.'

The estate: More sales

As part of the overall financial plan, Sir Augustus and his trustees put the Rosehill estate on the market in 1902 and in the same year began the sale of outlying parts of the Battle Abbey estate. In July that year properties and land totalling close to 1,500 acres in Ewhurst, Northiam, and Pett were put on the market, followed in May 1903 by a number of residential, sporting and agricultural properties totalling 828 acres in and around Bexhill, described as 'a favourite and rising Watering Place.' Further sales on a smaller scale followed later in the decade and in the years leading up to the first world war.[15]

Attempts were also made to extend the exploitation of the natural resources of the estate. In May 1907 headlines in the *Sussex Daily News* announced 'A big Battle scheme. The shale discoveries at the Abbey. A syndicate formed.' It gave news of the sanctioning by a judge in the Chancery Division of a

SUSSEX.

THE PARTICULARS AND CONDITIONS OF SALE

OF THE OUTLYING PORTIONS OF

THE BATTLE ABBEY ESTATE

INCLUDING

FREEHOLD

Residential, Sporting and Agricultural

PROPERTIES,

ACCOMMODATION LANDS AND BUILDING SITES,

Situate in the picturesque Parishes of

EWHURST and NORTHIAM,

About Six Miles to the North of the Town of Battle,

And in the Parish of PETT, about Six miles from Hastings, in the County of Sussex.

COMPRISING ABOUT

1497 ACRES

(MORE OR LESS)

OF EXCELLENT

Arable, Pasture, Hop, Wood and Marsh Lands

WITH APPROPRIATE

RESIDENCES, FARMHOUSES, BUILDINGS and COTTAGES,

Producing a Rental of

£930 PER ANNUM.

Exclusive of the Woodlands in hand and portion of the Sporting Rights.

For Sale by Auction by Messrs.

EDWIN FOX and BOUSFIELD

AT THE MART, TOKENHOUSE YARD, BANK OF ENGLAND,

On WEDNESDAY, the 2nd day of JULY, 1902,

SALE COMMENCING AT TWO O'CLOCK PRECISELY,

IN LOTS.

May be viewed by permission of the Tenants. Particulars may be obtained at the Mart ; of Messrs. EDWIN FOX and BOUSFIELD, 99, Gresham Street, London, E.C. ; and of the Vendor's Solicitors—

Messrs. HASTIE,

65, Lincoln's Inn Fields, London, W.C.

proposed agreement to explore whether the shale deposits which had recently been discovered contained oil, natural gas or minerals in commercially-viable quantities. A company with a capital of £40,000 had been formed in the hope that this would be the case. Local people were both surprised and somewhat concerned by the news. But they need not have feared, for as with similar hopeful discoveries nearby at Heathfield, the early promise of industrial development soon petered out. Once again, commercial success eluded the later Websters.[16]

The Abbey: A tourist attraction...

By contrast, the number of visitors to the Abbey site continued to provide a steady if modest income for its new owner. The fact that the former family residence was now leased out did not affect the arrangements for visiting established by the Clevelands – except that the entrance charge introduced by their immediate successor now became a permanent feature. As before, the public was admitted every Tuesday throughout the year for conducted tours around the Abbey ruins. These arrangements continued to be criticised by some: an account published in 1907 gave an unflattering account of a typical guide – 'At last, with evident relief, he conducts the crowd to the gate, and saying "That's all I can show you today, ladies and gentlemen", dismisses them.' Nevertheless, 'Once a week great crowds of visitors come from Hastings by rail, by waggonette, or a-foot, and pay their sixpences to be conducted over the place.'[17]

In the aftermath of the sale there was a surge of interest which took the number of visitors for 1902 to over 17,000. In the following year this fell back to around 14,500 – a figure which remained much the same over the following decade. Each year only a few hundred came in the first and last three months, but from Easter numbers rose substantially to over a thousand a month, reaching a peak in August which in 1902 was just over 4,500, and in 1913 just under 4,000. The entrance fee for the great majority was 6d, but members of school and similar parties paid only 3d a head, and a similar low rate was also introduced for railway employees – no doubt in recognition of the contribution made to numbers by special railway excursions. On a rough calculation, annual entrance fees for this period totaled in the region of £5-600.[18]

Souvenir Normand memorial stone

ROY PRYCE

...and a symbol of peace

During these years there was a significant increase not only in the number of foreign visitors (for instance, a group of seventy Hungarians, Austrians and Poles in August 1913) but also in foreign interest in the symbolic significance of the Abbey. In the early years of the century this played a part in the growing rapprochement between Britain and France which led to the Entente Cordiale of 1904. It was then that a group of French aristocrats with Norman connections and internationalist convictions conceived the idea of using the site as a symbol of Anglo-French amity rather than conflict.

In 1896 they had set up an organisation called Le Souvenir Normand with the aim of cultivating relations between peoples from countries which had experienced the influence of the Normans. This they saw as a contribution to their ideal of universal peace. Their supporters included all the reigning monarchs in Europe who could claim descent from William the Conqueror. Contact was established with a British group based in Hastings who together with Lord Brassey and Sir Augustus invited a delegation to come over in August 1903. To mark the occasion, and to underline its political significance, a stone memorial was unveiled close to the spot in the Abbey grounds where Harold was reputed to have fallen, with an inscription (in French) which recalled the 11th century battle and declared that 837 years later 'the Souvenir Normand has joyously proclaimed the Peace of the Normandies soeurs'.

Visitors today to the Abbey may find the wording of the inscription rather curious and archaic, but the French gesture was part of the process of reconciliation which led shortly afterwards to the signature of the Convention establishing the Entente Cordiale on 14 October 1903, a date said to have been chosen by Edward VII in memory of the Battle of Hastings and 'in honour of the

Monument of Hastings (ie, Battle Abbey) where the Souvenir had set the seal on the Entente' by the installation of the Norman Stone.[19]

Sir Augustus was present at the unveiling ceremony but otherwise seems to have played only a marginal role in the initiative, inhibited no doubt by the fact that although he was the owner the Abbey he was not living there. Nor does he seem to have shared the concerns of others about the international scene – though this was later to impinge in a direct and dramatic way on the Webster family. His interests were firmly anchored closer to home.

Masonic activities

Shortly after his repurchase of the Abbey Sir Augustus was asked whether he was interested in becoming a Conservative candidate for Hastings but unlike several of his predecessors he does not appear to have been tempted by a parliamentary career. Instead he devoted a great deal of his time to his activities as a Freemason. In October 1901 the Duke of Connaught appointed him Grand Master of the Provincial Grand Lodge of Hampshire and the Isle of Wight. He was installed in this post on 20 February the following year at a special meeting held in the great hall of Winchester castle and in late July presided over his first annual meeting in the town hall at Andover. Before the official business began, and as a reflection of the close links between the masons and the Crown, Sir Augustus moved a resolution to offer to the King (Edward VII), the Protector of their Order, 'their sincere congratulations on his recovery from his serious illness and the happy progress he has made towards convalescence.'[20]

The previous evening Sir Augustus had also visited the Lodge of Peace and Harmony at Southampton where, according to the *Hampshire Advertiser* he 'highly pleased a large attendance of brethren...by his working of the Third Degree.' After the conclusion of their business, about sixty of them sat down to an excellent banquet, punctuated by toasts, speeches, and part-singing by a vocal quartet. As was habitual on such occasions, judicious philanthropy also figured in the proceedings. Sir Augustus urged support for a scheme of 'perpetual presentation' to the Royal Masonic Institution for Girls which would allow them to claim a place there for a candidate of their choice. Apart from 'the sentimental view of its being a memorial of a brother who had presided over the province since 1869', he told his fellow masons that the 1,500 guineas needed for the scheme was also 'a perfectly sound business transaction.'

A few days before this event, on 23 July, Sir Augustus was at another 'large gathering of the brethren of the Craft', this time at the Dome in Brighton where he had been invited by the Sussex masons to install the Earl of March as their Provincial Grand Master. This ceremony too was followed by a banquet which was served in the Royal Pavilion. 'The customary loyal and masonic toasts were duly honoured, and a pleasing programme of vocal music was sustained... Recitations were also contributed by Bro Eric Williams.'[21]

Such events kept Sir Augustus regularly in the local news, and from time to time aided no doubt by gentle nudges on his part – in the national press as well. On 10 February 1912, for instance, the London *Evening Standard* reminded its readers that it was his forty-eighth birthday in an article which also surveyed his life and the Webster family past and present.

The onset of war

A little over two years later the outbreak of the first World War ruptured the calm tenor of their lives, as it did of almost everyone else in the country. Sir Augustus was abroad when war was declared, but although he was then fifty he hastened back to rejoin his old regiment. He was posted as a Captain in the Grenadier Guards on 4 October and was assigned to the training battalion at Chelsea Barracks. This enabled him to frequent his clubs in London but it was no sinecure, especially as casualties mounted and fresh recruits had to be hastened into the front line.[22]

The following year, 1915, brought new problems and anxieties. In September his tenant at the Abbey, Mr Grace, intimated that he intended to leave within the following twelve months – an understandable but very inconvenient decision with costly implications, given the difficulty (and in the event, the impossibility when he left in September 1916) of finding another tenant in the midst of a war. More immediately, there were also Zeppelin raids on the capital. Writing to his wife on 14 October Sir Augustus reported 'another terrific air raid here last night...suddenly several violent explosions of bombs evidently not far off. We all went outside and shells were hurtling everywhere and down by the

R.M.I.G., 1916.

CAPTAIN SIR AUGUSTUS F. WEBSTER, Bart.,
Grenadier Guards,
R.W. Provincial Grand Master, Hampshire and Isle of Wight.
CHAIRMAN.

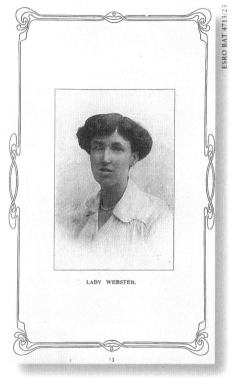

LADY WEBSTER.

The Websters in Wartime

barracks one could see lots of little flames all along the front, and a bright glare behind – that time I believe there were three Zeppelins.' Bombs were dropped on the barrack square, the cookhouse, the stables, a shed and the front parade ground 'which smashed every window including the mess plate glass.'[23]

Soon there were other, and more serious, worries. The Webster's only son, Godfrey, was anxious – like so many young men of his class at the time – to join in the war. In spite of his father's attempts to hold him back, he left Eton in December 1915 and entered the Royal Military College at Sandhurst in February 1916 as a gentleman cadet. About the time he arrived the Germans began their assault on Verdun, and in early July the British and French took the offensive on the Somme. Both resulted in fearful carnage. The British lost almost 420,000 men. The training of new officers had to be speeded up in an attempt to make good these desperate losses. No doubt to boost their morale there was a steady stream of important visitors to Sandhurst. In June these included George V and

Queen Mary. 'I was unable to get home as the King suddenly decided to come and inspect us on Sunday,' Godfrey wrote. 'The show went off very well except that the Commandant forgot his speech and stood with his mouth wide open for quite half a minute trying to think what to say. However, he got going in the end and the King said he thought we were very good. The Queen and Lord French came round with him on 2 March.'[24]

In November, after only some eight months at Sandhurst, Godfrey was posted as a subaltern in the Grenadier Guards, his father's regiment. The following March, after a brief home leave, he was despatched to join the British Expeditionary Force across the Channel. A fellow officer wrote to Sir Augustus:[25]

> 'My dear Gussie,
>
> I want to tell you how much I felt for you this morning saying goodbye to your splendid boy. I am going through all the anxiety myself with my only son in Macedonia and I know what it all means to us.
>
> Please God your boy will be all right. He is one you may well be proud of and I pray he may return safe and sound to you. From all accounts he is the best we have had for a long time and I know he will be a credit to the Regiment we both love.'

The Colonel in command of the Grenadier Guards, Sir Henry Streatfield, was also seriously concerned for Sir Augustus. He wrote to him on 2 March:[26]

> 'My dear Gussie,
>
> You look so awfully tired and played out. Wouldn't you like to go right away for a month? ... It seems to me that at your age the work with a training company is really too severe after two and a half years of it. I know you never spare yourself. You have worked so awfully hard and loyally...'

1917: Annus horribilis

Much worse was to follow in what turned out to be for Sir Augustus an annus horribilis. At around 7.30pm on the evening of Friday 15 June his wife went with his elder daughter Evelyn for a swim in Farthing Pond close by their home at Powdermill House. The two of them first helped the children's governess, Charlotte Kensington, pull a boat into the water and Lady Webster then said that she intended to swim across the lake, a matter of a hundred yards. A few moments later, while Miss Kensington was baling water out of the boat, she heard a cry from Lady Webster who was then some seven or eight yards away: 'The boat, Miss Kensington, quick.' Evelyn was in difficulties. Playing with a piece of wood she had found herself out of her depth, and she barely knew how to swim. Her mother reached her, and Miss Kensington saw the two of them struggling in the water. She pulled the boat round as quickly as she could with one oar, the other having slipped out of its rowlock. Seeing Evelyn sink under the water, she pulled off her skirt, plunged in, was able to get the girl on her back, and brought her safely to land. She then lost consciousness for a moment.

Farthing pond

When she came to, and looked around, there was no sign of Lady Webster. She had drowned in the rescue attempt. At the inquest, held on the following Monday, her doctor said that she easily got out of breath, and had suffered a sudden heart attack. The jury returned a verdict of accidental death. Its foreman proposed that Miss Kensington's brave conduct should be brought to the attention of the Royal Humane Society.

'Deep indeed was the gloom into which Battle was plunged on Saturday morning when the news was made known of the death of Emily Mabel Webster the previous evening under tragic circumstances,' reported the *Sussex Express*. In its lengthy report she was described as 'a gracious lady who was ever ready with help and assistance.' The paper added 'She had taken such a kindly interest in everything that was for the benefit of the town and its inhabitants that there was not a family but felt that a personal loss had been sustained.' She was not limited by her own social circle, 'she was loved for her kindly manner as much in the most humble cottage as she was in the more pretentious household.' The town came to a standstill on the Tuesday afternoon when a memorial service for Lady Webster was held in the crowded parish church. All business premises were closed and blinds drawn in private houses. Her elder daughter, Lucy, was the chief mourner.[27]

In the meantime Godfrey had joined the 3rd Battalion of the Grenadier Guards in the British Expeditionary Force in Flanders. He wrote to his mother on 21 May to report that he had just arrived after more brief training:[28]

> 'The course was quite nice and we did not have to work too hard. I now know every screw and bolt in the Lewis gun by its pet name. In the Exam I was equal top with another fellow. I am now Lewis gun instructor in the company.'

He added that they were billeted in a village close by: 'it is quite intact and the villagers are still here'. Their mess was in a farmer's house: the garden was very well kept and the fruit trees were all in bloom. He had seen a crested lark. He had received the parcels; 'the cake is very good.' He would soon be sending back a lot of his possessions 'as we have to lighten our kit considerably on account of moving.' He added, 'we are doing a lot of training here. I don't expect we shall be here long.'

In early June he was nevertheless able to take part in a dinner to celebrate the 4th of June attended by some 300 old Etonians, mostly from the Brigade. They had a great time, broke a good deal of furniture, and he and his commanding officer had difficulty in finding their way back to their billets. It was a rather typical gesture when a new offensive was in the offing. For Godfrey Webster it was a moment of relaxation in comparative safety. But by mid July he was at the front in Flanders, and in the thick of what became known as the third battle of Ypres. On 16 July he scribbled a letter to his aunt Rous: it was in pencil on small scraps of paper torn from a notebook . He tried to be reassuring, in spite of appearances. 'I am safely here and most awfully busy, scarcely a moment to oneself.' The great heat of the previous month ('I think we shall all melt soon') had given way to rain. One night he woke to find that he was lying in about two

IWM Q5935

Stretcher-bearers struggling through mud during the Third Battle of Ypres, August 1917

inches of water in his tent. 'I wonder if you hear the guns now' he asked.[29]

By then he had already made a name for himself in the battalion and the brigade. Put in charge of a 'very important reconnaissance' of a crossing of a canal which lay in the path of a projected 'push' he brought back valuable information in a report which was published in detail not only at Brigade level, but also by the Division and the Corps. On another occasion he was leading a party of ten men back from the front, and had reached the second line of trenches, only to find it blocked by a party of some thirty Scots Guards who were trying to dig out another guardsman who was buried up to his thigh and in great pain. They had been at it from some one and a half hours without success. Godfrey took control, got the men to work with their entrenching tools, and had him out in fifteen minutes. His commanding officer earmarked him for future promotion.[30]

At the end of July the main assault began, which as the Menin Gate memorial at Ypres records, 'quickly became a dogged struggle against determined opposition and the rapidly deteriorating weather.' On the 31st the Guards succeeded in gaining some ground which took them to a position some three-quarters of a mile beyond Pilkem Ridge, near Langemark, a few kilometres north of Ypres. On the night of 3 August Godfrey was with the 13th platoon,

No 4 company of the 3rd battalion of the Grenadier Guards being led by a Scots guardsman to relieve men in the front line there. As they reached slit trenches close by it a heavy barrage fell on them – 'a hurricane of din and bursting of shells all around our crouching position' as one of the survivors later recounted. One man was wounded, and their guide went missing, but led by Webster, the men continued to advance in single file. They had hardly gone fifty yards when a shell landed in front of him, hurling him into the air. He was killed instantly.[31]

Godfrey's body was recovered the next day, and was buried close to the front line. His commanding officer and military colleagues of Sir Augustus hastened to express their deepest sorrow at his loss. The only meagre consolation they could offer was that his death had been instantaneous: he had at least been spared the agony of prolonged suffering. They all expressed great admiration for him: 'a splendid young fellow…a bright and promising young life.' The King, George V, also sent a message 'to say how very truly the Queen and he sympathise with you in your irreparable loss.'[32]

Godfrey's death must have been a shattering blow to his father, especially as it came so soon after the loss of his wife – and at a time when he was clearly exhausted by his self-imposed wartime duties. It also had very serious consequences for the future of the Webster family. Godfrey had been the only male heir: with his death the baronetcy was destined to come to an end. There were many other titled families which suffered the same fate during the war: the *Morning Post* compiled an annual list of them under the heading 'Hereditary titles and the war.' These were still being updated after it was all over. A copy of the issue dated 28 December 1918 is preserved in the family papers: the Webster title is included in the list of 'Baronetcies left without living heirs.' Such reminders must have been very hard for Sir Augustus to bear.[33]

Awarded an OBE in June 1919 for his wartime services, he had by then returned to Powdermill House and civilian life. He continued to be active in the higher echelons of the Freemasons, as he had been during the war also, and its camaraderie no doubt brought some solace, as well as frequent contact with members of the royal family. In early May 1919, for instance, he took a prominent part in the ceremony initiating the Prince of Wales into 'the secrets and mysteries' of freemasonry, and in July that year was also involved in the installation of Prince Arthur of Connaught as Master of the Royal Alpha Lodge.

That same month Sir Augustus was voted 'Grand Elected Knight of the XXXIII Degree', which was followed in May 1921 by his appointment as 'Grand Inspector Inquisitor Commander.'

Lucy and Evelyn

In the meantime his married sister Amelia Sophia Rous (Mrs Askwith), who was living in Chelsea, had taken over responsibility for his two daughters. Lucy, the elder of the two, was fifteen when her mother died; her younger sister Evelyn (known to family and friends as 'Pickle') twelve. In a series of letters Rous (as she was known in the family) kept Augustus posted of their development – and their constant financial needs. As she approached her coming of age, Lucy was having a busy time attending balls up and down the country. She had grown up to believe in true Webster fashion that money would always be available. 'She rushes to me at the last moment,' wrote Rous, 'for fivers to go here, or send things "pay on delivery" there and I don't know where I am. What she does not understand is that if you want to do a thing very much and can't afford it, you don't do it. So far someone has always paid and all is well...But it can't go on for ever.' She suggested that her brother should pay 'her tenner direct – neither more nor less each month.'[34]

Rous admitted however that Lucy's tendencies 'were extravagant not from any intention, but mostly because she tried to do too many things at once.' She was showing some signs of an awareness of the need for economy – and had also mentioned the possibility of going to work. 'I really don't think it would be a bad idea,' wrote Rous, 'as Lucy on the loose is like a steam engine with the valve blown off.' It was a somewhat exasperated but also affectionate view: Lucy was clearly capable of charming her aunt. In a letter of 21 June 1921 Rous wrote:[35]

> *'I had a really wonderful letter from Lucy, looking back over the last four years and all it had meant to her – She's still very young and rather erratic, but she is the right stuff and after all she is only 20...She is not fit for responsibility yet, but she is learning and best of all, she wants to learn.'*

The immediate question later that summer was whether the money could be found to send Lucy off to Italy for the winter. ('With the exchange rate as favourable as it is, it may be the cheapest method of disposing of her'). In the

R.W. Bro. Sir AUGUSTUS F. W. E. WEBSTER, Bart.,
Prov. G.M., Hants and I.W., 1901.

meantime, Evelyn at the age of seventeen, had been despatched to Paris. 'To have her much with you', wrote her aunt in October 1921, 'is the most utterly exhausting effort...I wouldn't mind Pickle being wild and irresponsible if only her mental powers were more developed.' But, she added, there were three and a half good years to work in – a reference no doubt to her commitment to see both girls through to their coming of age.

Reporting back the following month on a visit she had paid Pickle in Paris, Rous told Augustus that she had found her 'extremely well, very fat, and much improved at any rate to all outward appearances.' But her French governess, who had earlier said her development was that of a child of ten, had told her that it was 'only under constant supervision that she maintains any sort of continuity of improvement.' She was however taking an intelligent interest in the Louvre and 'for the first time I gather that she really does want to improve, which up to now she never did.'[36]

Unfortunately the correspondence does not reveal any more about this period in the life of a member of the Webster family who was later to become a powerful presence in Battle. What is clear is that she formed a lifelong attachment to the Abbey, as was also the case for her father in spite of the fact that he never lived in it himself.

After the war Sir Augustus stayed on at Powdermill House. But it must have been a rather melancholy experience. For several years the Abbey itself remained empty. 'I am sorry you have still got no tenant for the Abbey,' wrote Rous in July 1921. 'These times don't help, do they?' Sir Augustus had the ivy stripped off the Gateway, but otherwise was mainly interested in the grounds, where he added some rare plants and shrubs to its gardens, at a cost according to one estimate of some £3,000.[37]

BATTLE MUSEUM

The East Sussex Hunt on Abbey Green, early 20th century

Arrival of the school

The Abbey, however, continued to be open to visitors, and it was one of them who in 1922 at last produced a new tenant for it. In May that year a young girl, Margaret Jacoby, came with some school friends. Her parents were Charles and May Jacoby the owners of St Etheldreda's, a girls' school at Bexhill who happened to be looking for larger premises. 'Who lives here?' she asked the guide. 'Oh', he replied, 'Nobody lives here; it has been empty for several years.' The moment she got home Margaret told her mother: 'There's the Abbey, we must move into that.' 'Nonsense,' her mother replied – but, having slept on it, changed her mind. Eight weeks later a lease was signed, and the school moved in on 22 September.[38]

The letting of the Abbey must have been a great relief to Sir Augustus, both financially and otherwise. But it marked the end of the Abbey as a country house and a private residence. It was the end of the era which had begun with the dissolution of the monastic house, and lasted for almost four hundred years. Up and down the country many country houses were experiencing a similar fate as families ran out of money or heirs (so many, like the Websters as a result of the war). Conversion to institutional use was one of a number of options: better certainly than neglect, decay or destruction – though in some cases it meant quite brutal change. The Abbey was spared this: the arrival of the school involved only a gentle and genteel conversion. The outward fabric remained virtually unaltered; so too did the arrangements for visitors to the site. The last of the Webster baronets could be pleased with the outcome as he pottered about the grounds.

But Sir Augustus had little time left to enjoy the Abbey. In January 1923 the East Sussex Hunt ball was held there before the school returned from Christmas vacation. It was his last public appearance. About a month afterwards he suffered a stroke, and later a second. He spent the last few months of his life in the home of a masseur in Brighton, where he died on Tuesday 13 August at the age of fifty nine. According to his daughter Lucy the cause was 'general paralysis of the insane,' the name then given to an advanced stage of syphilis – a disease which had also accounted for the early deaths of two previous Websters.[39]

On the afternoon of Saturday 17 August, 'amid every sign of respect' and after a service 'of a Masonic nature' attended by a large number of Masons as well as his tenants and others, the ashes of Sir Augustus were interred in the family vault under the altar of the parish church. His daughters Lucy and Evelyn headed the Webster family mourners.[40]

10

HANGING ON: LUCY, EVELYN AND GODFREY

After the death of the last Webster baronet, the family hung on to the Abbey for another fifty-three years. This final period of their ownership between 1923 and 1976 was a time when many owners of country houses were forced to sell or abandon them: in the case of the Websters the end-game proved particularly prolonged.

None of the three members of the family most closely involved was able to live at the Abbey, and the hopes they all nurtured of being able to secure their future there were destined to be disappointed. Their fate ultimately was decided not by them but by family trustees and judicial authorities. Towards the end of the period both Evelyn and her eldest son Godfrey were living in Battle. Like many of their Webster predecessors, they continued to behave in a lordly manner although saddled with debt, to the astonishment and amusement of local people. But a rift between the two Websters had a corrosive, and ultimately disastrous impact on their dreams of continued ownership of the Abbey. There was a darker side too to this final act of the family saga. In the background, largely hidden from sight but the source of much speculation and gossip, was yet another personal tragedy, this time of a Webster heiress who was locked away for most of her life, an embarrassing ghost at the final rites of the family's tenure of the Abbey.

Lucy prepares to inherit

Under the terms of her father's will Lucy Webster, the eldest daughter of the last baronet, was to inherit the Battle Abbey estate for her lifetime. At his suggestion she had spent some twelve months from the autumn of 1920 as a 'mud pup' on the Yorkshire estate of Lord and Lady Harewood learning about estate management, as well as visiting local steel-making and engineering works. Although confessing near the end of her period there her 'absolute ignorance and incapability,' she had in fact shown a keen interest in the financial management of the estate, and back in Battle she was clearly preparing herself to take over as her father's condition worsened in the early part of 1923.[1]

In addition to inquiring about the details of the estate, she began to reflect on its future and whether she might sell off some further parts of it, and develop the rest. During this period she also came to the decision, largely it would seem as a result of a misunderstanding with her aunt Rous (Mrs Askwith), to transfer her legal business away from the firm of Hasties which had been the Webster family solicitors for several generations. She soon regretted this and returned to them – but in the meantime she had to face a considerable wait of more than two years before the legal formalities could be completed and the estate handed over to her. For a rather impetuous young woman this must have been a very frustrating experience. Eventually, by June 1925, the paperwork had almost been completed: on the 19th she wrote 'I am now quite capable of managing my own Estate, which I intend to do'.

Estate sales

In the meantime the executors of Sir Augustus had decided to sell off substantial parts of the estate, like many other landowners at the time. Agricultural prices halved between 1920 and 1922, heralding a long period of decline in the countryside. The ownership of agricultural land was no longer profitable, and in addition the Webster executors needed to free capital to pay off the outstanding mortgage on the Abbey, and to meet death duties. Hampton and Sons advised them that these obligations could be met over a ten-to-twelve year period if the Bexhill part of the estate were sold off, leaving a profit from the rest of £3-4,000 a year 'for all time'.[2]

The response of the executors was not only to follow their advice in December that year, when the Bexhill part of the estate was put on the market, but also to embark on much more radical surgery. On 11 March 1924 at an auction held at the George Inn in Battle, 2,365 acres were offered for sale in 73 lots. These included twenty-one dairy farms, many smallholdings, accommodation and building land, together with 32 houses and cottages. The sale was advertised as 'the outlying portions' of the Battle Abbey estate, though the first 21 lots which included the Wellington Inn were mainly located in Battle itself, between

By order of the Executors of Sir Augustus Webster, Bart., decd.

SUSSEX.

In and around the Historic Market Town of BATTLE.

Particulars, Plans, Views and Conditions of Sale

OF

Valuable Outlying Portions of the

Battle Abbey Estate

CONSISTING OF

TWENTY-ONE DAIRY FARMS

With Good Houses and Buildings, held Yearly.

Numerous Small Holdings. Valuable Accommodation and Building Lands. Thirty-two Houses and Cottages. The Wellington Inn, Battle, a Fully-Licensed Market House. Ground Rents. The Battle Fruit Farms. Corn Warehouse. Coal Stores and Wharfs. Allotments and Extensive Woodlands.

The Whole extending to about

2,365 Acres.

WHICH

HAMPTON & SONS

Are instructed to Sell by Auction,

At THE GEORGE INN, BATTLE,

On Tuesday, the 11th day of March, 1924,

At 11 o'clock precisely, IN 73 LOTS unless previously disposed of privately).

VENDORS' SOLICITORS—Messrs. HASTIE, 65, Lincoln's Inn Fields, W.C. 2.

Particulars, with Plans, Views and Conditions of Sale of the Auctioneers,

HAMPTON & SONS, Ltd., 20, St. James' Square, London, S.W. 1.

Mount Street and North Trade Road and up Caldbec Hill. Later in the same year, on 25 September, another sale was held in the same location of 'valuable town properties' in Battle. On this occasion the 21 lots included 26 cottages and two butchers shops, as well as tithes in Battle and Ewhurst – the latter yielding £1,450 and £1,600 p.a. respectively.[3]

In June 1926 a fourth big sale took place, this time covering a total of 1,174 acres. Its 45 lots included Battle Cattle Market and Drill Hall, but consisted for the most part of land and properties in outlying portions of the estate, as well as some marshland which had failed to sell earlier. Taken together, these sales marked a radical reduction in the size of Battle Abbey estate, which this time was to be permanent.

An unfortunate heiress

By then Lucy Webster had become the titular owner of Battle Abbey and its estate. But it was not an inheritance she was destined to enjoy. Although she was very intelligent and shrewd, as her preparations for assuming ownership demonstrated, there were other and more negative aspects to her personality and behaviour. Like many of the Websters before her, she had grown up in the belief that money would always be available, and had easily acquired the habits of a spendthrift. At the same time she was highly strung, impulsive and rather unstable. From about the age of sixteen these elements in her personality became more pronounced, and fused with her developing strong sexuality – another familiar Webster trait. She began to question conventional attitudes to sex, wrote what she later described as 'crazy stuff', and became subject to periods of abnormal behaviour. For part of this time she lived in Battle at Tollgates, a house which had been built by her father: she began to acquire a reputation for promiscuous behaviour, and the story circulated of her running naked down the High Street.[4]

In her early twenties she had the misfortune to become deeply involved with a religious psychoanalyst, Homer Lane, who had very advanced ideas for the time about sexuality and sexual behaviour, which he argued should be freed from the constraints of conventional morality. She became a follower and financial supporter, even spending over £1,000 on a fur coat for his wife. In the course of

1925 Lane was charged with writing improper letters to various women patients, was found guilty and deported. Lucy hired a private detective to discover his whereabouts in France and set off to Nice after him. A period of intense religious and sexual experience followed which included two days naked on a nearby mountain and sex with a succession of strangers on the Riviera. On her way back to England, Lane having departed for the United States, Lucy spent some time in Paris where she did the rounds of various night clubs of ill-repute, and at one time thought of investing money in one of them.

She was to pay a high price for this extraordinary adventure. As a result of her sexual promiscuity she contracted a venereal disease which, on her return to England in October 1925, led to a serious illness. She was admitted to a nursing home for urgent treatment. While she was there she was seen by a doctor who concluded that she was also suffering from religious mania and nymphomania, and considered that in terms of the prevailing legal regime she was certifiably insane. Once the necessary formalities were completed this meant she was placed under the protection of the system than applied to those suffering from mental instability, the management of her affairs being entrusted to her aunt, Mrs Askwith, under the supervision of the grotesquely-named 'Master of Lunacy' appointed by the Supreme Court.

There is good evidence that at this stage Lucy herself was a willing participant in these decisions, even though the stigma attached in the public mind to being certified was undoubtedly very considerable. Nymphomaniacs are often distressed by their own behaviour, and that was certainly the case with Lucy Webster. Earlier in the same year, in April 1925 during the legal proceedings against Homer Lane, she had herself already taken the initiative to see a doctor and asked to be certified. There is no suggestion that she was coerced later that year, though no doubt her aunt, her sister and the family trustees favoured the same course of action, and for good reasons. Although the Websters were no strangers to sexual adventures and their unfortunate consequences, the clamorous way in which Lucy was flouting prevailing conventions was a serious embarrassment. Her behaviour was also a source of deep concern for a different reason. The financial recklessness which she had displayed was as alarming as her unconventional sexual activities. Lucy was no ordinary member of the family: she was its heiress. Her family and its trustees feared that were she allowed unfettered financial control over the estate it could again sink deep into debt, and their whole future, including ownership of the Abbey, once more be put at risk.

The legal regime applied to Lucy answered these concerns. Its function was to protect and manage the property and financial affairs of a person who, by reason of mental disorder, was incapable of dealing with such matters. Although still described at the time by the archaic term 'lunatic', the law defined such a person as someone who was mentally ill but who might enjoy lucid intervals and even recover (in contrast to 'an idiot' who had no prospect of recovery). The Court did not attempt to prescribe treatment for the condition, and although its procedures for approving expenditure were cumbersome and slow, the regime allowed Lucy to retain her freedom of movement – she was then living in London – and to continue to deal with her day-to-day affairs.

During the following twelve months there was a steady improvement in her mental state. In May 1926 she again saw the two specialists who had examined her the previous year, this time in the hope of being able to regain control over her own affairs. They both concluded that while her condition had certainly improved it would be imprudent to grant her wish, but after a spell as a voluntary patient at a sanatorium in Surrey she was de-certified in the middle of 1927 in time to take a hand in the preparations for, and to be present at, the wedding of her younger sister Evelyn in September that year. Her expenditure was still subject to the jurisdiction of the Court – she was allowed £50 a week – but that did not prevent her buying a car and, towards the end of the year, looking for a flat of her own in London.

Sadly, however, her condition then deteriorated again and by mid 1930 she was back as a patient in a mental home, this time at Ticehurst not far from Battle. There the regime was quite liberal – she was able to go riding and hunting, and pay visits to the theatre – but her period there proved to be the prelude to a permanent withdrawal from the world, other than brief visits to a friend at Christmas. The remainder of her long life was spent in similar institutions elsewhere in the country, her financial affairs being managed by successive agencies of the Supreme Court, as the legislation relating to mental illness was revised, and from 1947 by the Court of Protection. It is not clear how far she continued to be a voluntary patient, or what part other members of the family played in her continued incarceration. Evelyn, it seems, rarely if ever mentioned her, other than to remark that her removal from the scene 'was a great loss for the men of Battle'. Godfrey, for his part, was more sympathetic but he was in no position to be of much help. For both of them, as well for the family trustees, it was in any case far better for Lucy to be out of the way and looked after by others. It was a tragic fate for a lively and intelligent – if wayward and impulsive – young woman which might well have been avoided had modern techniques of treating her type of condition been available and her own family more sympathetic and supportive.

The Webster-Harbord marriage

Evelyn Webster's marriage in September 1927 was a big affair. The ceremony itself took place in Battle parish church, where she was attended by fifteen bridesmaids decked out in Tudor costume. Afterwards the wedding party processed across the road for a reception at the Abbey. The groom was Charles R Harbord, a member of an Anglo-Portugese family with interests in the port wine trade and hotels, and the brother of the theatre and set designer Felix Harbord. A few years older than his bride, Charles was a tall, slim and handsome man who had already spent a number of years working for the British American Tobacco Company in

BATTLE ABBEY BRIDE AND OLD WORLD RETINUE

Like a picture from some romantic story, and blending with dignified beauty in the setting of historic Battle Abbey, Sussex, is this photograph of the bridal party at yesterday's wedding of Miss Evelyn Webster, daughter of the late Sir Augustus Webster, and Mr. Charles Harbord. On the left is Miss Lucy Webster, owner of Battle Abbey who gave her sister away.—(Sunday Graphic.)

The wedding of Evelyn Webster, 1927. Lucy is on the far left.

India. The couple sailed for there on the P&O liner Rawalpindi that autumn. By the time they arrived Evelyn was already pregnant, and they had a 'beastly journey' overland to Assam. But having arrived she pronounced it 'lovely': there was wonderful shooting, riding and tennis. ('The people here are absolutely nil, but it does not matter'.) They enjoyed a quiet life, and their daily routine which began at 6.30am when Charles went riding before breakfast. After the day's work they played tennis between 4.30 and 5.30pm before tea, and then sometimes went to the club to play billiards and bridge before dinner and an early bed. For the summer of 1928 they rented a bungalow in Shillong where their first child, Godfrey Vassall, was born on 16 June.[5]

Something however happened to Harbord's job; he failed to find a satisfactory alternative in India, and in the Spring of 1930 they decided to return to England, after a stay of less than three years. They arrived by the end of the summer and a second son, Simon, was born in August 1933. But within a few years the marriage foundered. Evelyn moved back to Powdermill House in Battle while Charles Harbord went off to Portugal and joined the family's hotel business.

May Jacoby

The school and visitors

In the years immediately following Evelyn's marriage there was only a faint Webster presence in Battle, the affairs of the estate being in the hands of the family trustees and the judicial authotities acting on behalf of Lucy. In the meantime it was the school which took centre stage at the Abbey. Although it had only 35 girls when it first moved in on 22 September 1922, by the following year numbers increased to a hundred. It flourished under its imposing and dynamic headmistress, May Jacoby, the married daughter of its founder and proprietor, John Raymond Sheehan-Dare. Some changes were made to the existing buildings to meet the needs of the school. An old racquets

BATTLE ABBEY SCHOOL

School Assembly, 1928

court (formerly the court house) in the gateway, for instance, was converted into a gym and in 1924 some wooden buildings were erected in the ground to provide a science room, studio and sanatorium. But money was tight. In correspondence with Lucy Webster in 1925 May Jacoby confessed that a school was a 'curious financial proposition' and that the Abbey was 'a most frightfully difficult and expensive house to run.' She was not sure whether they would want to stay after the first twelve years.[6]

Visitors to the Abbey were another source of some concern as well as extra expenditure. Their annual number had risen from around 13,500 in 1913 to over 22,000 in 1923. Some local people were, it seems, rather sniffy about them. It was reported in the *Sussex Express* that intending visitors often went to Hastings thinking they would see the site of the battle there – a misconception which was not confined to the lower orders (see p.166). The report continued, 'then they wake up to the fact that the battle was fought a few miles up the road. So they take a shilling bus, come out and see the spot, spend ninepence on the fee, and go back to Hastings.'[7]

After the death of Sir Augustus arrangements to deal with visitors

An art class in the Abbey grounds, 1920s

were in the hands of his executors, but continued to be unsatisfactory. In the early summer of 1925 Mr Sheehan-Dare wrote to Lucy to explain the problems. 'Visitors to the grounds often enter without paying, carve their names on the ruins, pick flowers and in the season, help themselves to fruit etc.' The gateway could not be used as an entrance because of its condition, and the guides were unsatisfactory. They exchanged ideas about improving the situation. He agreed that a standard entrance fee of a shilling should be introduced and that an extra 3d to view the battlefield 'would prove an attractive idea' to the majority of visitors. He offered to take control of the guides: there were a sufficient number of them, but 'the "story" they tell to visitors can certainly be made more entertaining.' He also suggested that something should be done to provide better facilities. In talks with charabanc proprietors he had discovered, for instance, that after a visit to the Abbey they hurried on to Robertsbridge 'because they cannot obtain a good tea in Battle.'[8]

While the school continued to develop – its academic standards were steadily improved and in 1928 it was granted the coveted 'Recognition' after an inspection by two of His Majesty's Inspectors – finances remained tight. In 1930, together with the Webster estate trustees, it sought a reduction in the Abbey's rateable value. It was argued that the building was 'not altogether suited for the purpose of a school,' that the dining room was dark, and the kitchen, though nice to look at, was 'very difficult to work economically.' It was also argued that the flow of visitors around its part of the Abbey buildings added to its costs by increasing the degree of supervision required to safeguard its pupils.

Trustees plead poverty

In the same hearing it was argued on behalf of the Webster family trustees that its revenues from visitors were in decline. Although reductions in the entrance charge on certain days introduced by their steward had increased the number of visitors, this had caused 'some irritation to the tenants' without increasing revenue. Moreover, the ruins had just been scheduled as a National Monument by the Office of Works and this had 'practically compelled' the trustees to secure the services of an eminent architect, Mr Harold Brakspear, and to envisage an expensive programme of repairs over the coming years. Gross receipts from visitors had been £1,843 in 1927, £1,888 in 1928, but had fallen to £1,661 in 1929. At the same time, the cost of repairs had suddenly escalated from £294 in 1928 to £1,068 in 1929, which together with other expenditure on upkeep and guides reduced net receipts from £1,087 in 1928 to a mere £85 the following year.[9]

BATTLE ABBEY SCHOOL

Webster portraits look down on a class in progress

Panorama of the school grounds in the 1930s

A few years later, in the early thirties, the family trustees sought to increase their revenue by enclosing the Green in front of the entrance to the Abbey. Notices were put up declaring it to be private property, the grass was removed, the whole area covered with tarmac, and surrounded by a spiked chain fence carrying a notice 'Car Park 6d'. Great was the indignation of the townspeople. The notices were pulled down; the Urban District Council protested and threatened legal action. In the end an amicable settlement was reached which recognised the rights of both the family and the public. But the Green remained a parking area for cars and buses: it was later to take many years of argument before it was restored – more or less – as an open space. [10]

A fire at the Abbey

In the meantime, far larger sums were required for repairs than had been anticipated as a result of a dramatic discovery at the school early on the morning of Saturday 31 January 1931. At around 4.30am one of the young pupils who had gone to the bathroom for a drink of water smelt smoke and realised there was a fire. Fortunately the girls had been trained in what to do. She blew her whistle to raise the alarm, roused her dormitory, and led them to safety down the Tower. In a very short time everyone safely evacuated the building. But the fire took hold behind the thick wall of a bedroom and, fuelled by a great deal of wooden

panelling, quickly spread, defeating attempts to douse it with extinguishers. Mrs Jacoby's daughter Margaret was dispatched up the High Street to the fire station but the fire crew had to be summoned by telephone. Accounts of how long it took for them to arrive with their fire engine differ, but by that time – when they were shortly joined by the Bexhill and Hastings brigades – the Abbot's Hall was fiercely ablaze, and the best they could do was to contain the damage. The library and north wings were saved but the Hall itself was gutted, and its roof fell in.

The staff of the school coped admirably with the emergency. They quickly found alternative overnight accommodation, and on the Tuesday the whole school was able to resume lessons in the undamaged part of the Abbey. They soldiered on for the rest of that term, but then moved to Bolney Court in West Sussex while repairs were carried out. Planned and supervised by Harold Brakspeare (who was subsequently knighted) these took some eighteen months.[11]

In the meantime the town of Battle went ahead with its plans to stage a pageant in the grounds and amid the ruins of the Abbey to celebrate and commemorate its history. This was a very ambitious affair, directed by Gwen Lally (who specialised in such productions), with performances spread over the first fortnight of July 1932, each of which involved some three thousand participants. In spite of much criticism and pessimism in advance of the event, it was a popular (though not a financial) success, with an audience of some

The Abbot's Hall after the fire

6-7,000 for the final Saturday matinee, and a further 3-4,000 that evening. Sheila K Smith, the well-known Sussex author, wrote the prologue, and many other local notables took part, some of them playing their ancestors. The pageant consisted of nine episodes in the history of the Abbey. The periods of ownership by the Montagues and Clevelands both figured among these, but not that of the Websters. Evelyn Harbord (née Webster), dressed in 'a charming Tudor costume', had a modest part in the pageant, sharing the role of Queen Matilda. It was no doubt much less than she would have wished, but the family was no longer a prominent feature of the local scene, and it was only quite recently that she herself had returned to Battle.[12]

After the festival the work of restoring the Abbot's Hall continued for another twelve months. In the course of it a number of discoveries were made – including the piscina of the abbot's chapel – and some discreet improvements were made. More spacious windows were installed at the western end of the Abbot's Hall, which it was claimed were more in keeping with those originally there; the walls were stripped of plaster; and the huge fireplace was rebuilt to a different design. The works were carried out on the instructions of the Webster family trustees, who in July 1933 had to apply to the Chancery Division of the High Court for permission to use part of the capital of the trust fund to help meet the costs. They asked for, and were granted, around £3,350 for that purpose which the trustees said would help to maintain and increase the number of visitors, from whom a considerable income was raised. Gross takings from this source were said to be between £1,500 and £1,600 per annum, yielding a net income, after payment of wages, of around £800 a year – a sum almost ten times higher than the figure quoted only three years earlier when the estate was pleading poverty and a reduction in the Abbey's rateable value.[13]

The formal ceremony marking the completion of the work of restoration took place on Saturday 27 May 1933 and was carried out in heavy rain by Princess Alice, the Countess of Athlone, and her husband the Earl, together with the Bishop of Chichester. Evelyn Harbord was among the 400 or so guests, but it was Mrs Jacoby and her husband who were photographed with the royal guests after the ceremony. The school had returned from exile on 25 March, and it was May Jacoby, its Principal who once again presided at the Abbey. On the following day, for instance, it was she who hosted the "At Home" there for the local Battle residents who had helped at the time of the fire. Similarly, it was Mrs Jacoby who on Sunday 25 June was at the Abbey Gateway to welcome 700 limbless ex-servicemen, members of the St Martin Association, on a visit which included a service on the site of the altar of the original Abbey church.[14]

Royal visits

For the pupils, Mrs Jacoby was a figure who inspired awe. As one of them recalled, 'each morning she appeared in a black coat buttoned to the waist over a black and white dress, descending the staircase at a quarter to nine. Then she would take prayers, beginning with "Good morning girls". We all replied, "Good morning Mrs Jacoby", and we literally all bowed to her, she was so regal'.[15]

Even Mrs Jacoby was momentarily flustered, however, when on 1 March 1935 Queen Mary paid an unexpected visit to the school. She was called out of her sitting room where she was interviewing parents – wearing ankle socks to keep out the cold – to find the Queen in the Abbots Hall. She subsequently accompanied her royal visitor on an extensive tour of the school which included the kitchen and all the bedrooms. Rather typically, the Queen remarked on observing ivy growing outside the library wall that it ought to come down before

Visit of George V to the school, March 1935

it ruined the stonework. (It was duly removed the following day). When she came across a group of girls in a room close to the kitchen she asked them what they were all doing. 'Waiting for tea your Majesty', they replied. The Queen was amused and said, laughing, 'Oh, I thought you were all working hard!'

Five days later King George V also turned up, again without warning. The first person he met was one of the Abbey guides, Philcox, to whom he confessed that he had been told that the famous battle had been fought at Hastings, and was duly corrected – to their mutual amusement. Mrs Jacoby was resting and had to dress hurriedly. Arriving in the sitting room she found the King playing with her cat Marmalade. They each soon found out that the other was somewhat deaf, so they had to shout at each other: their subsequent conversation was heard all over the Abbey. The girls were hastily lined up, and as the King prepared to leave, Mrs Jacoby yelled 'Curtsey, curtsey!' A member of staff reported, 'As he went down the drive they were all tottering into a curtsey which looked very nice, but we nearly had hysterics because we stood behind watching them and none of them knew how to do it properly.'

These visits may well have been made with the educational needs of the royals' granddaughter, Princess Elizabeth, in mind. The following year, in March 1936, she and her parents, the Duke and Duchess of York, came when they were staying at Eastbourne to see the school and Battle church. This was the occasion for another royal confession of ignorance. The Duke (the future George VI) said that he did not know about the monk's curse on the Brownes. 'But I do, Daddy', Princess Elizabeth is reported to have said.[16]

In the event the future queen did not attend the school, but it certainly continued to occupy centre stage at Battle Abbey in the period up to the second world war. At least one observer thought that this was quite inappropriate. In a tone of high indignation a well-known and respected author and commentator, AV Morton, wrote in 1942:[17]

> 'Only in England perhaps could Battle Abbey become a girls' school. Indeed it might seem to a foreigner to be one of the baffling inconsistencies of English life that the place where the future of England was changed should be devoted to the education of young ladies; for here, if anywhere, is a sacred national shrine. But when you approach the fine gateway of Battle Abbey it is soon made clear to you that Battle is a girls' school first and a national shrine a long way after'.

In the meantime Evelyn Harbord was struggling to make ends meet at Powdermill House. Her modest income was stretched with two boys being educated privately, and the bank was unhelpful. It was a familiar problem for a Webster, but she was determined to keep up appearances. There was a steady stream of quite prominent visitors – including Lillian Bayliss and Ninette de Valois – but when, for instance, two ambassadors came to stay Evelyn saw to it that holes in the stair carpet were disguised by a lick of matching red paint – applied at her command by the daughter of a family friend. She also took in various paying guests, including young foreigners wishing to learn English, who included one of Mussolini's grandsons, Fabrizio Ciano, whose father was then Italian Foreign Minister. (Fabrizio was later to write an account of his father's death at the hands of Mussolini under the title of *Quando il nonno fece fucilare papa* – When Grandpa had Daddy shot). In the autumn of 1939, after the outbreak of war, Evelyn advertised in *Nursery World* that she would take children aged between one and eight to share a governess and nurse with her own children in a 'Country house, safe zone.'[18]

Wartime in Battle

In the same belief scores of evacuees from Greenwich had arrived in Battle two days before war was declared on 3 September, and were accommodated in the blackout by members of the local Women's Institute. The period of apparent safety, however, came to an abrupt end in May 1940 when the German army arrived, victorious, on the other side of the Channel. Sussex was now in the front line, as it had been on other occasions, though not since the Napoleonic wars. The evacuees departed (some to the south-west, others to Canada), houses were requisitioned, and 'the previously quiet town of Battle became suddenly full of soldiers'. In June the school was given just forty-eight hours to quit the Abbey when it was taken over by the War Office. It departed for the duration to Killerton Park in Devon. In its place first came units of the British 55 Division, including the Devonshires, hastily deployed in the face of the imminent threat of invasion, and later, from the middle of 1941, Canadian troops who took over from them.[19]

The first of the new arrivals were elements of the 2nd Canadian Division, which from October 1941 included the 8th Canadian Reconnaissance Battalion. It was men from this Division who provided the bulk of the five thousand troops who were used in the disastrous raid on Dieppe in August 1942; a frontal assault which cost the lives of more than nine hundred of them out of a total of 3,367 casualties. Many of those stationed in Battle did not return.[20]

For most of this time the Abbey was used as a billet and mess for Canadian NCOs, the officers being housed at Beauport. Churchill and Smuts paid them a visit, but it was in 1943 that one of the most extraordinary wartime incidents took place at the Abbey. On 1 February three German fighter bombers strafed the High Street, killing the owner of a shop and his wife, wrecking some other business premises and badly damaging two hotels. The Abbey itself only narrowly avoided severe damage. One of the bombs landed on Abbey Green at an acute angle immediately outside the gatehouse and ricocheted at great speed past a sentry, relieving him of his rifle. He fainted, the bomb shot through the archway, hitting the porter's doorway on its way but failed to explode, breaking up on the lawn beyond the gateway. Had it detonated the consequences could have been devastating as Royal Engineers had stored two tons of gelignite in rooms in the gate house. It was a narrow squeak for all concerned.[21]

As the time for the re-conquest of the continent drew near, the Canadians were replaced by British troops but they left some permanent reminders of their presence both in the town, in the area along the London road which became known as 'Canadia', and in the Abbey where two dormitories kept the numbers (25 and 27) given to them by the troops. Even after the invasion forces had left, the town remained in the front line along with the rest of East Sussex which became known as 'Doodlebug Alley' as it lay under the flight path of V1 and, later, V2 missiles.[22]

Re-emergence of Evelyn Webster

After the ending of hostilities with the surrender of Japan in August 1945, it took time for the Abbey to be handed back to its civilian owners. The school returned in March 1946 to find the buildings scarred with the ravages of military occupation, the gardens overgrown, and German prisoners of war still working on the farm associated with the Abbey. But the greatest change it faced was the absence of Mrs Jacoby as Principal. She had fallen ill during the war and given up the running of the school, returning to Battle where she was to die in September 1948 after a long illness.

Evelyn Harbord now assumed a more prominent role both at the Abbey and in the town. On 1 June 1946, having become chair of the Rye Division of the Liberal Association, she gave a garden party at Powdermill House as part of a celebration of 'Liberal Foundation Day'. With the writer Sir Shane Leslie (a cousin) and the prospective Liberal parliamentary candidate as chief guests, this provided the main story that week in the local paper. Mrs Harbord also played a significant part at the resumption of the traditional celebration of Guy Fawkes Day later that year. Having given permission for the procession to pass through the Abbey Gates before returning to the Green, it was she who lit the bonfire there, and subsequently distributed the prizes for the best costumes.[23]

Her role at this annual event was one she evidently savoured: it has been vividly described by June Parker who became Headmistress at the School in 1968, by which time it had become a familiar spectacle – and Evelyn had reverted to her original family name:[24]

Evelyn Webster at the Festival of Britain celebrations in the Abbey, 1951

> '*The Battle Bonfire Boys have a reputation comparable to that of Lewes: dressed in fantastic costumes, historical, whimsical, ferocious or funny they form a great procession and move from the top of the High Street down to Lower Lake and finally arrive at the Abbey. Suddenly the Gates are opened and with flaming torches held high and led by the band comes the invading army; at their head walked for many years their President, Mrs Webster, clad in black with an enormous wide black hat...Torches flare, some are flung smoking to the ground, squibs explode and unflinching in the centre of it all stands Mrs Webster waiting for the great crowd to fall into silence whilst she addresses them.*'

Like her father, Evelyn was keen on amateur dramatics: she built a stage in a converted stables at Powdermill House where both adults and children put on plays. Like him, too, she also enjoyed dressing up. In 1951 she appeared in Tudor costume on horseback as part of the Festival of Britain celebrations in the Abbey. She also played a prominent part, though this time in more conventional garb, in the ceremonies held in 1966 to mark the 900th anniversary of the Battle of Hastings.

The celebrations, which were accompanied by the issue of special commemorative stamps, were spread over three days and attracted many distinguished participants and huge popular support. On Friday 14 October, the anniversary of the battle itself, a lunch attended by the great and the good was followed by the unveiling of a plaque on a wall in the Abbey grounds by the French foreign minister, the Prince de Broglie 'to commemorate the fusion of the Norman and Saxon peoples.' The occasion, attended by a large crowd, began with a procession to the site headed by the Battle Abbey choir. This was 'received and greeted' by Mrs Webster, standing on a platform beside the plaque. That evening a reception was held in the great hall of the Abbey.

The following day more than 40,000 people, it was claimed, from all parts of the country descended on the town for the 1066 pageant held in the Abbey grounds. There was a three-mile traffic jam on

Speaking at the 900th Anniversary celebration

either side of the town, and the official guests only arrived after the main event. Over 24,000 people paid to watch the pageant, organised by the Bexhill Round Table. Its centrepiece was a re-enactment of the battle, fought between students from Sussex University (the Normans) and two hundred from the University of Kent. It was a lively encounter: 'Some scuffles that were not in the script broke out! Several people received bleeding noses.'[25]

On Sunday eight hundred people crowded into the parish church for a commemorative service at which Evelyn Webster read one of the lessons, and the Archbishop of Canterbury gave the sermon. This was followed by a ceremony around the Norman Stone in the Abbey grounds, to which participants were welcomed by Evelyn who also delivered a speech on the theme of the unifying of the French and the British after the battle. To the amusement of girls from the school, the Archbishop was seen stamping his feet because of the cold.[26]

Twelve days later the importance of the occasion was also recognised, if rather belatedly and briefly, by a visit from the Queen and the Duke of Edinburgh. The gateway to the Abbey was decorated with huge banks of flowers, and Mrs Webster was among those presented to the royals who visited the Abbot's Hall before crossing the road to the parish church. They then departed, after spending barely half an hour in the town, for the remainder of their day's visit to 'the Conqueror's coast'.[27]

Several local people who knew Evelyn Webster at this time have commented on her imposing appearance, enhanced by a variety of suitably large hats, and how she liked playing the 'grande dame'. She was driven about the town in a Rolls Royce, and behaved as to the manor born. She was proud of her Webster forebears, whose history she researched, and like her father she had a serious commitment to the Abbey and its place in the national life. In 1952, at the suggestion of a close friend, Richard St.Barbe Baker, founder of the 'Men of the Trees', a programme of tree-planting in its grounds was undertaken, which blossomed the following year into a project for the creation of a 'Forest of Thankfulness' to commemorate 'our deliverance at Dunkirk', for which the first oak was planted on Remembrance Sunday that year.[28]

Evelyn also encouraged and befriended Eleanor Searle, the North American academic and author of an important study of the medieval Abbey. In the preface to her book she was effusive in her thanks to Mrs Webster: 'Wandering scholars were no doubt often received at Battle Abbey when her ecclesiastical predecessors presided there, but none can have been welcomed more hospitably than I, nor left with a greater debt of gratitude and affection.'[29]

Others, however, were treated quite differently. The Woodhams, father and son, who were long-serving estate managers whom she had known all her life would be summoned to her presence, even in the middle of the night, and treated with hauteur. They were never offered a drink. Evelyn also took pleasure in summoning the Dean of the parish church to a weekly meeting at her residence. But it did not escape notice that money was evidently in very short supply. Powdermill House was in a very run-down condition, there was little domestic help, and language students were taken in as paying guests. The tennis court was in a poor state, its surface undulating with mole hills and its net full of holes.

Substantial unpaid bills accumulated with local suppliers. And although social life was maintained, it was only with difficulty. On one occasion, for instance, Evelyn brushed aside the concerns of her cook who pointed out mould on the soup, adding 'It will add to the flavour.' In short, behind the façade, Evelyn was struggling to make ends meet.

Godfrey Harbord

So, too, was her eldest son Godfrey who reappeared in Battle in the mid 1960s. He was another imposing figure, some six feet six inches tall, who often sported a monocle. But like many of his mother's Webster predecessors, his early life had been marked by considerable turbulence. Expelled from Eton, he had lasted only six weeks in the Grenadier Guards as a National Serviceman, and had left Trinity College Dublin – where he affected the name Harbord-Webster (dubbed by some 'Cardboard Lobster') – without a degree. In the early fifties he found a job for a while with the Festival of Britain, and another

PAUL PETROVITCH

Godfrey Harbord in later life

on a cable-laying ship which took him to Canada where he became a disc-jockey at a radio station. In an attempt to find a more settled future for him his father then persuaded Godfrey to follow in his footsteps and embark on a career in the catering and hotel trade. He enrolled at a prestigous catering college in Lausanne, and followed this by a spell as a trainee in two up-market hotels in Munich.[30]

In the late fifties or early sixties his mother called him back to England, where apparently he expected to take over the running of part of the Battle Abbey estate. But this did not happen. Instead, he took a succession of other short-lived jobs, including working for an animal feed manufacturer in the north of the country, and – back in London – for Peter Evans Steak House, Fuller's Tea Rooms, and an egg distribution business.

When he returned to Battle, Godfrey – who by then had adopted Webster as his surname – went to live in Tower Hill farm on the Battle estate, built of concrete by his grandfather, Sir Augustus Webster, for his farm manager. The conditions there were extremely primitive: 'appalling' according to one observer. The rooms were very small and full of dogs, the dining room had an open fire which smoked, and the furniture was battered and sparse. One guest, invited to take a seat on a sofa whose innards were prominently poking out of its middle, asked him: which side of the spring? Most young women who came to visit fled in disgust. Regular guests learnt to bring their own provisions and drink – and to appreciate their host's expert cooking. Like his grandfather Sir Augustus he was also an excellent musician. He had a good voice and played the guitar very well – but he never used a plectrum and his nails were always unkempt.

Godfrey was also always very short of money. According to one account the family trustees, who were well aware of his spendthrift habits, made him an allowance of only £20 a week and suggested that if he wanted more he should register as unemployed. To supplement his meagre income he shot and sold pheasants and pigeons, delivered eggs and, more seriously, trained gun dogs. He was very good at that, and had a number of distinguished clients, including the actress Susannah York and the novelist Mary Norton. He was also a considerable linguist: from time to time in the summer he took on the role of a courier, escorting groups around Europe and making money on the side from currency transactions.

He could be charming, but he was arrogant and had a very short fuse. Like his mother, he assumed a lordly air and behaved as though he owned the estate. Those who strayed on to it without permission were roughly treated – so much so that on several occasions he appeared before local magistrates accused of threatening behaviour, backed up in one case by a loaded gun.

Godfrey was also a bitter man. From an early age his mother had shown a marked preference for his younger brother Simon, in part perhaps because Godfrey took his father's side after the breakdown of his parents' marriage. Evelyn, in turn, was wont to refer to him as 'my idiot son'. She did not organise a celebration of his coming of age, as she did later for Simon, nor did she invite him to her table at Powdermill House when they were both living in Battle. For his part, Godfrey resented the frequent presence in his mother's life of other men. Their mutual dislike was intense and deeply-entrenched: it also proved to be disastrous for the hopes which both nurtured of holding on to the Abbey and its estate.

Family conflict

In 1969 relations between Godfrey and his mother became even more tense when the family trustees embarked on a radical revision of the trusts relating to the Battle Abbey estate. These had been established under the will which Sir Augustus had made as far back as 1905. They had not been modified either by the time of his death or subsequently, though changes both in the structure of the family and in the taxation of estates meant that there were many respects in which they had become outmoded and an impediment to the efficient management of the estate.

Following the death of her brother in the war, Lucy had acquired a life interest in the estate, but as she was still unable to deal with her own affairs, that meant that many decisions relating to the management of the estate were subject to the approval of the Court of Protection and the Official Solicitor acting on its behalf. This involved laborious, time-consuming and expensive procedures. Moreover, the trustees were not allowed to borrow money or invest capital in other than gilt-edged stock. This meant that money was tight for repairs and maintenance work on the estate which was becoming progressively more run-down.

The solution was found in a Disentailing Deed under which the Court deprived Lucy of her life interest, and Evelyn and Godfrey surrendered their reversionary life interests in the estate. A new set of trusts was then put in place. The detailed provisions of the new settlement were extremely complex, but in essence they meant that Lucy was provided with an income for life from a modest portion of the estate, while the income from the bulk of the rest was divided between Evelyn and Godfrey. It was not, however, an even division: Evelyn's share was just over 65%, Godfrey's just under 35%. He was furious at the outcome, and especially angry that he was not given access to any capital, and that he would require the written assent of the trustees for many decisions regarding his use even of the income he had been allocated. Godfrey sought to overturn the new provisions in the High Court, and appeared in person to plead his case. But this was a disaster. He insulted the judge, was literally thrown out of the court, and almost went to prison for contempt.

It was Evelyn who appeared to emerge as the real victor from this bruising encounter, and she was in buoyant mood when she told the new headmistress of Battle Abbey school, shortly after her appointment in September 1968, that she was going to take over the Abbey, and that the school would have to go. She would then live in the library wing. In the meantime she sought a place on the school's governing body – an initiative which was repulsed; questioned the way the school dealt with visitors (the numbers of which she was anxious to increase); and, in 1975, rather brutally asserted her rights over the grounds around it. She decided, 'to the dismay of all the school' that 'it was not appropriate for an Abbey to be surrounded by flower beds'. As a result 'the herbaceous border, the flower bed east of the Sixpenny lawn and the dahlia beds in the maze were all replaced by grass, and at the same time the oak tree planted by the Duke of Athlone in 1933 beside the front drive was cut down'.[31]

Evelyn Webster had not, however, reckoned with the trustees of the Webster Settled Estates. They were confronted with the hard fact that the management structure of the estate provided virtually no income to maintain it, and that the family was running out of money. They were also irked by the constant feuding between Evelyn, Godfrey, and his brother Simon. In spite of earlier assurances which Evelyn claimed had been given to her, they announced in July 1975 that they were considering its future. This could only mean one thing: the trustees were contemplating selling Battle Abbey and its estate.[32]

11

THE 1976 SALE

The announcement by the trustees did not at first attract widespread attention, but it confirmed the worst fears of the immediate members of the Webster family, and alarmed people in Battle. Evelyn was furious. For her it threatened not only to extinguish hopes of being able to regain control and occupation of the Abbey, but also to put an end to the family's long-standing period of ownership. Godfrey was also very angry with the trustees – whose chairman was a cousin – though in his case anger was accompanied by a determination to attempt to raise the sum needed to exercise the option offered by the trustees of the purchase of the Abbey and its estate for £600,000 (some £6-8 millions in today's money).[1]

In Battle there was concern, and not only on the part of the local business community whose commercial interests were closely bound up with the flow of visitors to the Abbey, that a change of ownership might mean either that it would be closed to the public, or subjected to some undesirable form of development. The local Round Table took the lead in voicing these fears, and discussing what action might be taken. Already in late August it was considering a national appeal if the Abbey and its estate came on the market so that it could be bought for the nation. It recognised from the beginning that this would be an immense task, but as a first step it set up the '1066 Fund' and followed this in October by establishing the '1066 Trust' as a charity with the twin aims of safeguarding the Abbey and the battlefield for the public benefit, and fostering public awareness of its importance. It made it clear, however, that it had no wish to be involved in the future management of the Abbey. The chairman of the Trust was Richard Compton, owner of a dress shop in the High Street, and his fellow trustees Robert Emeleus, proprietor of a pharmacy, and Michael Clark, a solicitor. It was the first time in the history of the Abbey that local residents had an opportunity – and sought to exploit it – of having a say about its future.[2]

During that autumn, Evelyn revealed that she had known about the proposed sale since April. 'I was so shocked and upset that I had a mild heart attack' she told the local paper. 'For reasons of their own, the trustees have decided to sell it. I am very distressed.' She went on:[3]

> 'I care passionately about the place. It is so beautiful and is such an important part of our heritage. It marks the beginning of English history – the last time England was conquered.'

Speculation grew about the likely fate of the Abbey, including rumours of an Arab buyer. The estate trustees met again just before Christmas but deferred a final decision, their spokesman, Angus Gordon, saying that 'If we are going to sell, I think it is generally agreed that the property market is getting better so it would be in our interests to defer a decision.' Few close observers doubted what that decision would be. But everyone had to wait until Thursday 11 March 1976 before a formal announcement was made at a press conference held by Strutt and Parker at their West End office in London.[4]

An auction announced

The estate was to be put on the market at an auction on Friday 24 June, said George Judd, the agent's senior auctioneer. He explained that the trustees had decided to sell for financial reasons. 'Taxation policies, including the proposed Wealth Tax, make it inevitable that the estate will have to be broken up within a few years.' He added that it would be offered in 26 lots, but he expected it to be sold as a whole. It was hoped that it might fetch more than £1 million. The beneficiaries would be Evelyn Webster, her two sons and two grandsons. (No mention was made of Lucy Webster, who by this time had apparently become a non-person). Mr Judd added that he hoped that the estate would be bought by 'the right person' but did not elaborate on who or what he meant by this.[5]

The sale particulars described what was on offer as 'one of the most important historic estates in Britain'. In addition to the Abbey itself and the site of the battle the estate included Powdermill House ('an attractive 17th century house with lake and 42¾ acres'), Down Barn Farm with its farmhouse and 152 ½ acres, the Pilgrim's Rest restaurant, several houses and cottages in the town, building sites, the town cricket ground, Powdermill Wood (93 acres), Farthing Pond, and George Meadow. In all it amounted to some 573 acres. The income

BATTLE MUSEUM

The Battle Abbey Estate
For sale by Auction on 24th June, 1976
Particulars of Sale

The Battle Abbey Estate
One of the most Important Historic Estates in Britain

Battle Abbey, dating from the 11th Century
The Site of the Battle of Hastings, 1066
Powdermill House
An Attractive 17th Century House with Lake
and 42¼ Acres

Down Barn Farm
with Farmhouse, Buildings and 152¼ Acres

Farmhouse, 2 Cottages, 2 Areas of Land,
Former Allotments, 2 Potential Building Sites,
Lake and about 93 acres of Woodland
Mainly with Vacant Possession

Battle Abbey School, Various Areas of Land,
14th Century Restaurant, 7 Cottages,
Garages and Cricket Ground
Let and Producing about £4,109 p.a.

About 573 Acres in All

Solicitors:
Lots 1-20
Stephenson Harwood and Tatham
Saddlers Hall, Gutter Lane, Cheapside,
London EC2V 6BS
(01-606 7733)

Lots 21-26:
The Official Solicitor to the Supreme Court
48-49 Chancery Lane, London, WC2A 1JR
(01-405 7641)

Auction 24th June 1976
by

and

ST. JOHN SMITH & SON

at the Mayfair Hotel, London, W1 at 3.00 pm
(unless previously sold)

Joint Auctioneers:
St. John Smith and Son
194/198 High Street, Uckfield, Sussex
(0825 4111)
and at Heathfield, Crowborough and Horam, Sussex

Strutt and Parker
13 Hill Street, Berkeley Square, London, W1X 8DL
(01-629 7282)
41 Milford Street, Salisbury, Wiltshire (0722 28741)
and at Bedford, Canterbury, Chelmsford, Cheshire,
Edinburgh, Grantham, Ipswich, Lewes and Southend

Price £2 per copy (to include Conditions of Sale)

1

Powdermill House (1976 Sale catalogue)

from those parts of the estate which were rented out amounted to about £4,109 per annum, of which some £1,870 was accounted for by Battle Abbey School.

Curiously, the income from what was described as 'The Tourist Business' was not specified, but it was claimed that well in excess of 100,000 visitors now paid to visit the Abbey each year, 'with a minimum of promotion and commercialisation.' (The figure quoted was somewhat exaggerated: according to Evelyn Webster the total for 1974 was 93,000). The particulars went on: 'There is very considerable scope for this aspect to be built up into a substantial and profitable business, with improved and expanded visitor facilities, along the lines that have been adopted at other leading national tourist attractions. Sufficient land is available for such expansion.' As far as the battlefield itself was concerned, this was 'ideally suited, subject to negotiation with the tenants, for incorporation in the visitor enterprise, with interpretation and re-enactments of the Battle, jousting tournaments and other events with a medieval or historical flavour.'⁶

The news of the impending sale was only reluctantly carried by the Press

Association and was largely ignored by the national press. Locally, however, it made big front-page headlines the following day in the *Sussex Express*. Evelyn and Godfrey Webster were both quoted. 'I am furious', said Evelyn. 'I have never been consulted, only informed. In October 1974 I was told that it would not be sold. All I know is what I read in the papers.' Her first inkling of what was in the wind had been when her solicitor informed her that he could no longer act for her. When Godfrey was asked if he was in favour of the sale he replied 'Don't be ridiculous, of course I'm not.'[7]

Contending interests

Behind the scenes, the prospect of the sale brought into play an array of different interests – local, national and international – which led to a complex set of pre-sale manoeuvres, some of them of a distinctly cloak-and-dagger nature. Although the 1066 Trust had made an early start, it had been hampered by the absence of a firm decision about the sale, and the worry that any target it set for a fund-raising initiative would inevitably become the reserve price for either a private sale or public auction. A study group it set up in January failed to produce any clear answers to these and other problems about financing the purchase of the Abbey. The Trust then turned for advice to a firm of professional fund-raisers, Wells International, which in April told it that there was no way that a sum of half a million pounds or more could be raised by June. The Trust's main aim then became to arouse sufficient interest and concern in the right quarters to bring forth a bidder in sympathy with its aims.

The government itself was an obvious target, but an approach made on behalf of the Trust, against the better judgment of some of its members, by the local (Conservative) Member of Parliament, Godman Irvine, received a brisk negative from Lady Birk, the Minister in the (Labour) government responsible for Ancient Monuments and Historic Buildings in the Department of the Environment. The Government, she wrote, saw no need 'to incur additional expenditure in buying the estate.' She did add, however, that the Department 'would be willing to cooperate with any new owner over the maintenance of the ruins and would be able to intervene if they should be in jeopardy from neglect.' For the 1066 Trust this reply meant that it had to re-double its efforts to seek a

private purchaser. With this in mind it sought to mobilise an array of the great
and the good for a letter to *The Times*, but this foundered on the hesitations of
some of its intended signatories.

The 1066 Trust also sounded out the two local authorities with the most
immediate interest in the fate of the Abbey. Rother District Council made
supportive noises but offered no money. East Sussex County Council was an
altogether bigger player but had its own interests to pursue. As a result of a recent
re-organisation of local government the county council had greatly increased its
size, resources and importance, taking in Brighton and the county boroughs of
Eastbourne and Hastings. Its internal administration had also been reorganised
with the appointment of a new-style and ambitious Chief Executive, Robin
Beechey. He was a Battle man himself, and so had an especial interest in the fate
of the Abbey. For both him and the County Planning Officer, Andrew Thorburn,
the Abbey was also of interest in the context of the development of tourism in
the county, a hitherto-neglected policy area offering substantial potential benefits
for the local community. Like the 1066 Trust they wanted to 'save the Abbey
for the nation'– but their ambition was to run it themselves. So although there
were discreet discussions with representatives of the Trust, and some exchange
of information, this was mainly a one-way affair. The officers of the Council had
their own strategy, and played their cards close to their chest.

In the meantime others were getting involved. One of the earliest was
a Canadian leisure and entertainments company based in Toronto, Ripley
International Limited. Its portfolio included the Tivoli museum in Copenhagen
and a waxworks on Blackpool's Golden Mile. One of its Vice-Presidents was
quoted as saying 'If we can go ahead with this scheme, it will be very serious and
tasteful. We promise not to sell little souvenirs of King Harold plucking an arrow
from his eye – not at least if they are made in Japan.'[8]

The prospect of this type of outcome was discounted early in April in the
Sussex Express: 'There is no reason to suppose that the new owner will be any less
vigilant in the protection of the estate than the present one has been' it wrote. It
added, however, in an editorial entitled 'Oh, for Harold !' that it was depressing
to note the almost total lack of public interest in the future of the Abbey. There
was no fierce campaign to acquire the Abbey and battlefield for the nation, and
no rallying posters or lobbying of MPs. 'Harold marched his army half the length

The Abbey viewed from the battlefield

of England to defend Sussex soil against the Normans. Alas it seems that no such fighting spirit lives today.'[9]

There were, however, stirrings in the face of continued rumours of interest on the part of American companies as well as rich Arabs. These were just the sort of potential buyers most feared by the 1066 Trust and its allies. The latter included the Council for the Protection of Rural England (CPRE), and the National Trust, whose representatives at both local and national level expressed concern about the future of the Abbey. They wished to see it remain open to the public but without it becoming 'a razzmatazz operation'. Neither, however, could offer any immediate financial help. The chairman of the Sussex branch of the CPRE admitted that it was hardly the time to be asking the government to spend money, but said he believed that if the government were willing to take a lead, the public would be ready to offer financial support. The south-east regional centre of the National Trust, for its part, decided to organise petitions to the Department of the Environment and East Sussex County Council 'urging them to take steps about the abbey and battlefield'. It also indicated that if the estate were not sold at auction the Trust would ' take a strong lead in any appeal.'[10]

Although these expressions of help were welcome, they offered little comfort to those fearful of the issue being decided at the auction in favour either of a rich individual who would in future exclude the public from the Abbey or an entrepreneur who would convert it into a mass tourist attraction. A major difficulty from the point of view of those opposed to such an outcome was the declared intention of the Webster trustees to sell the whole estate as a single unit. Pressure was put on them by a number of interests in an attempt to persuade them either to exclude Lots 1 and 2 (the Abbey and the Battlefield) from the auction, or to offer them separately from the rest of the estate. The trustees, however, held to their intention. The Sussex Chairman of the CPRE lambasted them for their refusal, describing it as 'a breathtakingly irresponsible way of dealing with the future of a historical site and a building without parallel in the country.' But the trustees no doubt wished to simplify their task as much as possible, and also, as their spokesman Andrew Gordon explained, 'We have an absolute duty to obtain the best possible price for the whole estate.'[11]

Towards the end of May tempers began to fray. *The Daily Mail* published a two-page article in its property section under the provocative heading 'Battle of Hastings 1976 and this time the invaders have no opposition.' Strutt and Parker were quoted as saying that they had alerted 'several historical organisations' at the time of their October announcement: 'We thought that would give them time to get organised. But nothing has been done.' The 1066 Trust was also criticised for not having launched an appeal. Referring to what had happened to Harold at the famous battle, the writer added ' Maybe they are asking for one in the eye too...'[12]

The article also reported that Ripley International had withdrawn from the contest, and cast doubt on the viability of the Abbey as a tourist attraction. It quoted Eric Morley, chairman of Mecca Ltd: 'As a patriot I feel it would be nice if an English company developed the site. But as an entrepreneur, I wouldn't touch it with a barge pole in these economic times. It would cost too much to set up, and I don't think there are enough potential customers to get a good return on the investment.' This view was echoed by the company secretary of Pleasurama Ltd: 'I suppose it could be turned into a sort of Disneyland...But it would be difficult to make it pay all the year round.'

Enter a White Knight

As June approached the temperature continued to rise – literally, as this was to be one of the hottest summers for many years – and so too did the tensions surrounding the sale. But just two weeks before the auction, a white knight at last appeared. He was the 53 year-old Earl of Lonsdale, one of Britain's wealthiest peers with an estimated fortune of £8 millions, and the owner of a 30,000 acre estate in Cumbria. Much of this was open to the public, and he had an excellent track record for providing facilities for visitors as well as good management and care for the environment. On 10 June he and his entourage paid a visit to Battle where he met a variety of local people, including members of the 1066 Trust committee, on whom he made a very favourable impression. He also met Evelyn and Godfrey Webster. The latter pair made quite an impression on him, but of a different sort. 'What a family! What an incredible family!' he kept saying. Evelyn, for her part, was pleased and gratified by his visit – but rather grand about it. 'Weren't they in coal a couple of generations back?' she asked.[13]

Lonsdale's appeal to the 1066 Trust lay in his reputation as a caring landowner, his willingness to buy the whole estate and to enter into a covenant with the National Trust to safeguard its future, and his evident sympathy and concern for it. 'The Abbey and its ruins,' he was quoted as saying, 'are of major archaeological and architectural importance and should not only be preserved but should be made more acceptable.' He quickly became in the words of the Sussex Express 'a popular runner with many people.'[14]

In the two days before the auction there was an increasing flurry of activity. On the Tuesday a petition with 5,466 signatures, collected in haste in the previous two weeks, was presented at the House of Commons to the two local MPs, Godman Irvine (Rye) and Kenneth Warren (Hastings) on behalf of the South-East Sussex Centre of the National Trust by its chairman, Mrs Frances Adams. It asked that 'urgent steps be taken to prevent the desecration of Battle Abbey and its historic battlefield.' A similar petition was put before the Planning Committee of the East Sussex County Council. The Sword of Asgard Medieval Society, which organised re-enactments of Viking and Saxon battles, also weighed in with another petition bearing a thousand signatures.

On that same Tuesday, however, those in the 1066 Trust with their ears close to the ground were told some disquieting news. Having been assured that a substantial offer in advance of the auction would be acceptable, Lonsdale had been dismayed to have his bid of £640,000 rejected by the Trustees. He now feared that this sum, which was close to his financial limit, would become in effect the reserve price, with a serious risk of others offering more. Although a Canadian foundation was ready to top up his bid, it was doubtful of being able to produce the money in time because of currency exchange restrictions. Others with larger pockets were also believed to be circling around, and the County Council was being suspiciously secretive about what it was up to.

On the Wednesday, the eve of the auction, Godfrey Webster sprang a surprise. His attempt to raise funds for a purchase having foundered a few weeks earlier, he applied at the last minute to a High Court judge for an injunction to stop the sale. He did this without the consent of his mother, Evelyn, and against the advice of his solicitor, whom he promptly sacked. The judge refused his application, but on the following morning, the day of the auction, some newspapers presented him as 'the man who is leading the Save the Battle Abbey campaign', and he held a press conference at which this belated initiative was launched.

A mystery bidder

That afternoon, Thursday 24 June, the auction took placed in the Mayfair Theatre in the West End. It was a boiling hot day and the temperature soared as heat from batteries of television lights added to that generated by press photographers, the attendant horde of journalists, and the crowd of the various interested parties as well as relatives, friends and locals who gathered in the stalls of the theatre. Lonsdale, in the second row, looked tense and nervous.

Before the opening of the formal business, and unusually, the auctioneer gave the floor to a spokesman for the newly-launched campaign who made a passionate plea to save the Abbey for posterity and from the danger of 'the alienation of the British heritage'. This drew a warm ripple of applause from part of the audience, but was received in silence by those, like the 1066 Trust, who had been fighting for the same cause for months rather than a few hours.

The serious business got under way shortly after 3pm. Once the preliminary formalities were over, the auctioneer called for opening bids. A dead silence followed, which was broken by a bid from the back of the auditorium of £450,000. The price at first rose in large amounts, with bids from many quarters. Lonsdale's representative, Victor Sandelson, joined in at £500,000. The proceedings then advanced by bids of £10,000 to reach £595,000 at which point the bidder from the back dropped out, but another mystery figure on the right, a tall man with a white beard, joined in. The battle was now between him and Lonsdale. The price rose by more modest amounts of £2,500. As the tension increased, the auctioneer himself got into a muddle about the bidding. But when it reached £670,000 on a bid from Lonsdale, there was a pause. The auctioneer began a countdown in his favour. But the man with the beard came back with a higher bid. The price then rose jerkily through the £670,000s and into the £680,000s. Sandelson once or twice shook his head, but after a conference with Lonsdale went on again. He raised his bid to £687,000. But the man with the beard went one better. Suddenly it was all over. The estate was knocked down to him for £690,000.

But who was he? There was a buzz of uncertainty as a crowd of photographers surged around the auctioneer. He struggled to free himself. He said he had an announcement to make. 'The Battle Abbey Estate,' he began, 'has been bought by the Government.' There were gasps and clapping, but he went on '…with generous assistance from American donors who wish to remain anonymous at present.'

There was a spontaneous burst of applause and cheering. Pandemonium then ensued. Everyone crowded round in search of more information. The identity of the mystery man with the white beard was soon revealed. Some people from Battle, greatly concerned at rumours that an Arab was going to buy the Abbey, had at first assumed from his tanned and hirsute appearance that these were about to be confirmed. Then suddenly the penny dropped. They realised that it was a Battle man they knew well, just back from a holiday in the sun. He was David Bowyer, a surveyor and civil servant working for the Department of the Environment.

Not very much was disclosed, on the other hand, about the American involvement in the deal. Neither their identity nor the extent of their financial contribution was revealed by the auctioneer. The solicitor who was representing them, Jeremy Francis, was only a little more forthcoming. He said the donor was

3rd Edition

DAILY EXPRESS

EXPRESS EXTRA TODAY

No. 23,638 Friday June 25 1976 Weather : A scorcher Price 7p

The Battle of Hastings is fought again and this time America wins it—for Britain

1976 AND ALL THAT!

Express Staff Reporter Alan Cochrane

A DAPPER civil servant paid out £690,000 yesterday to help England win the second Battle of Hastings.

The man in the dark flannel suit stepped in at a crucial moment of the public auction in London. And, backed by a large goodwill cheque from America, he was able to outbid his only rival and save the site of the battle—and the historic Battle Abbey—for the nation.

Lord and Lady Lonsdale after the sale

It was only after the hammer fell that the other bidder, Lord Lonsdale, found out that 55-year-old Mr. David Bowyer was from Whitehall.

Both the Earl and the Department had the same aims — to make sure that 1066 and all that stays in British hands.

Nobody would say how much money had been donated by an American trust as a gesture in their country's bi-centennial year, but it was thought to have been about half the purchase price.

Secret

Lord Lonsdale was "delighted," but the 53-year-old earl added: "It does seem a pity that Britain could not save the battle site without outside assistance.

"Had I known who that other chap was I would not have kept bidding against the nation. As it is I got what I wanted — without paying for it."

Last night there was speedy defence for the Government's action in keeping their interest secret.

Mr. Richard Compton of the 1066 Trust, set up to fight the sale, said that if Government interest had been known it would have attracted speculators, particularly if they knew that an American academic trust was also involved.

He said of the Americans' participation: "We knew of their existence, and they approached us about buying only the abbey and the battlefield.

"We contacted the Department of the Environment, who took it from there."

The 900-year-old Abbey was built by William the Conqueror to celebrate his victory.

Refused

The need for a second "battle" over the historic site in and around the Sussex village of Battle was simply mounting costs.

In 1912 a trust was set up to administer the 573 acre estate, which had been owned by the Webster family since 1719.

A last-minute attempt by the latest in the Webster line 51-year-old Mr. Godfrey Webster, to put a stop to the proceedings failed on Wednesday night when a High Court judge refused to grant him an injunction.

Even as the sale got under way in the theatre of London's Mayfair Hotel Mr. Webster was still campaigning to stop it. But when he discovered who the mystery buyer was he said: "I'm content."

The Government intends to retain the abbey and the battlefield site. The rest of the estate will be sold off.

Secrets on my doorstep

By Michael O'Flaherty

THE MAN at the centre of the Cabinet leak row talked yesterday of secret papers in shopping bags left outside his office. Mr. Frank Field also claimed classified information had been passed to him in the street.

The 33-year-old director of the Child Poverty Action Group was speaking after a 55-minute interview with Sir Douglas Allen, who is investigating the leak.

Mr. Field . . . Quizzed

There will be an emergency Commons debate on Monday over the Cabinet minutes used for an article by Mr. Field, in the magazine New Society, on the scuttling of the child benefit scheme.

Mr. Field refused to identify his source — codename "Deep Throat" just like a similar informant in the Watergate affair — when Sir Douglas questioned him.

But he did reveal the six-year supply of classified material to his London office.

Shelf full

He said later that some arrived in brown paper carrier bags "stuffed to overflowing," some documents were left at the door of the charity's attic office in Macklin Street, and others came by post.

The supply started in 1970 when the Tories were in power.

He now had a shelf full of documents. Many were 4in.-thick green-backed files marked "For official use only." They detailed how extra supplementary benefits could be claimed by the poor.

Mr. Field stressed: "I don't know who the informants were, but they are all heroes. They were not Deep Throat—he was only involved in the Cabinet leak."

The anti-poverty campaigner had told Sir Douglas that Government of both parties, as well as senior civil servants, knew the classified information had been passed on.

This claim was later denied by both Tory and Labour spokesmen.

He also said he knew the documents were covered by the Official Secrets Act. But they had been used by his group in booklets and publications sent to Ministers, civil servants, the Press and the poor.

THE LABOUR split over postponing the child benefit proposals re-opened last night with former Social Services Secretary Barbara Castle delivering an angry warning to Ministers.

Mrs. Castle, architect of the scheme which would give mothers about £2.50 a week for each child, said Left-wingers might abstain in a debate on the leaks demanded by the Tories for Monday.

Opinion—Page 16

Boy loses arm and walks home

Bid to sew it back on again fails after spin drier accident

By Don Mackay

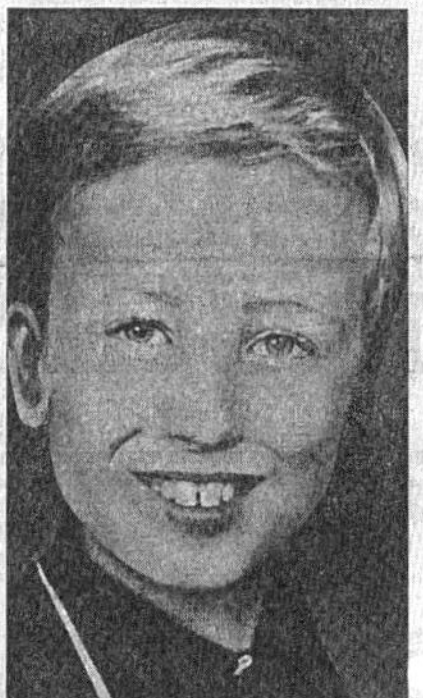

Mark the brave—he never cried on way to hospital

A MOTHER told last night how she saw her little boy walking home after his right arm had been ripped off in the spin drier at a launderette.

As a motorist took her son to hospital she and her husband dashed to the launderette to find the arm still in the drier. They rushed it to the hospital, where surgeons tried to sew it back on. But the operation failed.

Last night as the boy, 10-year-old Mark Cameron, was "fairly comfortable" in Macclesfield Infirmary, factory inspectors and police were trying to find out what happened.

The launderette's part-time attendant was not present at the time of the accident.

It was tea time on Monday when Mark set off from his home in Lord Street, Macclesfield, to do his mother's washing at Mr. John Lee's launderette in Mill Lane, a quarter of a mile away.

He had been before and knew how to operate the drier—a Bendix extractor.

In the accident his arm was wrenched off midway between the elbow and shoulder.

Brave

Mark's mother, Mrs. Carol Cameron, 31, said last night: "When I saw him walking home minus his arm I was just horrified. I shouted 'Oh God' and ran to my sister-in-law."

Neighbour Mr. John Barrett, who stopped a passing car and went with Mark to hospital, said: "All he said on the way to hospital was 'I can't feel my fingers.' He was really brave and never cried."

Mark's father, 34-year-old contractor Derek Cameron was too upset to talk about his son's injury.

Above the drier that trapped Mark's arm is a notice signed by Mr. Lee. It warns people not to take washing out until the machine is stopped.

Mr. Lee, who lives at Hawk Green, near Marple, had no comment to make last night.

At the hospital a spokesman said: "Mark is doing very well. He is a brave little lad and an ideal patient."

A British Medical Asociation spokesman said it was surprising Mark had been able to walk after the injury. "But he may not have felt the injury because of shock," he added.

Pub bomb injures 30

A bomb exploded without warning at the Glenowen Inn in the Glen Road, Catholic area of Belfast last night, injuring about 30 people.

A few minutes earlier, a soldier was seriously wounded in the chest by a sniper's bullet at Rodney Parade, also in West Belfast.

Same again . . .

Cinemas may be forced to keep showing the same films to avoid blank screens because of a strike by drivers at Film Transport Services. They deliver new films to nearly all cinemas in the country.

£5 million offer to save jobs

Express Staff Reporter

A £5 MILLION loan has been offered to a Lancashire-based textile firm to buy and run Brentford Nylons factories and some of its shops.

The unsecured loan, revealed yesterday, has been offered by the Department of Industry to David Whitehead Ltd., of Rawtenstall.

It was recommended by the Industrial Advisory Board.

Brentford Nylons went into receivership in February, putting about 1,600 jobs at risk.

The David Whitehead company was founded 180 years ago and employs several thousand people. It has several subsidiaries based abroad.

The light touch

The Queen ate by candlelight last night, at a dinner given by President and Madame Giscard D'Estaing at the London home of the French Ambassador.

Ninth tremor

An earth termor—the ninth in the past eight days—shook the Hanford area of Stoke-upon-Trent yesterday.

Cricket fans hurt

Four boys and three men were hurt last night when a car went out of control while leaving the Northants-West Indies cricket match at Northampton.

A police spokesman said: "There is nothing sinister and, fortunately, no really serious injuries."

Union pension power?

By John Warden

TRADE UNIONS are to be given a 50-50 say in £20,000 million worth of company pensions.

A White Paper yesterday laid down that they will have a right to 50 per cent control of occupational schemes. The Government will introduce the necessary legislation.

It means the Cabinet has overruled the occupational pension board and sided with Mr. Len Murray, T.U.C. general secretary.

Earlier this year, Mr. Murray declared: "The size of these funds, and their implications for the economy make them a matter of interest to trade unions.

"Workers regard these pension funds as belonging to them and not the employers."

But yesterday Tory spokesman Mr. Patrick Jenkin pledged that the Tories will fight "this monstrous extension of trade union power."

He said the Government's proposal would mean middle management and others would have their pensions at the mercy of trade unions.

He added: "Millions of pension scheme members are not trade union members. Why should they have to watch their pension schemes handed over to the unions?"

The White Paper says the Government intends to have further discussions with unions, employers and the pension interests before legislating.

It rejects the suggestion that employee representatives should be elected by scheme members, not appointed by trade unions.

INCREASES in social security benefits announced last April will be paid from November 15, M.P.s were told early today.

About 12,500,000 people will be paid more in pensions, sickness and unemployment and supplementary benefits. Total cost: £1,386 million a year.

Financial Express—Page 16

An order melts away

AS temperatures in the North reached the 80's yesterday, a Manchester ice-cream factory turned down a 1,000 gallon export order from the Middle East because it was already working non-stop to meet home demand. Elsewhere, a drought order was introduced in South West Yorkshire, where reservoirs are down to a critical 66 per cent of capacity.

Labour votes axed as they win poll

By Derek Hornby

LABOUR regained its overall majority in the Commons yesterday with victory in the Rotherham by-election.

But in a low poll — the turn-out was just 46 per cent—their majority in the town was slashed from 17,000 to less than 5,000.

The figures show a swing to the Tories of 13.3 per cent, and early today jubilant party chiefs were claiming: The Government's days are numbered.

But the Labour Party's general secretary, Mr. Ron Hayward, put the swing down to complacency among Labour supporters.

Their views

"Labour voters told our canvassers that they need not bother to turn out because the result was in the bag," he said.

The by-election followed the death of Social Services Minister Brian O'Malley, who had a majority of 17,034 at the General Election.

The Tory vote yesterday was almost 1,000 up on the General Election and candidate Douglas Hinckley said: "The people of Rotherham have said exactly what they think of this Government."

But Labour's man, Councillor Stanley Crowther, said: "The voters have supported the Labour Government and its policies."

The Liberal vote fell from 5,350 to 2,214 and their candidate, Miss Beth Graham, lost her deposit.

One by-election is pending—at the safe Labour seat of Thurrock, made vacant by the death of Mr. Hugh Delargy who had a majority of 19,080 in 1974.

Voting figures: Stanley Crowther (Lab) 14,351, Douglas Hinckley (Tory) 9,824, Miss Beth Graham (Lib) 2,214, George Wright (National Front) 1,696, Peter Bishop (World Grid Sunshine Party) 129, Robin Atkinson (Eng Ind) 99. Labour majority 4,527.

LATEST

'COPTER CRASH KILLS 8

United States Marine Corps helicopter crashed in isolated training area of Hawaiian Islands, killing eight of 10 marines on board.

HOW QUICKLY CAN YOU SPEAK ANOTHER LANGUAGE?

Very quickly: ask Linguaphone

The Linguaphone method is the most natural way to acquire a new language. It *really* works: and you can *prove* it!

Just listen—in private!

With the exciting Linguaphone Language Course (choose records, cassettes or tapes to suit yourself) *you listen, you understand,* and *you begin speaking immediately.*

And what is more, speaking well and unaffectedly, with an authentic accent; absorbing the grammatical rules naturally and without effort as you go along.

Something you've always wanted

To be fluent in another language is a wonderful asset. You know it's something you've always wanted: believe us that it is so much easier than you think. *Millions* of people learn their second language the Linguaphone way.

FREE RECORD OR CASSETTE AND BROCHURE

show you how to:

- Learn a language in only 30 minutes a day.
- Grasp grammar and vocabulary effortlessly.
- Acquire an authentic accent.
- Help your children with examinations.
- Be a success in business.
- Really enjoy your holidays abroad.
- Open up new cultural horizons.

Choice of 34 languages

Take your pick of 34 different language courses. You can have a FREE record or FREE cassette and brochure that tell you in detail how you can master another language. These are yours for the asking. There's no cost or obligation. All you need to do is complete the coupon and post it to the address below.

Name .... Age ....
(Block Caps) (if under 18)
Address ....

The Linguaphone Institute (Dept. DE/16),
207-209 Regent Street, London, W1R 8AU.

Please send me your FREE record ☐ or FREE cassette ☐ and illustrated brochure of the new language courses. (Tick as applicable)
There are Linguaphone courses in 34 languages including:
FRENCH ☐ GERMAN ☐ RUSSIAN ☐ SPANISH ☐
(Put a cross beside the language which interests you)
Other languages: ....

Personal demonstrations in London: Linguaphone Showroom, 207 Regent Street; Foyles; Harrods. Also: Rare Records, Manchester and Readers Digest Centres in Selfridges, Rackhams, Birmingham; Rushworth & Dreaper, Liverpool and other stores nationwide.

TV Radio Page 12 | Weather Page 2 • Target Page 7 • Hickey Page 9 • Large Crossword Page 11 | Better Jobs Page 16 • Sports starts on Page 17 • Small Crossword Back Page

PHONE STD CODE 061 236 2112 TELEX 668773

an American academic institution which preferred to remain anonymous. The money had been raised by a number of university figures across the nation. He could not say how much, but it had provided the bulk of the purchase money for Lots 1 and 2 (the Abbey and the battlefield) 'with a view to the whole of this site being preserved in the British national interest.' He added: 'It is also a real and tangible token of the enduring link between the USA and the UK in this, the bicentennial year of the United States.'

Reactions to the sale

The immediate reactions both to this aspect of the purchase, and the government's involvement, varied a great deal. Some were stunned and bemused, others pleased or exultant. Lord Lonsdale himself, the under-bidder, was philosophical. 'I am delighted with the outcome, of course,' he said , 'but it does seem a pity that Britain couldn't save the site of the Battle of Hastings without outside assistance. Had I known who that other chap was I would not have kept bidding against the nation. As it is, I got what I wanted – without paying for it!'

The chairman of the 1066 Trust, Richard Compton, expressed relief that the Abbey had been preserved for the public, but added that it was a pity that a British person who had been prepared to buy it was not allowed to, and that public money was used which could have been devoted to other purposes. Some members of the Trust expressed their disappointment in stronger terms, part of their ire being directed at representatives of the County Council whom they suspected of having done a deal behind their backs.

There was certainly no attempt on the part of the latter to disguise their satisfaction at the outcome. It emerged that they had been in secret talks with the Department over a period of three or four months, and that they confidently expected to be rewarded for the £30,000 which they had put up towards the purchase price – a sum which had been discreetly provided with the approval of the Chairman of the Council without going through the usual budgetary procedures.

It also emerged that the governmental coup had been carefully, and secretly, prepared. The Department of the Environment had learnt of the American interest (of which the 1066 Trust had also been indirectly aware) and had made contact with those concerned – later revealed to be members of the Philosophical Society of America, based in Philadelphia – through the British embassy in Washington some three or four weeks before the auction. The prime movers on the American side were Mr Eugene B Power of Ann Arbour, Michigan who had been the Library of Congress representative in London during the second world war, and Professor Julian Boyd, emeritus professor of history at Princeton university. Mr Power made it clear that they were only interested in the Abbey and the battlefield, but were told that it was unlikely that these lots would be sold separately. A deal was then struck by which the Department undertook to bid for the whole estate in return for a substantial contribution to the cost of Lots 1 and 2. This was much later revealed to be $380,000 – over £200,000 at that time.[15]

The crucial importance of this remarkable act of American generosity was underlined in the press coverage of the event the following day. The story made the front page in a number of major daily newspapers, most prominently in the case of the *Daily Express* which made it the main item for the day under banner headlines. This was echoed by the *Daily Mail*, also on its front page: 'Britain (with some help from America) wins Battle of Hastings.' More decorously *The Times* gave prominence to a photograph of the Abbey ruins in its own front-page account of the sale.

For the most part, the coverage concentrated on the cloak-and-dagger aspects of the negotiations which had preceded the sale. But a critical note was struck by the *Daily Express* which underlined the fact that Lonsdale had not known of the government's interest, 'and that their bidding had been, to say the least, counter-productive.' Local reaction in Battle was also rather mixed. The following week the *Sussex Express*, for its part, while noting that 'a sigh of relief echoed round Battle on Thursday last week when it was announced that the Government had bought Battle Abbey Estate,' went on to add 'But since then a feeling of resentment has grown in some quarters that the purchase was accomplished with American help.' It was indeed ironic that the final phase of the Webster period of ownership, which had been greeted with such applause in 1901 because it had defeated an American bid for the Abbey, should have been brought to an end with the generous help of American money. But if there was local resentment, it was certainly misplaced as on this occasion the funds were crucial in securing the Abbey for the nation.

Some members of the local 1066 Trust had other grounds for being critical of the outcome. They could not understand why the government had not welcomed the willingness of Lonsdale to buy the Abbey, and had bid against him, especially as it had initially ruled out a purchase. To these questions they were given no clear answer. They also noted, ruefully, that whereas Lonsdale had scrupulously not been willing to take account of proffered Canadian charitable funds to augment his own bid because they were not immediately available, the government itself had had no such hesitation with regard to the American funds which still had to clear the bureaucratic hurdles of exchange control regulations. In fact, the transfer was to take some time, and recourse was had to another American charity, the Royal Oak Foundation, as an intermediary to hasten the process – somewhat to the indignation of some of its staff.

There was also concern locally when it was revealed that both the government and the County Council aimed to recover the cost of their investment by the subsequent re-sale of the rest of the estate. But on this issue the Department of the Environment hastened to give reassurances about its readiness for a dialogue. The government also agreed to set up an Advisory Committee with local representation as a forum in which the management of the Abbey could be discussed, a unique departure from the usual practice of the Department of the Environment.

But what of those most immediately affected by the sale – the Webster family itself? Although Evelyn Webster had opposed the decision by the trustees of the estate, had continued to complain about them during the run up to the auction, and publicly said that she considered the price obtained 'on the low side', privately she was wholly delighted with the outcome. As one of the main beneficiaries of the sale she could now contemplate the future free of the financial worries which had been her constant companion for many years. Her two sons were equally pleased.

Shortly afterwards Godfrey organised a celebratory and farewell occasion at the Abbey. Two hundred and fifty guests were invited to a ball in the great hall. 'It will be white ties, champagne and diamonds all the way,' said a friend. 'It's Webster's swansong.' It was indeed a memorable, and bibulous, evening. Godfrey enjoyed a last chance to occupy the Abbot's throne and made an emotional speech to mark the occasion. But it was noticed that some twenty uniformed Securicor guards, hired by the Department – which had taken out a huge insurance for the event – were on duty and the atmosphere, according to one of the guests, was tense and the gaiety enforced. There were fears that to mark the end of the Webster ownership, the great hall might be set on fire, fulfilling the monk's Dissolution curse. But the night ended without so dramatic a finale. The Websters departed in some style leaving, it was said, a scatter of unpaid bills in their wake.

POSTSCRIPT: FROM PRIVATE TO PUBLIC OWNERSHIP

Evelyn and Godfrey Webster were the main beneficiaries of the proceeds of the sale of the Abbey, which provided both with some immediate capital (partly used in Godfrey's case to pay off his accumulated debts) as well as continuing income. Provision was also made for Lucy – then well into her seventies, and still confined in a mental institution – as well as for Godfrey's younger brother Simon and the latter's two children by successive marriages, Antony and Marcus Harbord.

For both Evelyn and Godfrey the sale meant departure from Battle. In the immediate aftermath Evelyn Webster was asked whether she was interested in staying in the town and buying Powdermill House. 'Its too big,' she replied, 'I shall get a flat in London'. Godfrey, for his part, had already made it known that he intended to leave the country for good and settle in Brazil. His choice was dictated partly by language – through the Harbord connection with Portugal he was fluent in the language of the country – and even more by the prospect of cheap land and labour. Brazil

Godfrey Webster in Brazil

offered the opportunity of at last being able to realise the dream of his own estate and a style of living to which he had aspired, and believed himself to be destined, all his life.[1]

The place he chose for this venture was a remote location in the province of Minas Gerais, a four-hour journey along a dirt track (until it was improved) from the nearest airport. There he acquired a huge estate of many thousands of acres in an idyllic spot at the foot of the mountains, to create what he called "a proper English Georgian estate". He cleared the land and built a palatial house with a swimming pool and an extensive garden, naming it Faz Quinta da Nova Vita (Estate of the New Life). On his estate Godfrey raised cattle, grew coffee and bred German pointers. He employed a staff of seventeen, of whom twelve worked on the estate farm, and three in the garden. He charmed the locals, not least because of his eccentric habits, which included a refusal to have a telephone installed: he could only be reached at 3pm one day a week when he drove to a bar some two hours away. This created some problems. One friend arrived from London expecting to be met at the airport by Godfrey who failed to show up. In the absence of any rapid means of communication, he took refuge in a local hotel – where Godfrey eventually turned up, having mistaken the date of his guest's arrival.

He ran the place as a benevolent despot; built a school for the local community (which he named after his grandfather) and on one occasion organised a mass wedding for his staff and other locals whom he had decreed should get married. Not for the first time, he also contemplated marriage himself, but withdrew at the last moment after the wedding invitations had been sent out, claiming his intended had turned out to be a gold digger. He eventually took Brazilian citizenship, having initially been obliged for the first four years to cross into neighbouring Paraguay every 90 days to renew his visitor's visa.[2]

Public ownership: new energies and resources, but new problems

The sale also opened a new chapter in the history of the Abbey. The transition from private to public ownership brought a whole new set of actors into play, launched an intense debate about the future of the Abbey, prompted new thinking about how it could be made more attractive to visitors, and provided much-needed new resources for restoration and improved facilities. All this was very much to the good. But it was not without its downside. The transition was also marked by significant tensions between the organisations now involved with, or concerned about, the ownership and management of the Abbey. It was to take over twenty years, and some bruising encounters, before the new regime settled down.

Three months after the auction, completion of the sale of the Abbey was announced on 29 September 1976 by Baroness Birk , Parliamentary Under-Secretary at the Department of the Environment. 'I am delighted,' she said, 'that Battle Abbey and the site of the 1066 battlefield have now been formally secured for the nation. We intend to ensure that this historic site is preserved as a national monument and continues to be accessible for the inspiration, instruction and enjoyment of our people and for visitors from all over the world.'

The statement went on to say that the Department was already working on 'long-term plans to provide better arrangements for the public and give them more appreciation and understanding of both the abbey ruins and the battlefield.' A joint working party to make recommendations about their future had been set up with representatives of the Countryside Commission, East Sussex County Council and Rother District Council. Local organisations had also been invited to join an Advisory Committee to give their views 'on the improvement and use of Battle Abbey and grounds in relation to the town of Battle.'

As far as the immediate future was concerned the ruins were 'currently' being administered by East Sussex County Council on behalf of the Department. The statement also reaffirmed the government's intention to sell off the remainder of the estate other than the Abbey and the battlefield, but added that it had now decided to keep the freehold of the Pilgrim's Rest, a medieval building opposite the Great Gate, because of its historic association with the Abbey, and that it had no plans to alter its use as a restaurant. (Later on it also agreed to retain the Stumblotts, an area of rough land below the Abbey grounds much enjoyed by walkers, which it subsequently donated to the Town Council as a public open space.)[3]

The bland prose of the Department's press release gave the impression – as it was no doubt designed to do – that the transition from private to public ownership was proceeding smoothly and purposefully towards a better future for all concerned. It was certainly true that the changeover meant a serious and critical examination of what the site offered, and how its facilities could be improved. It also released and mobilised new energies. But behind the scenes family squabbles had been replaced by tensions within and between public bodies and voluntary organisations, some of them quite as sharp as those of the past.

Already during the summer the first engagements had taken place, some partial victories secured – and some casualties sustained. East Sussex County

The Pilgrim's Rest

Council, for instance, had been duly rewarded for its modest (and temporary) financial contribution towards the cost of the government's purchase of the Abbey by the Department's decision to delegate to it responsibility for its administration. But this was only for a year, pending a decision about the long-term future of the ownership and administration of the Abbey. So this was at best a partial, and conditional, fulfilment of the County Council's ambitions.

The 1066 Trust, for its part, had also experienced mixed fortunes in its dealings with the Department. Its proposal that responsibility for the administration of the Abbey and battlefield should be delegated to a Development Trust under local authority control but with strong local representation and fund-raising powers had been firmly rebuffed, as had its arguments casting doubt on the expertise and sensitivity of the County Council. On the other hand, the creation of the local Advisory Committee – the first of its kind for one of the Department's properties – went some way to meet its wishes, and the decision to withhold the Pilgrim's Rest and the Stumblotts from the re-sale was largely due to the pressure it had brought to bear.

After these preliminary skirmishes all was sweetness and light at a reception attended by Peter Shore, the Secretary of State at the Department of the Environment, held at the Abbey on 13 October – the eve of the famous battle in 1066 – to celebrate the new ownership of the Abbey, and to thank the eight American donors, all of whom came over for the occasion. But the intensive discussion then under way about the future of the Abbey had revealed a number of contentious issues. Some of them, including a suggestion that the school should quit the Abbey, had come to light in the response to the 1066 Trust's initiative in canvassing views among local organisations; others were aired at a public meeting held on 9 November. The role of the Trust itself, and its support for local management of the Abbey, was also questioned at the first meeting of the local Advisory Committee. One participant argued that 'the average local person doesn't give a damn' [about the Abbey] and that it was far better that it should be run by the Department. Some members of the Town Council, at its meeting on 19 November, were also critical. They demanded to see the Trust's accounts, and one proposed that it should be wound up. Not surprisingly this was stoutly resisted by the Trust.[4]

While these arguments were rumbling on, the auction of the remainder of the estate took place on 16 December, the ten lots being sold for a total of £220,000. This meant that the net cost to the government of the Abbey and the battlefield, taking into account the American contribution, was rather less than £270,000 – a modest sum for so important a part of the national heritage.[5]

A plethora of plans

At the beginning of the new year, there was an optimistic mood in the town. The president of the Chamber of Commerce said he expected a boom. It was estimated that as a result of the publicity surrounding the sale and change of ownership numbers visiting the Abbey in 1976 had risen to 120,000. There were many new plans afoot which promised to bring even more people into the town. The possibility of a new hotel close to the battlefield on the site of a derelict market garden on the south side of Powdermill Lane was being explored; a centre for the study of Anglo-French was proposed for Pyke House as an extension of its educational work; and the Department offered to undertake new excavations at the Abbey.[6]

Proposals had already been put forward towards the end of 1976 by the County Council and Rother District Council to improve access to the Abbey and parking facilities in the town. These focussed on enlarging the Abbey car park in Park Lane, converting Abbey Green into a pedestrian area, and building a new road from the market car park to the Abbey to relieve pressure on the High Street. Three alternative routes for this were suggested for discussion, all running to the west of the High Street. Although highly controversial, these proposals were also evidence of new and positive thinking about how to adapt the town's facilities to the expected large increase in visitor numbers.[7]

Work had also been undertaken jointly by the Department of the Environment and the County Council to analyse the problems that had to be tackled to improve facilities for visitors to the Abbey, and to draw up proposals for what in the jargon was called an 'Interpretive Plan'. In a paper submitted in February 1977 its authors first analysed the constraints that had to be overcome. They noted, for instance, that visitors had to follow a specified route to meet the needs of the Abbey school for privacy but that this prevented them seeing the site in its proper historical sequence. They were in any case unable to walk over the battlefield which was let out on an agricultural tenancy. Little or no attempt was being made to explain the battle or even to say where it took place, and there was a general paucity of explanatory material. 'These arrangements,' the report observed tartly, 'at least have the merit of not confusing the visitor with too much information'. More was clearly required, but there was no habitable building available for a display and existing income from visitors was insufficient to finance more than marginal improvements.[8]

Various solutions to these problems were proposed the following month by the representative of the Department at the next meeting of the Advisory Committee, including re-roofing the Courthouse next to the Gatehouse so that it could be used for interpretive facilities and a sales area. But this was a long-term project and in the meantime substantial and expensive repair work had to be carried out to both.

As the extent of the problems became apparent, earlier optimism gave way to irritation. In July 1977 the 1066 Trust, still under attack by some members

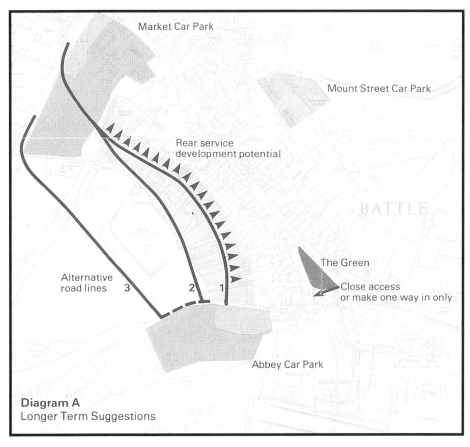

Market Car Park

Mount Street Car Park

Rear service
development potential

BATTLE

The Green

Alternative
road lines   3   2   1

Close access
or make one way in only

Abbey Car Park

Diagram A
Longer Term Suggestions

Map of options for proposed relief road, 1976

of Battle town council, expressed concern about the future fate of the Abbey
beyond the end of September when the County Council was due to relinquish its
responsibility for the management of the Abbey. Trust members picketed meetings
of the relevant county council committees to press their case for an independent
management company. But the Department decided to resume direct control
itself of the Abbey. There had been conflicts between County officials and those
of the Directorate for Ancient Monuments of the Department, disagreement
about plans put forward by the County Council for the future of the site, and
little progress in discussion of the terms under which the County Council might
assume long-term responsibility for the Abbey.

The '1066 Country' proposals

The County Council, however, regarded the Department's decision as only a temporary setback. It had up its sleeve what it hoped would be a trump card: an ambitious plan which was unveiled to a considerable fanfare in June the following year. This proposed the creation of 'a new tourist territory – the 1066 country' centred on Battle Abbey but 'spreading out to other parts of England and the

© East Sussex County Council
Lewes
East Sussex

This leaflet describes proposals for the creation of a new tourist territory, centred upon Battle Abbey in East Sussex, but spreading out to other parts of England and the Continent.

The emphasis will be upon Anglo-Norman culture and the history of our environment.

A future for the 1066 Country

Continent'. The Abbey itself, it argued (rather tactlessly) was 'only a minor part of the story'. The aim was to 'seek to capture the essence of all that 1066 means for us' and to put it in the context of the changes which have happened in subsequent centuries: 'the emphasis will be upon Anglo-Norman culture and the history of our environment.' The detailed proposals, a very mixed bag, included holiday tours of battlefields in southern England, Belgium and northern France; a scholarship for US citizens to study the conservation of historic buildings in Battle; and special banquets organised by the Hastings College of Education. This 'future for the 1066 country', it was claimed, was expected to bring between 150,000 and 200,000 more visitors each year to Battle within five years, and eventually double that number.[9]

This was a prospect which dismayed many people in the town. Local reactions to the proposals were distinctly hostile. One of the first to comment was the headmistress of Battle Abbey school who said she was 'appalled' at the prospect of so large an influx of tourists, adding that 'should there be any interference we have rights under our lease to stop it.' Battle town council was concerned about traffic congestion, and insisted that its support for the plan was contingent on the provision of a Relief Road – the financing of which rapidly became a source of disagreement between the County Council and the Department of the Environment. The Chamber of Commerce, for its part, opposed the conversion of a shop in the High Street into an Information Centre, saying that the loss of a retail outlet was a serious matter. Rother District Council agreed, but its refusal to grant planning permission was brushed aside by the County Council, a decision castigated locally as 'an example of bureaucratic power without conscience.'[10]

After a number of well-attended local meetings at which these and other concerns were voiced, the chairmen of Battle Town Council, the Chamber of Commerce, and the Civic Association issued a joint statement early in 1978 which sounded a general alarm:

> 'The immediate prospect for Battle is cause for concern. We appear to have
> a County Council which ignores the District and Town Council's views and
> intends to make this town, which for centuries served a wide area as its
> commercial and industrial centre, into a tourist attraction with little or no
> regard to what this will mean to the residents.'

An offer rejected

Over the next three years the fate of the plan hung in the balance as the Department of the Environment deliberated on the critical issue of the future role of the County Council with regard to the Abbey. Eventually, during the summer of 1981, it made an offer to transfer ownership to the Council. At first sight it was a generous offer. After selling off surplus land the Department proposed to make a free transfer of the remainder of the estate including the Abbey itself, the battlefield, West Park, Horse Lodge farm and the Abbey Green. But there were significant conditions attached to the proposed gift. The Council would be required to give an assurance that it would not sell it, and would maintain it 'appropriately and to a pre-arranged programme.' Otherwise the Department would itself resume ownership. Moreover, the Department proposed to contribute only 25% of the cost of 'approved consolidation work' on the monument itself . In other words, the bulk of the expense of maintaining the Abbey in good repair would have to be met by the County Council from its own resources.

It was this condition which proved to be the fatal stumbling block in the way of the ambitious Council officials. Some councillors were alarmed about the potential costs of ownership of the Abbey, and did not believe the claim that these would be covered by receipts from visitors. Others doubted whether the Council had the necessary expertise to cope with its management. After extensive deliberation, a narrow majority rejected the Department's offer. With this decision, much of the steam (if not the rhetoric) also went out of the '1066 Country' proposals. There were few tears in Battle at this outcome.

Arrival of English Heritage

Two years later, in 1983, as a result of a reorganisation of the Department of the Environment, responsibility for the Abbey was transferred to a new quango, English Heritage, which became responsible for all aspects of protecting and promoting the country's historic environment. One of its early initiatives was to establish management teams for individual properties with the aim of closer coordination between the various specialised services involved in their care. In the case of the Abbey, the team set about drawing up a long-term management plan, and also a ten-year conservation programme. Work was also put in hand on a set of more immediate priorities. These included a new ticket office to provide direct access to the site from the car park, a more visitor-friendly guide book and an audio-visual display.

The plan to create a shop and museum in the Courthouse was also revived. The idea was generally welcomed, but its realisation proved a very lengthy, difficult and costly operation. The school had ceased to use the gymnasium and art room there because the building was in a derelict and dangerous condition: nevertheless, prolonged negotiations were needed before it could be coaxed to liberate the space. Another lengthy wrangle followed about the type of roof that should be put in place: there were traces of three different configurations, and experts argued fiercely about which historical style would be the most appropriate. Beyond this lay problems of funding and planning consent, which was only secured after an appeal. It was not until 1998 that the new complex was finally opened.

A proposal too far

In the meantime a number of the more ambitious proposals put forward in the early days of the new public regime had either been shelved or were still to be carried out. The project for a relief road, for instance, perished partly because of funding problems, and partly because of local opposition. Shop owners argued that it would take trade away from the High Street; the cricket club that it would threaten their pitch; environmentalists that it would be an ugly intrusion on the landscape; and parents of pupils at the Abbey school that it would endanger lives.

The project for a 50-60 bedroom hotel also fell by the wayside, though the later conversion of Powdermill House into a hotel added significantly to existing facilities in the town. The eventual transformation of Abbey Green from a car park into an open space was only achieved after a very lengthy series of battles, and against the fierce opposition of most of the traders in the High Street.[11]

In 1998 English Heritage itself ran into serious trouble from the same quarter – and from many other local people – when it put forward an ambitious proposal for the Abbey. Its chairman, Sir Jocelyn Stevens, had decreed that during the year priority should be given to the improvement of catering facilities at its

Battle Abbey School from the Gatehouse

various properties. The Abbey itself had none, and the directive from on high was seen as a good opportunity not only to remedy this, but also to provide some additional facilities for visitors. Their numbers were steadily rising and an earlier project for a modest, and well-hidden kiosk offering refreshments was abandoned in favour of a much more ambitious project in the old walled garden, then being used only as a rubbish dump. Proposals were drawn up for a café and a Visitor Centre, together with a new service road from Powdermill Lane. With a view to securing local support, it was suggested that the Centre could be used for a display illustrating the links between the Abbey and the town – for which people in Battle were pressing.

The plan, which was to cost £600,000, soon ran into a storm of opposition. Once again local shopkeepers were amongst its fiercest opponents on the grounds that it would not only compete with existing tea rooms and eateries, but would also keep visitors away from the High Street. But they were not the only ones to object. Many also thought that the proposed building would be very intrusive, and not only detract from the site where Harold was reputed to have fallen, but also spoil the view of the Abbey from the town. Rother District Council planning committee gave the proposals such a cool reception when they were submitted in May 1998 that they were hastily withdrawn.[12]

A slightly revised plan submitted in October fared even worse. New and powerful voices were added to the chorus of protest. Their objections focussed on the new service road which English Heritage said would be necessary to get supplies to the new facility. Starting from Powdermills Lane, this would have cut right across the site of the battle which had recently been opened up to visitors. The proposal attracted the ire not only of the local Historical Society, but also of the Battlefield Trust, an association set up precisely to safeguard such historic sites. This proved particularly embarrassing, as the Trust's founder, Kelvin van Hasselt, was a member of English Heritage's advisory panel on battlefields – which it had omitted to consult. He lambasted the proposal as 'bizarre and totally inappropriate', and said that his colleagues on the panel were 'absolutely livid.' Other powerful voices also joined in the chorus of opposition, including English Heritage's own Inspector of Historic Buildings, the County Council's archaeologist, the Council for the Protection of Rural England, and the British Council of Archaeology.[13]

Confronted by such a force, English Heritage beat a hasty retreat. The proposal was withdrawn and its authors given a dressing down by Stevens who in late January the following year convened a public meeting at the Abbey to discuss what to do next. His original hope seems to have been to find a compromise, but at the meeting itself on Thursday 18 February 1999 he was confronted with such vehement opposition that he quickly changed tack. 'We got it wrong' he said, apologised profusely, and then declared the project officially dead.[14]

Achievements to celebrate

Following this debacle, English Heritage took greater care about its relations with the local community and the new regime of public ownership settled down. By the turn of the century it had achieved a great deal to improve facilities for visitors to the Abbey. They were now able to enter the site directly from Abbey

The school choir performs in the Abbot's Hall

Green through the Gatehouse complex, rather than by way of the car park and a miserable prefabricated building there. An individual audio guide and other explanatory material was now available in the shop on the ground floor, as well as a display about its history in a new museum on the first floor. The suggested circuit led by way of an audio-visual display about the Battle of Hastings to a tour of the battlefield marked with a series of panels describing the various phases of the conflict, and ending at the ruins of the Abbey itself. In deference to local interests, there were no refreshments on sale, and the Abbot's Hall was only open (as it still is) during the school's summer holiday. Even so, what was now on offer was a vast improvement on the amateurish arrangements during the Websters' period of ownership. There were also many more events for the public each year, including an annual re-enactment of the battle in mid October.

In response to this more vigorous promotion of the Abbey, visitor numbers climbed to to reach a peak of just over 186,000 in 2000. In October 2001 a special programme was devised to celebrate the 25th anniversary of the purchase of the Abbey for the nation, and to thank the Americans who had done so much to make this possible. Their delegation – much reduced in numbers in the immediate aftermath of the terrorist attacks of September 11 – was led by one of the benefactors, Lady Eccles, who took part in a series of events marking the occasion.[15]

But new problems arise

Since then, however, the achievements of English Heritage at the Abbey have been overshadowed by new problems. The major challenge is a quite sharp and continuing decline in the number of visitors. The facilities available to them have fallen behind both the range and standards now expected by the public, and generally available at other comparable sites. The lack of any catering provision has become more than ever a major issue. In addition, toilets are inconveniently located, and after more than twenty years in place the exhibition material is seriously outdated and in need of radical renewal.

In response to these problems, English Heritage has put forward plans for a new £2.3 million visitor centre and café. But once again it has run into local opposition led by the Battle Historical Society. Echoing the complaints made at the time of the ill-fated 1998 proposal, the Society is protesting against a lack of consultation, and also the proposed location, this time on a site backing on to the car park, which it asserts would be prejudicial to the historic environment of the Gatehouse. There is no doubt that new and improved facilities for visitors to the Abbey are urgently needed: it remains to be seen whether they can be achieved in a way that will appease opposition and gain local consent.

Farewell to the family

In the intervening years since the sale of the Abbey most of the Websters and Harbords who had been closely involved with it had departed the scene. Simon Harbord died in 1984 and his mother Evelyn four years later. She had spent her declining years in an apartment in Rutland Gate, Bayswater and latterly in a nursing home in Reigate, Surrey. She died aged 84 on 11 November 1988 and was buried in the family vault in Battle parish church after her funeral on 22 November. Her elder sister, Lucy, who had been transferred from North Wales to another psychiatric hospital in Northampton followed shortly afterwards. She was 88 when she died there on 29 April 1989. After a funeral service in Battle attended by only six people she was buried in the last remaining space in the vault. It was then sealed by Godfrey who came over from Brazil specially to 'box up' (as he said) the aunt for whom he had always had a special affection.

By that time these events had only a limited resonance in Battle: memories of the Websters remained among those who had known them, but were otherwise fast fading. Godfrey, for his part, returned to Brazil where in spite of a substantial income from the proceeds of the estate, he managed in true Webster fashion to live well beyond his means, and constantly complained of niggardly treatment at the hands of the family trustees, whose chairman was a cousin. It was his pressure which led to successive sales of Webster family portraits, of which the remaining 19 were purchased in 1999 for around £140,000 by English Heritage. Godfrey sought to lay hands on the capital so realised but the trustees reminded him that he had only a life interest in the proceeds.

In 1994 Godfrey suffered from two accidents – one from driving a tractor that overturned on him – which severely affected his mobility and general health, and which led to his death in July 2003 at the age of 75. In the meantime restorers at English Heritage had been working both on the huge Battle of Hastings picture which they had acquired as well as the Webster portraits. In the summer of 2002 the former was restored to its original position in the Abbot's Hall, and in January 2004 most of the family portraits were also returned to the Abbey. They now hang in the library there – rather high up, above the panelling – as a reminder of the Webster period of ownership: not perhaps the most glorious, but certainly one of the most extraordinary, in the long history of the Abbey.

Notes

Abbreviations

Brakspear	Sir Harold Brakspear, 'The Abbot's House at Battle', Society of Antiquaries of London (1933)
Boys Behrens	Lillian Boys Behrens, *Battle under 39 kings. Legends and records* (1937)
Brent	Judith A Brent, *A catalogue of the Battle Estate Archives*. ESRO Handbook No 6 (1973)
Cleveland	Duchess of Cleveland, *History of Battle Abbey* (1877)
Dolan	Brian Dolan, *Ladies of the Grand Tour* (2001)
ESRO	East Sussex Record Office
Farrant	John Farrant, *Sussex Depicted. Views and Descriptions 1600-1800*. Sussex Record Society Vol 85 (2001)
Guilmant	Aylwin Guilmant, *Bygone Battle* (1983)
HEH BA	Henry E Huntington Library, San Marino, California. Webster of Battle Abbey Archive
Journal	*The Journal of Elizabeth Lady Holland (1791-1811)* Ed The Earl of Ilchester, 2 vols, vol 1 1791-1799, vol 2 1799-1811 (1908).
Lowerson	John Lowerson, *A short history of Sussex* (1980)
Parker	June Parker, *Battle Abbey. The story of a school* (1994)
PRO	Public Record Office (Kew)
SAC	Sussex Archaeological Collections, Sussex Archaeological Society
SRS	Sussex Record Society
Thorpe	Thomas Thorpe, *Descriptive catalogue of the muniments of Battle Abbey* (1835)
VCH	Victoria County History
Whittick (Oxford DNB)	Christopher Whittick, 'Webster family (per. c.1650-1836)', *Oxford Dictionary of National Biography*, Oxford University Press (2004), vol 57, pages 871-874

2. AN AMBITIOUS ARRIVAL

1   For varying accounts of the demolition following the Dissolution, see *Gleanings respecting Battel and its Abbey* (1841) 122-123; L H Pyke, *Short Guide to Battle* 35-37; Cleveland 159 note 2, 162–163; Rose Graham, 'The monastery of Battle', *Journal of British Architectural Association*, October 1924; Eleanor Searle, *Lordship and Community. Battle Abbey and its banlieu 1066-1538* (Toronto 1974) 442; VCH Sussex vol 9 103-105; Brakspear 155. For the monk's curse, Cleveland 166. For the disasters which struck Sir Anthony's successors, *ibid* 194-204. For his yew avenue and flower garden, Cleveland 243.

2   For rebuilding carried out by Sir Anthony, Maurice Howard, *The early Tudor country house,*

1490-1550 (1987); Browne Willis, *History of Mitred Parliamentary Abbies (1718)*, quoted in Cleveland 193.

3   For the Montagues and Battle Abbey, Cleveland 172-193, C Roundell, *Cowdray, The history of a great English house* (1884) 34, Timothy McCann, 'Religious observance in the 17th century' in Kim Leslie and Brian Short, *An historical atlas of Sussex* (1999) 56-57.

4   Whittick (Oxford DNB) for the 1st Webster Baronet and his forebears; Cleveland 205.

5   Sir Godfrey Webster's Thames street properties, HEH BA 63/7 (Thorpe 186). For Nelmes, VCH Essex, vol 7, 26-29, 37. The house was demolished in 1967, with the exception of one of its outbuildings, now much remodelled and known as Capel Nelmes.

6   ESRO BAT 4651.

7   HEH BA 65/42.

8   For purchase of Copped Hall, HEH BA 66/99 (Thorpe 192). The 16th century Copped Hall was demolished in 1748 and rebuilt 1753-8. This survived until 1917 when it was severely damaged by fire, leaving only the shell of the building. VCH Essex, vol 5, 121-24.

9   E Cruickshanks, Stuart Handley & D W Hayton, *The House of Commons, 1690–1715*, vol 2, 186-192, vol 5, 821-822. R Sedgwick, *The House of Commons, 1715-1754*, vol 2, 241.

10   Details of property mortgages in HEH BA 66/7-9.

11   HEH BA 64/16 (Thorpe 188), Cleveland 205.

12   Thorpe 190.

13   Thorpe 190, 194; *Gleanings* 135.

14   Webster's commission, HEH BA 75/3; 66/21 for appointment as Deputy Lieutenant.

15   For the South Sea stock, HEH BA 75/17 & 76/45.

16   Horace Walpole, *Letters*, vol II, 299 26 August 1749.

17   *Gleanings* 135 for the need for oxen; Cleere & Crossley, *The iron industry of the Weald* (2nd ed 1995) 194; Roy Pryce, *Heathfield Park* (1996) ch. 5 for examples of the new money coming into the Weald.

18   Lowerson 97.

19   Sir Thomas's Sussex purchases ESRO BAT 273, 979; Brent 6-7; R F Whistler, 'The annals of an English family', SAC vol 35, 63; and *Gleanings* 133.

20   Visit of the Revd Jeremiah Milles, Farrant 22-23 and 88-98; a reproduction of Budgen's 1724 map ESRO AMS/6008/1/1/29; maps of the Websters' estates BAT 4421. Sir Thomas's alterations to the Abbot's House, Brakspear 144.

21   References to 'Battle House' in HEH BA 70/7 & 12; 'Battle Place' in 70/10,13 & 20.

22   For Sir Thomas's purchases from Jethro Tull, *Gleanings* 135.

23   Details of rents in HEH BA 70/ 7-32; contractual details, for instance, in 70/12.

24   Beech Furnace, HEH BA 70/10 & 11, 70/17/1 & 2; Robertsbridge HEH BA 72/41 & 42; Etchingham, Cleveland 206. See also C W Whittick, 'Wealden iron in California – a recent foray at the Huntington Library, San Marino, California', *Wealden Iron Research Group Bulletin*, No 12, second series, 1992, 29-62; and H Cleere and D Crossley, *The iron industry of the Weald*, 1995 ed, 352-3.

25 HEH BA 72/9.

26 The gunpowder works at Sedlescombe, HEH BA 70/30: the Toledo waterworks, 76/36.

27 John ('Vulture') Hopkins ESRO BAT 4651; Mortgages, ESRO BAT 869 and Thorpe 195.

28 The 1733 settlement, ESRO BAT 1115 & 6; sales of Sandford Orcas HEH BA 73/18; Ongar, VCH Essex vol 4, 177; and Copthall, ESRO AMS 2925. 1744 financial situation, ESRO BAT 1122.

29 Heather M Matthews, 'The papers of John Collier of Hastings - A catalogue' ESRO SAY (introduction); ESRO SAY 1749 & 1828.

30 For the accident to Godfrey Webster, ESRO SAY 1794.

31 ESRO SAY 1797 & 1799.

32 ESRO RAF 16/16.

33 ESRO SAY 115.

34 For Lady Jane Webster's will HEH BA 75/16.

3. BORN WITH A SILVER SPOON

1 Whittick (Oxford DNB) for the 2nd Webster Baronet; HEH BA 63/17 & 18 (Thorpe l95-6) for Deed of Conveyance dated 31 May 1733.

2 Cleveland, 209.

3 R Sedgwick, *The House of Commons 1715-1754*, vol 2, 527 for the 1750 rebuff to the Prince of Wales. For the East Grinstead constituency see also W D Cooper, 'Parliamentary History' in T W Horsfield, *The history of the County of Sussex*, (1835) vol 2, 40 and G H Nadel, 'The Sussex election of 1741' SAC 91(1953) 84-124.

4 HEH BA 75/14 for particulars of Whistler Webster's estates in East Grinstead and elsewhere in Sussex and Surrey. For his period in parliament, Sedgwick, *op.cit*; Sir Louis Namier & John Brooke, *House of Commons 1754-1790*, vol 3, 617.

5 Cleveland 207-8, 236.

6 *Op.cit* 229-230.

7 Farrant 54.

8 Quoted in Farrant 119. I share his uncertainty (note 35) whether the Godfrey Webster mentioned by Grose was the 3rd or 4th Webster baronet, but agree that the latter is the more likely.

9 ESRO BAT 2751.

10 Robertsbridge ironworks, HEH BA 71/27-30; lock on river Rother, HEH BA 72/26/1; Webster's involvement in Ticehurst to Hastings turnpike, ESRO SAY 1366.

11 For Lady Jane Webster's will and subsequent court case, HEH BA 75/8, 75/9/2-10, 75/16.

12 For Sir Whistler's will, ESRO BAT 1117 and 1330.

13 *The Fuller Letters 1728-1755*, ed David Crossley & Richard Saville, 179, and C L Shadwell, *Registrum Orielense*, vol 2, 1701-1900 for the education of the 3rd Bt.

14   ESRO SAY 2061 9 November 1751.

15   Will of 3rd Bt. ESRO BAT 1331.

4. AN UNFORTUNATE RAKE

1   For the 4th Webster Baronet, Whittick (Oxford DNB), Louis Namier and John Brooke, *The House of Commons, 1754-1790*, 617, and John Ingamells, *A dictionary of British and Irish travellers in Italy 1701-1800*, 985.

2   Diary of Francis Grose, quoted in Farrant 119.

3   *Journal* vol 1, xii; Brent 10 notes 1-4; VCH Sussex vol 7, 37.

4   ESRO ACC 5645. Letter of 9 Dec 1801 from James Inskipp to Thomas Chaplin. (Typescript based on documents whose present whereabouts are unknown, previously in the possession of Evelyn Webster.)

5   Namier and Brooks, *op.cit* 617, for Sir Godfrey's parliamentary career; vol 3, K-Y 258-259 for Baron (Thomas) Pelham (1728-1805) who subsequently became the 1st Earl of Chichester.

6   Quoted in Dolan 96.

7   *Auckland Journal*, I, 375 quoted in G E Mingay *English landed society in the 18th century*, 29.

8   ESRO BAT 1133.

9   *The Torrington Diaries*. Ed. C Bruyn Andrews, vol 1, 360-362.

10   R H D'Elboux, 'The Court House, Battle Abbey', *Sussex Notes and Queries*, vol 12, (1950-53) 198-9.

11   For Rose Green, also known as 'Mr Worge's house at Starrs Green', see Christopher Whittick in Farrant 156. The quotation is from Cleveland 210.

12   *Journal xi-xii.*

13   Dolan 113, quoting Granville I 52.

14   Dolan 98. Namier and Brooke, *op.cit* vol 3, K-Y 259-260 for the Hon Thomas Pelham (1756-1826), MP for Sussex 1780-1801, Home Secretary 1801-3, Baron Pelham (1801) and subsequently (from 1805) 2nd Earl of Chichester.

15   *Journal* 1, 3 note 1.

16   *Journal* 1, 5 & 159.

17   *Journal* 1, 6.

18   *Ibid.*

19   *Journal* 1,13.

20   ESRO AMS 5440/203.

21   ESRO ACC 5645. Letter of 30 January 1793. (See note 4).

22   ESRO AMS 5440/210.

23   *Journal* 1, 27, 38.

24 *Journal* 1, 53.

25 Dolan 111.

26 *Journal* 1, 96-97.

27 ESRO AMS 5440/221 Pelham to Sheffield 12 Nov 1793; *Journal* 1,103.

28 The Gauffier portrait was the most important in a collection of twenty-two Webster family portraits acquired by English Heritage in 1999; it was not re-hung in the Abbey in January 2004 but remained on display at Kenwood.

29 *Journal* 1, 117, Cleveland 210-211.

30 *Journal* 1, 117.

31 *Ibid* 121.

32 Dolan 116, *Journal* 1, 121.

33 *Journal* 1, 126; Sonia Keppel, *The Sovereign Lady: A life of Elizabeth Vassall, third Lady Holland with her family* 41, 51-52, 56.

34 Quoted in Ingamells, *op.cit* 986; *Journal* 1, 130-132.

35 *Journal* 1, 140.

36 *Journal* 1, xv.

37 *Journal* 1, 263-264, Dolan 118-119.

38 *Journal* 1, xvi.

39 *Journal* 1, xvi, 147.

40 Dolan 262-7, Cleveland 211-217.

41 ESRO ACC 5645. Letter of 18 May 1800.

42 *Journal* vol 2, 90, 98; *Gentleman's Magazine* (1800) I 594.

5. A DISASTROUS PROFLIGATE

1 For the 5th Webster Baronet, Whittick (Oxford DNB); quotation in *Journal* 1, 237.

2 ESRO BAT 4638 for baptismal record.

3 Cleveland 221, Byron to Hobhouse, 27 February, quoted in Leslie Marchand, *Byron. A Portrait*, 50. To the same, 15 April quoted in Marchand (ed), *Byron's Letters and Journals*, vol I, 165.

4 *Lady Bessborough and her family circle*. Ed Earl of Bessborough. (1940) 181.

5 Cleveland 57; the quotation is from John Williams Ward, 5 April 1810. *Letters to 'Ivy'* 162.

6 Quoted in Boys Behrens 115.

7 ESRO BAT 4769 & 4775.

8 Debrett (1936).

9 Cleveland 218-219. In her account the Dormitory is referred to, erroneously, as the Refectory.

10 Cleveland 219, Brakspear 153-154, ESRO BAT 3502.

11 Cleveland 265 note 1.

12 For the subsequent history of the painting, see pages 132-3 and 207.

13 'CEWC' (Lady Cleveland), *Guide to Battle Abbey* 55.

14 Cleveland 178-9, 220, 243-4.

15 Boys Behrens 115.

16 For a recent study of the development of Brighton as a resort, Sue Berry, 'Myth and reality in the representation of resorts. Brighton and the emergence of the 'Prince and fishing village myth' SAC 140 (2002) 97-112.

17 The quotation is from the important recent study by Rosemary Sweet, *Antiquaries. The discovery of the past in eighteenth century Britain*. (2004) 277.

18 Information about the Ticehurst family kindly supplied by David Sawyer, Archivist, Battle Museum.

19 Geoff Hutchinson, *Fuller of Sussex. A Georgian squire* 77-78.

20 R G Thorne, *The House of Commons 1790-1820*, vol 5, 500-501; Lowerson 112-114.

21 ESRO BAT 4763/19 &20. Affidavit of Sir Henry Webster, 23 May 1846.

22 ESRO BAT 1337.

23 For Henry Webster and Edinburgh university, *The Horner Papers*, ed Kenneth Bourne and William Banks Taylor (Edinburgh 1994) 231, 564-565.

24 For Henry Webster and the Peninsular war, *Lady Bessborough and her family circle*, 231, letter from Frederick Ponsonby to Lady Duncannon 21 November 1812. Webster's own account of his exploit at Waterloo is in J C Young, *A memoir of Charles Mayne Young* (1871) vol 2, 98-102. See also Elizabeth Longford, *Wellington. The years of the sword*. 502-508.

25 ESRO BAT 4821/18.

26 A portrait of Charlotte Adamson by Sir Thomas Lawrence was commissioned by Sir John Fleming Leicester Bt (later Lord de Tabley), she having lived for a while at Tabley House in Cheshire as a companion to Lady Leicester. ESRO BAT 1151 for details of the marriage settlement.

27 Cleveland 221.

28 For the lady in the pie, Battle Museum, Battle WI *Scrapbook*, (1952) 12.

29 Cleveland *Ibid*.

30 ESRO BAT 4718/2.

31 ESRO ACC 5645 Letter of 20 May 1803 to Messrs Frogatt & Robson. William Inskipp took over from his father as Steward in 1813 at a salary of 100 guineas a year, plus rent-free house and land.

32 Lowerson 127.

33 ESRO BAT 2610, 2629, 959-961, 1,004-1,008.

34 Cleveland 221.

35   Cleveland 221, ESRO BAT 2128, 2634, 2635, 2636, 4763/10.

36   J Manwaring Baines, *History of Hastings, (1955)* 50; speech of 12 March 1820 printed in *An account of the Sussex election including the poll*, 86.

37   W D Cooper 'Parliamentary History' in T W Horsfield, *The History of the County of Sussex*, vol 2, Appendix III, 36-37; for the bowl of punch, ESRO BAT 4859/4.

38   *Brighton Herald* 9 & 23 August 1823.

39   *Ibid* 30 August 1823.

40   Horsfield, *op.cit* 25 for election expenses.

41   ESRO BAT 4803/7 for Lady Webster's letter from Bern.

42   For the affray at Herstmonceux, Thomas Geering, *Our Sussex parish* (1884, reprinted 1925) 74, and *The Times* 22 November 1830. For a general account of the disturbances, Eric Hobsbawm & George Rudé, *Captain Swing* (1969) 89-91, 104-l09, 218.

43   Quoted in W H Hills, *History of East Grinstead* 223-224.

44   L F Salzman, *Hastings* (1921) 103; J M Baines, *op.cit* 50-51.

45   For the Websters' neglect of Bodiam, The Marquis Curzon of Kedleston *Bodium Castle, Sussex* (1926) 48-49, 80-81; for its sale, Geoff Hutchinson, *Fuller of Sussex* (1993) 107-113.

46   For the history of the Battle Abbey archive, Christopher Whittick, 'Wealden iron in California' 29-30. (See ch 2, note 24) For detailed calendars of its contents by the same author, *Webster of Battle Abbey archive*, 2 vols, Henry E Huntington Library, 1991 & 1993. These volumes supercede the earlier catalogue by Thorpe.

47   *Gentleman's Magazine*, 1836 vol 2, 426-7; ESRO PAR 236/1/5/1; Whittick Oxford DNB.

48   ESRO BAT 4751 and 4766.

6.   Two Websters at sea: a reluctant sale

1   ESRO BAT 4763/6.

2   ESRO BAT 4763/ 4 & 12 for the Robinson v Webster case.

3   Cleveland 222.

4   ESRO BAT 4807 & 4805.

5   ESRO BAT 2743 & 2744.

6   Dame Charlotte wrote enthusiastically to her son about another lady he was considering marrying, ESRO BAT 4807. ESRO AMS 6066 for the 6th Baronet's marriage settlement.

7   ESRO BAT 1225 for purchase of Rose Green.

8   Brent 14, Cleveland 169, 244.

9   *Sussex Express* 10, 14, & 21 February & 8 March 1853.

10   *Sussex Express* 14 & 21 May 1853: BAT 4817 & 4820.

11   ESRO BAT 4681, page 78.

12   Palmerston quotation in Keith Feiling, *History of England* 857-8.

13   ESRO BAT 4852 & 4807.

14   ESRO BAT 4807.

15   ESRO BAT 4699.

16   ESRO BAT 4807.

17   *Ibid*; also Cleveland 222.

18   ESRO BAT 4821/2 letter dated 20 April 1854.

19   Information on Dame Sarah Joanna provided by Mr E H Jones of Netherfield, *Rye and Battle Observer*, 14 February 2003. She lived into her eighties, dying on 19 December 1889.

20   ESRO BAT 4818.

21   Molly Beswick, 'The Battle Abbey Estate brickworks: 1853-1901', *Sussex Industrial Archaeology Society Newsletter*, No 42, April 1984. ESRO BAT 4821 & 1265.

22   ESRO BAT 4821/9, 2646.

23   Cleveland 222, 236.

24   Several other contemporary prints were also dedicated to Lady Charlotte, as was Marcus Lower's translation of the *Chronicle of Battle Abbey*, published in 1851.

25   Cleveland 222-3, quoting from Hawthorne's *English Notebooks*.

26   ESRO BAT 2646, letter dated 26 April 1857.

27   ESRO BAT 2646.

28   ESRO BAT 2646, undated drafts of 1857 sale particulars.

29   ESRO BAT 2646 for proceeds of sale; 4826 for Sarah Joanna's letter of 26 May 1858.

30   ESRO BAT 4825, undated letter.

7.   A PERIOD OF NOBILITY

1   *Sussex Express* 25 May 1901.

2   Description of the Duke given by Lady St Helier, *Memories of fifty years* (1909) 94 quoted in *Complete Peerage*, III, 286-287, note (c). The story is recounted by W E Allwork in 'Battle in the last seventy years', talk given to Battle Historical Society in 1952. (Text in Battle Museum.)

3   *Sussex Express* 5 September 1891.

4   *Sussex Express* 25 May 1901.

5   Cleveland 236-243, 246, 301.

6   'Country Homes: Battle Abbey', *Country Life* 6 November 1897; Brakspear. 145.

7   The Rev Edward Turner, 'Battel Abbey', SAC vol 17 (1865), 51; Cleveland 303, 224-261 for a detailed description of the Abbey buildings and its ruins at this time, and 262-307 for similar detail about the interior of their living quarters (including their collection of pictures).

8   *Sussex Express* 25 May 1901; Harry Taylor, 'The Brasseys of Catsfield' in *A tapestry of Battle* (Battle Writers' Group, 2002) 139.

9   ESRO BAT 1040 & 2150; W E Allwork, *op.cit.*

10 Cleveland 347-52.

11 *Country Life* 21 October 1899.

12 Cleveland 352-7.

13 George F Chambers, *Tourists' Guide to the county of Sussex* (4th ed. 1887) 65. See also 1898 edition of *Black's Picturesque Guide.*

14 Quotation from an advertisement on the back page of 'CLWC's (Lady Cleveland's) *Guide to Battle Abbey.*

15 *Sussex Express* 21 May 1901 for obituary of Lady Cleveland.

16 *Ibid*.

17 *Ibid* 28 May 1901.

18 Boys Behrens 117; ESRO BAT 4852/15, cutting from *Evening News & Post* 13 December 1901; BAT 4852/31, cutting from *Evening News* 18 January 1902.

19 *East Sussex News* 2 August 1901, *Sussex Express* 12 April 1902.

20 *Sussex Express* 3 December 1901.

8. THE WEBSTERS DISPERSED

1   ESRO BAT 1284 for loan application.

2   ESRO BAT 4828 for Arthur Webster's financial problems.

3   ESRO BAT 4807, 4803/4, 1253, 1256.

4   ESRO BAT 4823, 2 December 1855.

5   ESRO BAT 4826 & 4807.

6   ESRO BAT 4834.

7   ESRO BAT 1299, 4821/16, 4843-4846.

8   ESRO BAT 4821/16.

9   ESRO BAT 4829 & 4821/16.

10 ESRO BAT 4821/15 for Dame Charlotte's will; *Burke's Peerage* for date of Guy Webster's death; BAT 4836 for Dame Joanna's missive.

11 ESRO BAT 4843/6.

12 ESRO BAT 4852 contains an undated and unattributed press cutting describing the departure of the battalion. *Debrett* 1896 for Gussie's clubs.

13 ESRO BAT 4852/ 17 &19 for stories recounted in cuttings from *The Free Lance* 21 December 1901 and *Ladies Field* 16 December 1901.

14 ESRO BAT 4852/1 Cutting from *The Tatler* 30 October 1901.

15 ESRO BAT 4711. Cutting from *The Table*.

16 ESRO ACC 554 for Deed of Arrangement dated 26 April 1890.

17 ESRO BAT 4713/54 & 33.

18 ESRO BAT 1322; 4852 for cutting from the *Evening Standard* 10 February 1912. Curiously, both children were born on the same day of the year, the second of September.

19 ESRO BAT 4704; 4855 for a press cutting of the article dated 1 November 1890. Other details from obituary in *Sussex Express* 17 August 1923, and BAT 4852/2 cutting from *Masonic Record*.

20 ESRO BAT 4853/3-23.

21 ESRO BAT 4853/ 25-37; *Daily Telegraph* 15 February 1901 for notice of Godfrey's death. According to the obituary of Sir Augustus in the *Sussex Express* 17 August 1923 he rejoined the army and served throughout the Boer War, but I have not found any confirmation of this from other sources.

9. RETURN TO BATTLE: TRIUMPH AND TRAGEDY

1 ESRO BAT 2151. Abridged sale particulars.

2 *Sussex Express* 30 November 1901.

3 *Ibid*, ESRO BAT 4852/5 cutting from *Manchester City News* 7 December 1901.

4 ESRO BAT 4852/16.

5 ESRO BAT 4852/7 cutting dated 7 December 1901.

6 *Sussex Express* 26 November 1901.

7 ESRO BAT 4852/3 & 4, cuttings from *Sussex Daily News* 28 November and 4 December 1901.

8 ESRO BAT 4852/11 & 15.

9 ESRO BAT 4852/11 & 44.

10 ESRO BAT 4852/35-37, 39, 44 & 45 for cuttings relating to the *Battle of Hastings* painting. Its chequered history is recorded in a file in Hastings Museum and Art Gallery.

11 ESRO BAT 4852 /52, 55, & 64.

12 Biographical details of Mr Grace, apparently supplied by himself, are to be found in *Sussex. Historical, Biographical and Pictorial* (1907, published only for subscribers) and *Sussex in the 20th century*, ed W T Pike (1910). But they are scanty and uncertain. The first asserts, for instance, that his place of birth was Queen's County, Ireland, the second that it was Sheffield. ESRO BAT 2065 for loan agreement.

13 See www.battle-abbey.co.uk for extracts from Peggie Phipps Boegner, *Halcyon Days* (1986).

14 Charles G Harper, *The Hastings Road* (1906) 227.

15 Sale particulars in BAT 2153-8, 2167-2183.

16 ESRO BAT 4852 (unnumbered): for the abortive industrial development at Heathfield, Roy Pryce, *op.cit* 120-121.

17 Charles G Harper, *op.cit* 231.

18 Visitor numbers derived from detailed accounts in BAT 4936 & 7.

19 *A brief history of the Souvenir Norman* (1996) 4. The organisation, which has several branches in other countries, including Britain, was revived after World War II and a French delegation has for a number of years paid an annual visit to Battle in October for a service at the parish church and a ceremony at the Norman Stone.

20 ESRO BAT 4821/17 for letter from a member of the Crossley family about the Hastings parliamentary seat. For masonic activities, ESRO BAT 4713 and BAT 4852/62. Cutting from the *Hampshire Advertiser* 26 July 1901.

21 ESRO BAT 4852/56. Cutting from *Sussex Daily News* 24 July 1902.

22 *Sussex Express* 17 August 1923, ESRO BAT 4873/65.

23 ESRO BAT 4859/26, 31 & 33 for departure of Grace; 4859/18 for Zeppelin raid.

24 ESRO BAT 4873/50.

25 ESRO BAT 4859/34. Letter from Francis Scott, 5 March 1917.

26 ESRO BAT 4859/24.

27 *Sussex Express* and *East Sussex News* 22 June 1917.

28 ESRO BAT 4873/65 & 73. See also *Sussex in the First World War*, ed. Keith Graves, SRS vol 84.

29 ESRO BAT 4873/73 & 74.

30 ESRO BAT 4861 & 4682.

31 ESRO BAT 4862 & 4864.

32 ESRO BAT 4861 & 4863. On the anniversary of Godfrey's death six years later a lance corporal who had been with him in the platoon that night wrote as 'one of his devoted men' to recall 'his courage and brilliant example.' BAT 4864.

33 ESRO BAT 4880.

34 ESRO BAT 4865/15.

35 ESRO BAT 4865/18.

36 ESRO BAT 4865/2, 3, 6.

37 *Sussex Express* 17 August 1923.

38 ESRO BAT 4865/19, Parker 7.

39 ESRO ACC 455 3 May 1926.

40 *Sussex Express* 17 & 24 August 1923.

10. HANGING ON

1 ESRO ACC 554. Letter of 25 September 1921.

2 ESRO ACC 554. Letter of 6 September 1923.

3   Details of sales from auction catalogues, Battle Museum.

4   The information in this section is drawn from contemporary documents in ACC 554.

5   ESRO ACC 554. Letter from Charles Harbord to Lucy Webster, 11 November 1927; undated letter from Evelyn Harbord from Assam.

6   Parker 15-17; ESRO ACC 554, May Jacoby to Lucy Webster, 29 September 1925.

7   *Sussex Express* 28 June 1946.

8   ESRO ACC 554. J R Sheehan-Dare to Lucy Webster, 8 May and 9 June 1925.

9   ESRO ACC 554. Undated 1930 cutting from *Sussex Express*.

10 W E Allwork, *op.cit* Intervention by James Woodhams.

11 Parker 23-27.

12 *Sussex Express* 24 June & 15 July 1932.

13 *Sussex Express* 26 May, 10 June & 28 July 1935.

14 *Sussex Express* 26 May & 30 June 1933; Parker 32-34.

15 Parker 41.

16 *Idem* 35-37, *Sussex Express* 28 June 1946.

17 H V Morton, *I saw Two Englands*. Quoted in Parker xii.

18 R J B Bosworth, *Mussolini* (2002) 13.

19 Battle Museum: Battle WI *Scrapbook* 18, Parker 39-42 for the school during wartime.

20 For general deployment of Canadian troops, P Longstaff-Tyrrell, *The maple leaf army in Britain (2003)* 22, 25; for details PRO WO 166/140 War Diary, South East Command 13 October 1941; 3 December 1941, Location statement (SE/2003/OPS).

21 For the wartime bomb, *Daily Telegraph*, 2 February 1943; Battle Museum, 'Battle in war'; J G Coad, *Battle Abbey* (3rd ed. 1994) 22; Alan Gillet, *Battle and Robertsbridge in old photographs* (1989) 47.

22 Battle WI *Scrapbook* 220-222. For an interesting essay on wartime Battle, Andy Lawrence, 'The impact of world war two on Battle: change or continuity?' Copy of mss in Battle Museum.

23 *Sussex Express* 24 May, 7 June & 8 November 1946.

24 Parker 77.

25 *Sussex Express* 21 October 1966.

26 Parker 59-60.

27 *Sussex Express* 28 October 1966.

28 A plaque in the small plantation close to the building in the Abbey grounds housing the audio-visual display about the Battle of Hastings is all that now remains of the 'Forest of Thankfulness'.

29 Eleanor Searle, *op.cit.*

30 *Daily Telegraph* 23 August 2003 for an indiscreet obituary of Godfrey Webster. Other

material from interviews. Accounts of his life differ in some significant respects: I have done my best to separate fact from fantasy.

31   Parker 80.

31   *Sussex Express* 25 July 1975.

11. The 1976 sale

1   The account of the events leading up to the sale, the sale itself, and its aftermath is based on a variety of sources including the extensive and well-informed coverage given in the *Sussex Express* by its reporter Lee Pateman; the national press; extracts from a diary kept by Ann Moore, who was then a County Councillor and Press Officer to the 1066 Trust; and interviews with others involved in various ways with the events described.

2   *Sussex Express* 29 August 1975 'Knights of the Round Table!'; 1066 Trust leaflet, October 1975, *Early beginnings, present and future role.*

3   *Evening News* 12 November 1975.

4   *Sussex Express* 24 October 1975, 2 January & 19 March 1976.

5   *Sussex Express* 12 March 1976. 'Historic site may fetch more than £1 million. BATTLE ABBEY TO BE AUCTIONED'.

6   *Evening News* 12 November 1975 for 1974 visitor numbers.

7   *Sussex Express* 19 March 1976. 'Abbey sale angers family.'

8   *Guardian* 10 April 1976.

9   *Sussex Express* 9 April 1976.

10   *Sussex Express* 23 April & 7 May 1976.

11   *Sussex Express* 28 May 1976. 'No retreat in Battle site sale decision'.

12   *Daily Mail* 27 May 1976. The following day the *Sussex Express* was equally critical of efforts to save the Abbey in an editorial headed 'A botched job'.

13   Evelyn and Godfrey made a similar impression on a wider public when they appeared on a BBC 2 television programme. One viewer described them as 'upper class eccentrics indulging in flights of fancy.'

14   *Sussex Express* 11 June 1976 'Peer joins fight for the Abbey', and 18 June 'Earl will make bid for Abbey.'

15   Mr Power was subsequently made an Honorary Knight Commander of the British Empire, and Professor Boyd a CBE.

12. Postscript

1   *Sussex Express* 2 July 1976.

2   For Godfrey in Brazil, *Daily Telegraph* 23 August 2003 and private sources.

3   Department of the Environment, Press Release 29 September 1976.

4   *Evening Argus* 14 October 1976, *Sussex Express* 15 October & 19 November 1976.

5   *Sussex Express* 23 December 1976.

6   *Sussex Express* 30 January 1976 'Will it be a boom year for Abbey town?

7   *Battle Abbey and Town Centre. Access and Parking.* Leaflet published late 1976 by East Sussex County Council and Rother District Council.

8   *Battle Interpretive Plan*, draft dated 17 February 1977.

9   *A future for the 1066 Country.* Leaflet issued by East Sussex County Council, June 1978.

10 *Sussex Express* 16 June 1978. 'Teacher appalled at County scheme'.

11 See, for instance, *Sussex Express* 31 July, 28 August, 4 September & 2 October 1998.

12 *Sussex Express* 29 May 1998. 'Heritage café plan causing concern'.

13 *Sussex Express* 30 October & 6 November 1998.

14 *Sussex Express* 26 February 1999, 'Abbey plans scrapped'.

15 *Battle Observer* 19 October 2001. *The Guardian* 16 September 2003 for an obituary of Lady Eccles, American benefactress and widow of the former Conservative minister Lord Eccles.

Index

Acre (Akko) 86
Adams, Frances 185
Adamson, Charlotte see Lady
Charlotte Webster
Advowsons 76
Albermarle Street 56,83
Alexander, Henry 77
Anne, Queen of England 9
Antiquaries 1,3,15,17,66
Army
    10th Hussars 62
    14th & 18th Light Dragoons 62
    9th Light Dragoons 71
    Dragoon Guards 118
    Grenadier Guards 121-123,140-142, 144-146,173
    Scots Guards 145
Ashburnham, Lords 19,69,127
Ashburnham, Sir Anchitel Piers 115
Ashenden, James 18
Assam 158
Astor, William Waldorf 130,131
Athlone, Earl & Countess 165

Bancroft, George 93
Bank of England 9
Barkham Farm, Bexhill 18
Barton, Thomas 77
Battle
    Abbey Green 162,168,202,203,206
    Beech Furnace 19
    'Canadia' 169
    Chamber of Commerce 197,201
    Caldbec Hill 154
    Cattle Market 154
    Civic Association 201
    Cricket club 178,203
    Drill Hall 154
    Duke of Wellington inn 100,152
    Eighteenth century 16,17

Fire station 163
George Inn 82,152
George Meadow 178
Guide book 69
Guy Fawkes night 169-170
High Street 168,203,204
History of 69
Mount Street 152
'no good tea' 160
North Trade Road 104,154
Railway, arrival of 3,87,90-91
Relief road project 198-199,201,203
Round Table 177
Stumblotts 195,196
Tollgates 154
Town Council 195,197,198,201
Urban District Council 162
Wartime (WW2) 168-169
Battle Abbey
    Abbot's Hall 63,65,96,114,163-165,206,207
    Abbot's House 17
    Abbot's Parlour 63,106
    Advisory Committee 191,195-198
    American benefactors 4,189-191,206-207
    Brickworks 96,99
    Church 64,106,165
    Chronicle of 17
    Country house period 5-6,149
    Courthouse 41,47,63,198,203
    Dining room 106
    Dissolution of 4,5
    Dorter 42,63,64
    Drawing room 107
    East front 111
    Estate farms
        Almory 100
        Beech 100
        Course Barn 100,108
        Down Barn 100,178
        Horse Lodge 202

Little Park 100
Marley 100,108
Park 108
Tower Hill 174
Estate sales
  (Whole estate)
  1858 98-102
  1901 126-133
  1976 176-192
  (Part estate)
  1902 133,135,136
  1903 135
  1920-1922 152-154
Fire (1931) 162-163
'Forest of Thankfulness' 172
Gardens 64,75,106,109-110,111,129,176
Gatehouse 28,64,165,206
Guest range 6,7, 28-29
Lettings 77-78,134-135,148-149
Library 106,208
Monk's curse 5,167,192
Muniments, sale of i-ii,83
National Monument status 161
Pageant (1932) 163-164
Public ownership 194-208
Railway 87,89,95-96
Reversion to original name 17
Shale discovery 135
Stables 64,106
Staff 108,115
Terraces 7,28,129
Undercroft 7
Visitors to 3-4,66-69,89,110-115,116,137,
148,159-160,161-162,165,180,197,206, 207
Wishing Well 106
Battle Abbey School 4,149-150,158-167,168,
176,180,201,203
Battle House 17
Battle Parish Church 6,23,84,91,116
Battle Place 17
Battlefield Trust 205
Beaconsfield, Earl of (Benjamin Disraeli) 108
Bear, Rev 33
Beck RCA 95

Beechey, Robin 182
Bessborough, Caroline 60
Bessborough, Lady (née Spencer, then
Duncannon) 52
Bethune's Mounted Infantry 125
Bexhill
  Webster estate 31,135,152
Birk, Lady 181,195
Bodiam
  Castle 16,17,20,83
  Webster estate 31,83
Boer War 125-126
Bolney Court 163
Boodles 13
Bowyer, David 187
Boyd, Professor Julian 190
Brakespear, Sir Harold 106,161,163
Brassey, Lady Sybil 108
Brassey, Lord Thomas 114,127,131,138
Brighton College 117
British American Tobacco Coy 157
Browne, Sir Anthony 5,6,28
Brompton Park House 56
Brooke, William 65,97
Brussels 72-73
Buck, Samuel 17,18,97
Budgen, Richard 17
Bunyan-Bunyan, Ashton Yates 123
Burrell, Sir William 29,35
Byde, Elizabeth 26
Byng, Hon John see Torrington, Viscount
Byron, Lord 60

California, gold 92-94
Canadian troops 168-169
Canterbury, Archbishop of 171-172
Caprons 77,84,100,119-120
Casley, David 17
Chamberlain, Joseph 108
Chaplin, Elizabeth 59
Cheeke, Jane see Webster, Lady Jane
Chesterfield (Derbys) 7,9
Chichester
  Bishop of 165

Earl of 69
East Street 79,80
Parliamentary seat 79-81
The Anchor 81
Christ Church College, Oxford 124
Churchill, John 30
Ciano, Fabrizio 167
Clark, Michael 177
Cleveland, (née Stanhope) Duchess of (1819-1901) 3,27-28,104-116
Cleveland, 4th Duke of (1803-1891) 3,103-109, 110-112,114-115
Clothworkers Company 8,11
Clutton, Henry 106-107
Cobbett, William 82
Colchester
Parliamentary seat 11
Collier, Cordelia 21,22
Collier, Mary 21
Collier, John 18,21,23,33
Compton, Richard 177,189
Conyers, Edward MP 26
Cook, Robert 120
Cooper, Elizabeth see Webster, Lady Elizabeth
Copped Hall see Copt Hall
Copt Hall 10,12,20-22,26,33
Council for the Protection of Rural England 183,184,205
Countryside Commission 195
Courts
Supreme Court 155-156
Chancery 32,165
Common Pleas 76
Exchequer 76
King's Bench 76,81
Queen's Bench 123
Protection, of 156,175
Cowdray 6
Crimean War 99,117-118
Crofton (Yorks) 33,35
Crossley, Henry 124
Crossley, Joseph 124
Crossley, Mabel see Webster, Lady Mabel
Currie, Rev. Dean of Battle 130

de Broglie, Prince 171
De Lisle and Dudley, Lord 16
Devonshire, Georgiana Duchess of 46
Dieppe, raid on 168
Dissolution (of monasteries) 3,5-6
Dorset, Earl of 12
Dresden 46
Duncannon, Lord & Lady 46

East Grinstead
Webster estates 21,22,26,31,37
East Sussex County Council 182,183,185,189, 191,195-196,198-202
East Sussex Hunt 149
Eccles, Lady 207
Edinburgh, Duke of 172
Edinburgh University 71
Edward VII 138,139
Elizabeth I 6
Elizabeth II 166-167,172
Elliot, Sir Gilbert 51
Emeleus, Robert 177
English Heritage 202-207
Entente Cordiale 137-138
Environment, Department of 181,183,188-191, 195-199,202
Epping 20
Etchingham 19
Eton College 121,140,144
Ewhurst
Webster estate 16,31,76,135,154

Fairlight
Webster estate 76
Farthing Pond 142-143,178
Festival, of Britain (1951) 170
Fitzgibbon, Colonel 77
Florence 49,51,54,55
Forrester, Captain FW 116
Foster, Lady Elizabeth 46
Fox, Charles James 38
Fox, Charles Richard 56
Fox, Henry Richard see Holland, 3rd Lord
Fox and Bonfield 129

Francis, Jeremy 187
Frank Knight & Rutley 134
Freemasons see also Webster, Sir Augustus, 8th Bt.
   Grand Lodge of Hampshire and Isle of Wight 139
   Household Brigade Lodge 124
   Royal Masonic Institution for Girls 139
   Royal Alpha Lodge 146
   United Grand Lodge 123
French Revolution 44,54
Fuller, John 69
Furner, John 37

Gamelen, Thomas 86
Gauffier, Louis 51
George V 141,146,166
Gilbert, Mary 79
Gilpin, Rev William 29
Gordon, Angus 178,184
Granville, Lord 108
Grace, Margarita 134
Grace, Michael 134-135,140
Grace, Peggie (later Mrs Peggie Phipps Boegner) 134
Grimm, S H 41,42
Grose, Francis 29-30,35
Gunpowder works (Sedlescombe) 20

Hamburg 56
Hampton & Sons 153
Harbord, Anthony 193
Harbord, Charles R 157-158
Harbord, Evelyn see Webster, Evelyn
Harbord, Felix 157
Harbord, Godfrey Vassall aka Godfrey Webster 151,157,158,173-177,181,185,186,191-194,207-208
Harbord, Marcus 93
Harbord, Simon 158,174-176
Harewood, Lord & Lady 151
Harold, King of England 29,182-183
Harper, Charles G 135
Harrow School 59
Hastings 159

Battle of 166,170-171
Battle of (painting) 63-65,133,208
College of Education 201
Corporation 64,110,132
Parliamentary seat 26,38,77-79,81,83
Webster estate 31,100
Hawthorne, Nathaniel 98
Hay, Richard 19
Heathfield 135
Henry VIII 3,4,5
Heritage, National 4,66-67
Herstmonceux
   Castle 41
   Fracas (1830) 82
   Woolpack Inn 82
Hildon House 119,124,133
Holland House 58
Holland, 3rd Lord (Henry Richard Fox) 51-53, 56
Holroyd, Maria 44-45
Hope, Lady Mary 108
Hopkins, John ('Vulture') 20

Ingall, Isaac 40-41
Inskipp, James 37-38,47,58,76
Iron Industry, 15,16,19-20,30

Jacoby, Charles 148
Jacoby, Margaret 148,163
Jacoby, May 148,158,159,165-166,169
Jordan, Abigail 8
Jordan, Thomas 8
Judd, George 178
Jukes, William & George 19

Kensington, Charlotte 142-143
Kitchener, Lord 108, 115

Lally, Gwen 163-164
Lunacy, Master of 155
Lane, Homer 154-155
Lausanne 45,173
Law Benevolent Society 96
Leconfield, Lady 108

Legal & General Insurance 119
Leghorn 56
Leslie, Sir Shane 169
Leveson-Gower, Lord Granville 51-52
Liverpool, Lord 69,70
Lockington (Yorks) 7,33
London Life Association 133
Long's Hotel 70
Lonsdale, Earl of 185-187,189,191
Louis Philippe, (ex) King of France 87

Mary, Queen (1910-1936) 141,146,165-166
Mayfair Theatre 186
Menin Gate Memorial 145
'Men of the Trees' 172
Meppen, E 116
Milan 54
Milles, Rev. Jeremiah 17
Modena 56
Montague, Viscounts 6-7,14,20
Morley, Eric 184
Morton, AV 167
Mountfield 94
    Webster estate 31
Munich 173
Murray, Elizabeth 89,90
Murray, Sarah Joanna see Webster, Lady Sarah Joanna
Murray, William 89

Nairn, Martha see Webster, Lady Martha
Naples 46,47,52
Napoleon, Louis, later Napoleon III 87
Napoleonic wars 3,62,71-73,76
National Trust 183,185
Navy 12,85,86,91,92,94
Naylor, Hare 41
Nelmes 9,13,33,35,37
Netherfield 95
Newcastle, Duke of 27
Nice 45
Normanhurst 114
Northey, Edward 17
Northiam

Place 133
    Webster estate 135
Norton, Mary 174

Official Solicitor 175
Ongar, Manor of 20
Orange, William, Prince of Netherlands 71
Oxford University Dramatic Society 124

Paine, Thomas 47
Paris 44
Parker, June 169-170,176
Pelham family 18,27,38
Pelham, Baron, of Stanmer Park (1728-1805) 38,45
Pelham, Hon Thomas (1756-1826) 44-47,50,54
Peninsular war 62,71
Pera (schooner) 92-94
Pett
    Webster estate 135
Philcox, Mr 166
Philosophical Society of America 187,189,190
Pilgrim's Rest 178,195,196
Powdermill House 133,148,158,174,178,180, 203
Powdermill Wood 178
Powdermills
    Sedlescombe 20,100
Powell, Sir Christopher 16
Power, Eugene B 190
Prescott, Sir George 77
Primrose, Hon Everard 108
Prosser Hastings, Amelia Sophia see Webster, Lady Amelia Sophia
Prosser Hastings, Charles 119
Pyke House 197

Quatre Bras 71-73

Raby Castle 103
Railway, arrival in Battle 3,87,90-91
Redvers Buller, General Sir 108
Richmond, Duke of 69,73
Ripley International 182,184

Robertsbridge
  Ironworks 19,30
  Taking tea 160
  Webster estate 20,76
Robinson, Ann 70-71,85-86
Robinson, Henry 71
Rome 54
Rosebery, Lord (5th Earl) 108,116
Rose Green 41,96
Rosehill Estate, Stockbridge 119,135
Rother District Council 182,195,198,201,205
Royal Humane Society 143
Royal Military College (Sandhurst) 121,140-141

Sackville
  Charles, Earl of Dorset 10
  East Grinstead estate 26
St Barbe Baker, Richard 172
St Etheldreda's School 148
St Martin Association 165
St Mary Abchurch 26
Salehurst
  Webster estate 31
Sandby, Paul 28,29
Sandelson, Victor 187
Sandford Orcas 10,21
Saunders, Anne 79-81
Saunders, Maria 79-81
Saxe-Weimar, Prince Bernard 71
Seaford
  Parliamentary seat 38,45
Searle, Eleanor 172
Sedlescombe 20,100
Sheehan-Dare, John R 158,160
Sheffield, Lord 69
Shore, Rt. Hon Peter MP 197
Smith, Messrs Daniel and Son 99
Somerset, Charles Seymour, Duke of 13
Southampton, Earl of 6
South Sea Company 9,14-15,20
Souvenir Normand 138-139,171
Spenser, Lord Henry 46
Stanhope, Catherine Lucy Wilhelmina see

Cleveland, Duchess of
Stanley, H M 108
Stanmer Park 50,51
Stevens, Sir Jocelyn 203-205
Stower, Joseph 126,127-129
Streatfield, Sir Henry 142
Strutt & Parker 178-179,184
Sussex, Duke of 75
Sword of Asgard Society 185

Taught, Mark 23
Teck, Duchess of 108
Thomas, Sir Edmund MP 27,31
Thorburn, Andrew 182
Ticehurst 156
Ticehurst, Francis William 68-69,97,114
Toledo waterworks 20
Tories 69-70
Torrington, Viscount 40
Trust, 1066 177,181-186,189,190-191,196-197,198
Tull, Jethro 18
Turin 54
Turner J M W 68
Turner, John 30

Vane, (later Powlett) Hon George Harry see Cleveland, 4th Duke
Van Hasselt, Kelvin 205
Vassall, Elizabeth see Webster, Lady Elizabeth
Vassall, Sir Godfrey 55,58 see also Webster, Sir Godfrey
Vassall,Richard 39,54
Victoria, Queen (1837-1901) 83,103,104

Walpole, Horace 15, 27-28
Walpole, Sir Robert 12
Waltham 20
Wareham
  Parliamentary seat 57
Warren, Kenneth MP 185
Waterloo, battle of 71-73
Weald, The 15
Webster family 1-4

Executors 152

Family tree (facing) 1

Origins and rise 7-8

Portraits of 161,207-208 see also colour section

Trustees ii,161-162,174,178

Trusts 175-176

Webster, Abigail 17,31-32

Webster, Lady Amelia Sophia (née Prosser Hastings) 119

Webster, Amelia Sophia Rous (later Mrs Askwith) 121,144,147-148,152,155

Webster, Arthur (1822-1868) 117

Webster, Sir Augustus 7th Bt. (1819-1886) 91-102,117,119-121

Webster, Sir Augustus FWE 8th Bt. (1864-1923) 4,116,121-126,140-150,152-154

Webster, Lady Charlotte (née Adamson, d.1867) 73-75,81-82,83,85-87,89,92-95,97,119,120,132

Webster, Lady Elizabeth (1727-1807) 33,59

Webster, Lady Elizabeth (née Vassall) later Lady Holland (1770-1845) 2,39-58

Webster, Elizabeth (18th c) 17,31

Webster, Evelyn (1904-1988)134,142-143,146-148,150,151,157-158,164,167,169-173,174-178,181,185,186,191,193,207

Webster, Frederick (1821-1880) 90,91,94,96,119

Webster, Sir Godfrey (c1650-1720) 8-9

Webster, Sir Godfrey 3rd Bt. (1718-1780) 21,22,31,33-34

Webster, Sir Godfrey 4th Bt. (1749-1800) 33,35-58

Webster, Sir Godfrey 5th Bt. (1789-1836) 2,59-84

Webster, Sir Godfrey 6th Bt. (1815-1853) 85,86-91

Webster, Godfrey (1897-1917) 2,141-142,143-146

Webster, Godfrey Vassall (1872-1901) 121,124-126

Webster, Godfrey (1928-2003) see Harbord, Godfrey

Webster, Guy (1831-1868) 2,117-119,120-121

Webster, Harriet (1794-1849) 54,56

Webster, Sir Henry (1793-1847) 2,47,70-73

Webster, Lady Jane (1682-1760) 10,21,24,26,31

Webster, Jane (d.1772) 17,31

Webster, Lucy (1900-1989) 124,143,146-147,150-152,154-157,160,175,193,207

Webster, Lady Mabel (née Crossley, d.1917) 124,132,142-144

Webster, Lady Martha (née Nairn, 1729-1810) 2,30,32,36,38,40-43,62

Webster, Mary (d.1722) 17

Webster, Peter 8

Webster, Lady Sarah Joanna (née Murray, Ashburnham widow, c.1803-1889) 89,94-95,101,118,119,120-121

Webster, Sir Thomas 1st Bt. (1676-1751) 1, 7-24,27

Webster, Sir Whistler 2nd Bt. (1709-1779) 17,22,24,25-34

Whigs 11-12,27,38,69-70

Whistler, Henry 10-11,12,26,32

Wellington, Duke of 71-73

Wells International 181

Wiesbaden 115

Wilkin, Frank W 63-64

William III, King of England 9

Woodhams, James 172

Worge, Elizabeth 33

Worge, George 18,30

York, Duke and Duchess (later George VI and Queen Elizabeth) 167

York, Susannah 174

Ypres 144-145

Zeppelins 140-141

BATTLE ABBEY,
Ground Plan.

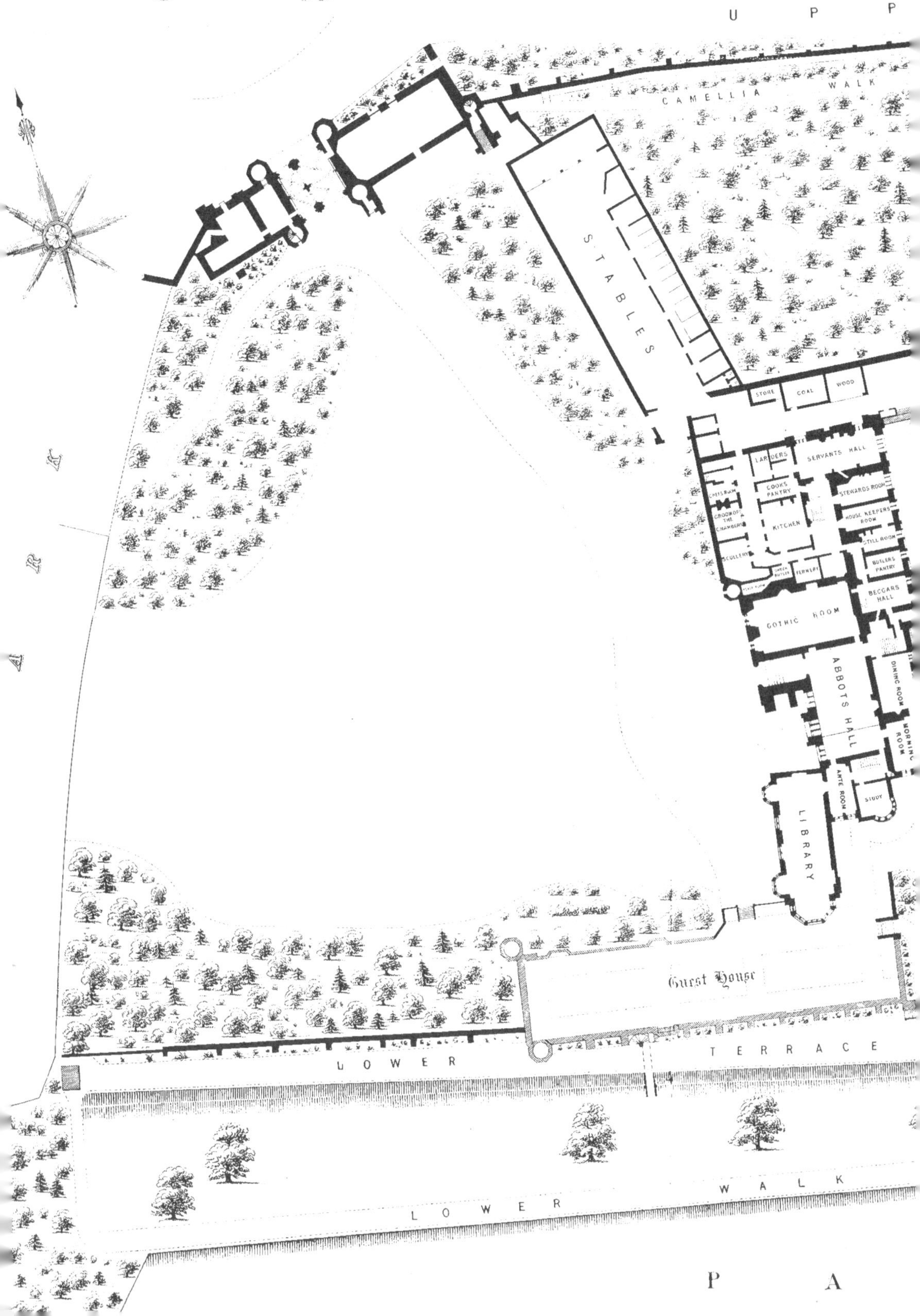

U P P

CAMELLIA WALK

S T A B L E S

STORE COAL WOOD

LARDERS SERVANTS HALL

CHEFS ROOM COOKS PANTRY STEWARDS ROOM

GROOM OF THE CHAMBERS KITCHEN HOUSE KEEPERS ROOM

STILL ROOM

SCULLERY BUTLERS PANTRY

HEAD BUTLER PEPKEEP BEGGARS HALL

GOTHIC ROOM DINING ROOM

ABBOTS HALL MORNING ROOM

ANTE ROOM STUDY

LIBRARY

Gurst House

TERRACE

L O W E R

L O W E R   W A L K

P   A